P9-ECP-993

Writing

for the

Orchestra

AN INTRODUCTION
TO ORCHESTRATION

Merton Shatzkin
University of Missouri—Kansas City

PRENTICE HALL, Englewood Cliffs, New Jersey 07632

Library of Congress Cataloging-in-Publication Data

SHATZKIN, MERTON
    Writing for the orchestra: an introduction to orchestration /
Merton Shatzkin.
      p. cm.
    Includes bibliographical references and index.
    ISBN 0-13-953431-8
    1. Instrumentation and orchestration. I. Title.
MT70.S466 1993
784.13'74—dc20
                                        92-32215
                                           CIP
                                         MN

Acquisitions editor: *Norwell Therien*
Editorial/production supervision
    and interior design: *Carole R. Crouse*
Copy editor: *Carole R. Crouse*
Cover designer: *Rich Dombrowski*
Prepress buyer: *Herb Klein*
Manufacturing buyer: *Bob Anderson*
Editorial assistant: *Lee Mamunes*
Artwork: *Ron Garnett*

©1993 by Prentice-Hall, Inc.
A Simon & Schuster Company
Englewood Cliffs, New Jersey 07632

Printed in the United States of America

10 9 8 7 6 5 4 3 2 1

ISBN 0-13-953431-8

PRENTICE-HALL INTERNATIONAL (UK) LIMITED, *London*
PRENTICE-HALL OF AUSTRALIA PTY. LIMITED, *Sydney*
PRENTICE-HALL CANADA INC., *Toronto*
PRENTICE-HALL HISPANOAMERICANA, S.A., *Mexico*
PRENTICE-HALL OF INDIA PRIVATE LIMITED, *New Delhi*
PRENTICE-HALL OF JAPAN, INC., *Tokyo*
SIMON & SCHUSTER ASIA PTE. LTD., *Singapore*
EDITORA PRENTICE-HALL DO BRASIL, LTDA., *Rio de Janeiro*

Contents

4

THE BRASS, 71

5

THE PERCUSSION, 94

6

THE HARP AND KEYBOARD INSTRUMENTS, 156

7

HISTORICAL SURVEY OF SCORING TECHNIQUES, 179

8

GUIDELINES FOR SCORING, 271

9

WIND–PERCUSSION AND STRING ENSEMBLES, 309

10

PREPARING THE SCORE AND PARTS, 319

11

UNUSUAL INSTRUMENTAL TECHNIQUES, 340

Appendix E: RANGES, TRANSPOSITIONS, AND CHECKLIST, 370

Illustrations

Preface

A single lecture years ago by Bernard Rogers sowed in me the seeds of a deep appreciation for the art of orchestration. Rogers's sensitive analysis elegantly brought out the sensitivity with which Weber handled his instruments in the overture to *Oberon*, and inspired me, years later, to search for similar wonders in other scores, hundreds of which I examined in preparation for the present book. It is my hope that some of that insight and inspiration will be transmitted to the reader.

Most writers of orchestration texts, like Rogers, are composers. Although I have also written music, the more important aspects of my career include over twenty years of experience as a violinist in professional orchestras, many of them at the first desk of the first violins under the nose of and advising the conductor, and a few recent years as conductor of a professional-amateur orchestra. Concurrently with these have been many semesters of teaching acoustics, history, theory, and orchestration at the college level. This many-sided experience with the orchestra, its musicians, its music, and students enabled me to approach the subject from a variety of practical and aesthetic viewpoints. The fallout from this experience can be found here and there in bits of information that may not be found in other texts.

The monumental task of bringing this book together was made possible with the kind and unselfish aid of colleagues and reviewers who critiqued the manuscript and offered information and advice. To them go my profound gratitude: Marita Abner, Joanne Baker, John Beck, Keith Benjamin, Nancy Cochran-Block, Richard Bowles, Carole Crouse, Wes Faulconer, Sara Funkhouser, Christopher Gallagher, Walter Halen, Gary Hill, Charles Hoag, Joel Hoffman, Donald Hummel, Lamar Hunt, Jr., Gerald Kemner, John Leisenring, Jennifer Liebnitz, James Mobberley, Stephen Multer, Walter Ross, Diane Schick, Reynold Simpson, Gaylen Umbarger, David Ward-Steinman, John Wiener, and others. I am also indebted to some of these, other individuals, and Explorers Percussion and

Calvary Baptist Church of Kansas City, Missouri, and the Kansas City Symphony for lending me instruments for the photographs.

This book is lovingly dedicated to those closest to me: wife Patricia, daughter Kate, and son Matthew.

Merton Shatzkin

CHAPTER 1

Introduction

The symphony orchestra has long proved its worth throughout the world. Many countries support their orchestras directly. Professional orchestras in the United States are nonprofit organizations that may receive some support from government grants, but they draw most of it from the private sector: Large businesses are important sources of support, since they see cultural associations as an important part of their image.

Besides the many professional orchestras, there are hundreds of amateur orchestras that fill the needs of doctors, office workers, salespeople, and others to develop their musical potential, to get a break from their careers, and to express themselves artistically in direct musical activity. Orchestras in schools provide not only a training ground for future professionals but also a means of adding social and cultural richness to the learning experience.

The present financial crisis of many American professional orchestras is daunting, but it can be seen as a consequence of a generally difficult economic climate rather than as a lessening of interest in orchestral music. The traditions are strong, there is no dearth of talented young musicians, and performance standards are steadily improving. In spite of fierce competition for funds and for places on concert programs, opportunities still exist for composers to write for the orchestra and be heard; the wealth of new music attests to the fact that the orchestral medium is far from having exhausted its potential.

This book is designed primarily for the use of college music majors and composers, arrangers, and conductors. A minimal knowledge of music theory is necessary for an understanding of most of the material, and for the rest, some competence in the subjects of harmony, counterpoint, and form is required. The book can serve a fairly compressed one-semester course or a more relaxed but in-depth two-semester course.

With the passing of time, new technologies and new fashions emerge. Instruments undergo modification, new ones are invented, and some obsolete instruments reappear. Composers restlessly look for new ways of making and combining sounds, and are constantly exploring the old and the new resources of the orchestra to expand their individual techniques. The subject of orchestration has therefore expanded so much that a single book dealing with every detail concerning the orchestra and related topics would amount to an encyclopedia. Therefore, it is necessary to make choices in what to cover or to stress.

The things not covered or stressed in this text are the histories of the various instruments, arranging (other than what comes under "Transcription," as defined in the next section), writing for specialized purposes such as film scores, and discussion of such media as the guitar, the voice, the choir, and electronic music. Excellent books are available that have information on these topics. They are included in the Bibliography.

It was the author's intention, given the limitations of space, to concentrate more narrowly on how composers have written for the orchestra and on the practical aspects of scoring—topics that are not always given their proper due. It is hoped that the book will replace the traditional "this is the way you do it" approach with a more open, and potentially more creative, "what is possible?" approach. The author also desired to avoid the habit of filling up pages with examples of orchestration that, effective as they may be, were used only once. Instead, certain "principles" of handling the orchestra that seem to have been handed down from composer to composer, but have not always appeared in textbooks, are cited as models for accomplishing certain results (see Chapter 7). Rather than being treated as rules, they are regarded as techniques, and you are encouraged to explore other possibilities.

Terms Defined

Symphony orchestra: An ensemble of at least seventy-five players, with representation of all the standard members of each instrumental family—woodwinds, brass, percussion, and strings.

Orchestration: The way in which the instruments are used, both individually and interactively.

Instrumentation: The list of instruments used in a composition; also the study of the techniques of the instruments.

Transcription: The rewriting of a composition not originally for orchestra so that it can be played by an orchestra, with the requirement that all the original pitches, rhythms, dynamics, and articulations are heard with nothing added except, possibly, octave or unison doublings and filling-in of harmonies.

Arrangement: A rewriting of a composition in any other form, allowing changes in harmony, rhythm, articulation, and form. The main requirement is that the arrangement be recognizable as another version of the original.

Range: The extent of pitches that can be produced by an instrument, expressed in terms of its lowest and highest pitches.

Register: A (any) portion of a range. With some instruments, registers are considered to be certain specific portions of the range, based on fingering.

Tessitura: The portion of the range that is most used in a composition.

Brightness: A character of tone quality that is associated with clarity and focus. Acoustically, it is associated with relatively strong overtones.

Darkness: A character of tone quality that is associated with the relatively soft and unfocused. Acoustically, it is associated with relative weakness of overtones.

Fullness, Volume: Projecting the effect of size. "Fuller" or "greater volume" implies that more instruments either are playing or seem to be.

Concert pitch: The pitch name that represents the pitch that sounds, as opposed to "transposed pitch," which does not.

Names of Pitches

There are two widely used systems of naming pitches: the Helmholtz system (named for a famous scientist of the nineteenth century) and scientific notation. Scientific notation assigns "C4" to middle C, "C3" to the note an octave lower than middle C, "C5" to the note an octave higher than middle C, and so forth. This book uses the more common Helmholtz system. See Example 1-1. In this system, all pitches from *c*-natural (second space, bass clef) upward are written in lower-case letters. Beginning with middle C, superscripts are added. Notes in the small octave are called "small c," "small c-sharp," and so on. Notes in the one-line octave are called "*c¹*," and so on. Notes in the Great, Contra, and Subcontra octaves use those names, respectively: for example, "Great C," "Contra C." All pitch names are given in italics in this book.

Example 1-1

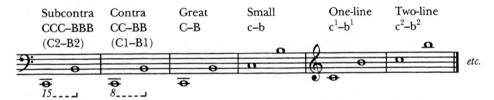

Clefs

The clefs normally used in orchestral scores and parts are the treble, bass, alto, and tenor clefs. Because the alto and tenor clefs are unfamiliar to most musicians who do not play an instrument that uses them, they will be explained here. These clefs are called C-clefs because they originally resembled the letter *C*. The present form of the clef has a shape that converges on *c¹*. The alto clef places that pitch on the third line, and the tenor clef puts it on the fourth line. Example 1-2a gives the treble-clef equivalents of some notes in the alto clef, and 2-1b gives the same for notes in the tenor clef. You are advised to learn these clefs well. Here is a suggested learning routine.

1. Find a part written in the clef.
2. Play the notes on your instrument, if it is not a transposing instrument. (If it is, play the notes on the piano.)
3. Read the names of the notes aloud in the Helmholtz system.
4. Transcribe them to the treble or the bass staff.

Example 1-2

Transpositions

Some instruments are not ordinarily written in concert pitch because they are built in such a way that their fingering is associated with transposed pitch. Most transposing instruments are identified by the "key" of transposition: The flute in G is "in G," the clarinet in A is "in A," and so on. Parts for such instruments are written consistently higher or lower than concert pitch by a transposing interval. That interval can be determined by a simple guideline: **A written C sounds the "key" of the instrument.** Thus, a C in a part for the clarinet in A sounds A; a C in a part for the saxophone in E-flat sounds E-flat; and so on.

Most transposing instruments sound *lower* than written. Only the smaller versions of the standard instrument sound higher: the piccolo, the piccolo clarinet in E-flat, and the small trumpets. Thus, for example, a written c^2 in an A clarinet part sounds a^1. From this, you can see that the transposition interval is a minor third *up* for this instrument—it must be *written* a minor third *higher* than it is to *sound*. (A few instruments sound more than an octave lower than written, most notably the bass clarinet in the treble clef.) The small instruments must be written *lower* than they are expected to sound.

The student should become proficient in both writing and reading transposed parts. First, memorize the guideline just given, and repeat it every time you must write or read a transposed part, until it becomes second nature. Write a series of random notes, most of which have sharps or flats, and then transpose those notes on a staff above them for instruments in various keys, especially B-flat, A, F, and E-flat, which are the ones most often encountered. After you have done that and checked the notes for accuracy, you can use the transposed parts for practice in reading by transcribing them on a different page into concert pitch.

Many musicians learn to transpose by thinking of a part in another clef. Although this method seems to be effective for those who use it, it requires the imagining of two things that are not there—a clef and a key signature—and this seems to have the potential for producing wrong notes. Two other methods of accomplishing transposition are by interval and by movable-*do* solfège.

The movable-*do* solfège method is good only for music that is in a key. It identifies scale degrees—*do, re,* and so on (whereas the fixed-*do* method identifies pitch names—*do* is C, C-flat, or C-sharp; *re* is D, D-flat, or D-sharp; and so on). To take an example, if an instrument is built in B-flat and the concert key is D major, the part will be written a major second higher than concert—in E major. Using the solfège method, the reader would read solfège in E major and transfer the pitch names to the same syllables in D major; for example, the notes $g\sharp^1$, a^1, b^1 in the part would be read "mi," "fa," "so." Transferring these to D major, the reader would imagine the pitches $f\sharp^1$, g^1, a^1, because these notes are *mi, fa, so,* respectively, in D major.

The interval method, which is the one explained earlier, may seem more difficult, but practice makes it not only feasible but also the most direct, and it is the most suitable for music that is not in a key. In addition, it reinforces a basic skill that is too often faulty—the recognition of intervals.

HOW TO USE THIS BOOK

The material in this book is presented in such a way that the most essential information is highlighted in some way: by headings, italics, lists, summaries, or appendixes. It should be easy to find and remember the important points that are explained at some length, and it should be possible to make outlines of the basic points for quick reference.

The emphasis is on the practical—the capabilities and limitations of the instruments and the consequences of combining them in various ways. The author has attempted to penetrate beyond the surface of how an instrument is played and what its problems and strengths are.

Although there is no separate section on scoring for nonprofessional orchestras, careful attention to the discussion of instrumental techniques (particularly the "Factors That Make . . . " lists) and the section on school bands in Chapter 9 should prepare the student to compose music that is playable by less skilled musicians.

Although this is not a book on arranging, those interested in that subject can use all the information on the instruments that is presented here. In addition, Chapter 8 indicates how arranging problems might be solved when working with miscellaneous groups.

When you study Chapters 2–4, refer to Appendixes A–C, which give fingering charts for the instruments discussed in those chapters. Appendix E gives the ranges of all instruments in one place and a checklist of things to remember when preparing a score—things that if overlooked or forgotten, can cause lost time and frustration when that first orchestral reading takes place; it would be helpful for the user to have this appendix at hand whenever scoring is done.

The material need not be learned in the order in which it is presented in the text. If the course lasts only one semester, it may be desirable to cover only the main points of Chapters 2–6, along with those of Chapters 7 and 8. If scoring of any of the instrumental families by themselves is undertaken, this sequence should be sufficient for the moment: Chapter 2 (or 3, and so on), Chapter 7, Chapter 8.

Chapter 10 should be added before full-orchestra projects are attempted. Study of Chapter 9 requires the knowledge of Chapters 3–5, with some attention to Chapter 2 for the string bass and possibly Chapter 6, if the harp, the celesta, or the piano is to be used.

The role of Chapter 7 is two-fold: to give a broad perspective of scoring practices by various composers and to introduce the time-honored techniques that are still used. It could be used selectively or in summary fashion, if time is limited. If time permits, it would be good to read portions of Chapter 7 while the earlier chapters are being studied so that the student can associate the instruments with their use in context. Similarly, it would be good to learn sections of Chapter 10 just before scoring exercises dealing with the instrumental chapters are assigned. Another use for Chapter 7 is a historical-stylistic approach to the study of orchestration, wherein students are asked to score in the style of Haydn, or Beethoven, or some other composer.

At many points in the book, certain compositions are mentioned as examples of what is being discussed. It would be helpful for the student to have many of these works at hand during the course. Here are some that are more commonly cited.

Mozart, Symphony No. 40
Beethoven, Symphonies No. 1, 6, and 9
Mendelssohn, *Hebrides* Overture
Brahms, Symphonies No. 1 and 4
Wagner, *Tristan und Isolde*
Tchaikovsky, Symphonies No. 4, 5, and 6
Rimsky-Korsakov, *Scheherazade; Capriccio espagnole*
Saint-Saëns, *Carnival of the Animals*
Franck, Symphony in D Minor
Strauss, *Don Quixote*
Mahler, Symphonies No. 1, 2, and 4
Debussy, *Nocturnes; Prelude to The Afternoon of a Faun; La Mer*
Ravel, *Rapsodie espagnole; Daphnis et Chloé;* Piano Concerto in G
Stravinsky, *Petroushka; The Rite of Spring; Agon*
Schoenberg, Five Pieces for Orchestra
Webern, Ricercare from Bach's *Musical Offering*
Bartók, Concerto for Orchestra
Copland, Symphony No. 3
Shostakovich, Symphonies No. 1 and 5
Prokofiev, *Peter and the Wolf; Lieutenant Kije* Suite
Varèse, *Ionisation*
Stockhausen, *Gruppen*
Carter, Double Concerto for Harpsichord and Piano
Tower, *Silver Ladders*

   As was mentioned earlier, a comprehensive book on the subject of orchestration would be encyclopedic in extent. For that reason, supplemental reading is offered in the Bibliography. Especially recommended are the books by Adler, Blatter, Burton, Carse, Del Mar, Kennan, Read, and Stiller.

   Beyond this, there is no substitute for extensive and detailed study of scores before, during, and after listening to *live* performances. It also helps to have as much experience with instrumental ensembles as possible, both as a player and as a conductor.

CHAPTER **2**

The Bowed String Instruments

ACOUSTICAL CONSIDERATIONS

The stringed instruments are alike in having the following features:

1. A wooden box, with top and bottom plates connected by ribs (the sides) and a small, cylindrical piece of wood (the sound post) that is wedged between the plates near the right foot of the bridge. A piece of wood called the bass-bar is attached to the underside of the top plate below the lowest string.
2. A wooden bridge that supports the four strings.
3. A bow.
4. Accessories, such as a tailpiece to hold the strings at one end and pegs to tune them at the other. The top plate has two openings, called the air holes or F-holes.

The normal tone is produced by the activation of one or more strings—usually by bowing or plucking. The string oscillates sideways and also somewhat along its length. Its vibrations are transmitted to the bridge, which transmits *its* vibrations to the top plate. The transference continues to the bottom plate, the sound post, the ribs, and the air within the box. The most flexible, and therefore the most critical, media in this system are the string, the bridge, the plates, and the enclosed air. The length, the mass, and the tension of a string interact to determine the pitch of a tone, and also affect its quality. On any given instrument, all strings have the same length (the bass extension is an exception), but the tensions and masses of the strings vary so that their pitches may be different.

As an example of how these factors interact, suppose that the player wants to produce a pitch on one string and then repeat it on another string. To do this, the player must make the vibrating portion of the lower-tuned string *shorter* than that of the higher-tuned string by stopping it with a finger at the appropriate spot. The shorter length of the lower-tuned string causes the string to sound thicker and less resonant than the higher string because its mass and tension are greater in pro-

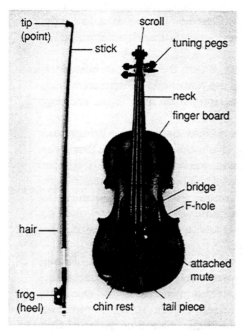

Ed Brown Studio

THE VIOLIN, ITS BOW, AND THEIR PARTS

Ed Brown Studio

THE STRINGS

Viola   Violin
   Cello   Bass

9

portion to its vibrating length than they are on the upper string. By the same token, any note played high on a given string will sound less resonant or bright than another note played low on the *same* string (because the vibrating length is again shorter).

Quality is also influenced by the point at which the string is bowed or plucked, the area of the string that is activated, the amplitude of that activation, the use of a mute, and the material and construction of the box. These are only some of the most important factors.

String players are taught to keep the bow midway between the bridge and the fingerboard to produce the "normal" tone. If the bow is moved farther away from the bridge, the tone becomes darker and weaker, since the overtones become less prominent. If the bow is moved toward the bridge, overtone strength increases, causing a brighter, more powerful sound. As the bow continues to approach the bridge, the resistance of the string causes the fundamental pitch to be lost, as well as some of the strength of the tone, and a "scratch" may result. (See "Sul ponticello," in the section on bowing styles.)

If the activation point is very narrow (for example, if the fingernail rather than the fingertip is used to pluck the string), overtones will predominate and a nasal, guitarlike tone will result. As the area of activation increases (for example, bowing with more and more of the hairs in contact with the string or plucking with the flesh of the thumb or with more than one finger instead of the usual first finger), the tone becomes darker. Greater pressure on the bow increases the *brightness* of the tone. Greater speed of the bow increases its *loudness*. A mute inhibits the smaller, faster vibrations of the bridge, lowering the intensity of the overtones and causing a muffled, dark, and distant tone.

Open strings (not stopped by fingers) are more resonant than those that are stopped, since the surfaces with which unstopped strings are in contact are less yielding than the fingertips of the player, which give a softer, less ringing sound.

Since the plates of the instrument are relatively flat, their vibration radiates air waves most strongly in a direction perpendicular to their plane. The higher frequencies produced by the instruments (both high pitches and the relative brilliance of the sound) are most affected by this radiation. Simply put, any listener who can see more of the area of the top plate than another listener is in a better position to hear the instrument at its most brilliant. This aspect of the stringed instrument's acoustics must be considered when deciding where to place the instrument on the stage. (This is discussed in "String Sections.")

Size and weight are factors that affect the responsiveness, quality, and resonance of the instrument. The larger instruments are generally slower to respond, darker in quality, and more resonant. Similarly, the higher-sounding strings on a given instrument are more responsive and brighter, but less resonant, than the lower ones. Fast staccato notes on the cellos and the basses tend to be noisier, but also more articulated, than on the upper instruments. A certain amount of buzz can be heard in the tone of the basses when they play sustained notes alone, but not when they are playing an ordinary bass line.

Each of the instruments in the string family has two especially resonant areas. One is the "air resonance," which is determined by the volume of the enclosed air and the area of the F-holes. The other is the "wood resonance," which is affected by the resonant frequencies of the plates. The air resonance of the violin is around $c\sharp^1$ and the wood resonance around bb^1 or b^1 (although one author places it on or just below a^1). Another wood resonance reinforces the low notes of the G string. The other members of the string family are not built in the same proportions as the violin (because if they were, they would be too large to manage), and their air resonances are higher with respect to their ranges: The air resonance of the viola is not on its lowest string, as it is on the violin, but on its third string—at about bb. Its wood resonance is about eb^1. The cello's air resonance is about d, also on its third string. The construction of basses differs from instrument to instrument, and air resonances may range from about $GG\sharp$ to about $C\sharp$ (sounding).

When an instrument is played at frequencies that are near these resonances, they sound fuller and richer. Knowing this, composers have written melodies with some of the more expressive notes in those areas.

On the other hand, some instruments, especially cellos, are afflicted with "wolf tones"—tones that, because of certain structural facts (there is some controversy over what those facts are), sometimes wobble uncontrollably in pitch. $F\sharp$ on the cello is the most notorious of these, which makes it a good note to avoid in an exposed passage. (Perhaps for the same reason, it is also a note that is difficult to get in tune.)

Scordatura. The tuning of the strings can easily be altered (*scordatura*), but this technique involves problems: (1) The alteration changes the quality of sound; (2) it may be difficult to keep the instrument in tune once normal tuning is reestablished; and (3) when a string's pitch is raised, there is extra strain on both the string and the instrument. Higher strings are most likely to be broken with higher tuning. The interval of a major second is a reasonable limit. Tuning a string down by a minor third or more can make the pitch less stable and the quality unacceptable; as with any unusual effect, though, it could be just what is desired!

The strings are named both by the pitch of the open string and by roman numerals: The highest-pitched string is I, the next II, and so forth. See Example 2-1. Professional players are familiar with both systems. The Italians and the French use solfège syllables for pitch names (see Appendix D); thus, to them the G string is "sol," and so on.

STRING SECTIONS

In today's symphony orchestras, there are usually about half as many basses as first violins; the second violins are one or more players fewer than the firsts; and the violas and the cellos each are somewhere between the second violins and the basses in number. A typical roster is about sixteen first violins, fourteen seconds, ten violas, ten cellos, and eight basses. (Several scores, from Wagner to the present, call for a ratio of 4–4–3–3–2, which is reasonably close to these figures.)

The first violins are always seated to the left of the conductor, with their top plates more or less facing the audience. In American orchestras, the seconds are often situated on the same side of the stage as the firsts, but more toward the rear of the stage, whereas in European orchestras, the seconds may be on the conductor's right. The cellos and the violas are usually to the right of the conductor, with one of these sections at the front of the stage and the other more toward stage rear. The section that is placed toward stage rear will "face" the audience more than if it is placed at stage front. This means that the arrangement with the cellos in front somewhat favors the violas and the placement of the violas in front favors the cellos. The basses are normally placed in a line behind the cellos and the violas, their top plates generally facing the audience.

All string sections have two players per stand—an "inside" player (the one farther from the audience) and an "outside" player. The inside player normally plays the lower notes when the part is divided, and turns the pages. (The latter factor should be considered when parts are being made—a divided part is not practical at the end of a page that must be turned, since the inside player must stop playing to turn.)

THE VIOLIN

The normal tuning of the violin is shown in Example 2-1. Orchestral parts go as high as e^4 and occasionally above. (Ranges for the strings, as well as other instruments, are given in Appendix E. These show suggested limits for elementary and high school players as well as professionals.) On the lower three strings, a practical limit is about an octave and a fifth above the open string. Generally, when one plays higher than an octave on a string, intonation becomes less accurate, the response of the string weaker, and the tone thicker and somewhat choked-sounding. (Except for intonation, this is least true of the violin E string.) For that reason, when very high string passages are called for, the same notes may also be given to wind instruments for security, as well as strength. Less advanced players are better restricted to a range of an octave or less on any string.

Example 2-1   Open strings of the violin

Each string has its own characteristic quality, partly because of the resonances of the instrument. For all stringed instruments but the viola, strings I and IV are usually called upon for very strong and expressive passages, and the inner strings are more used for secondary parts or leading lines that are thinly accompanied by other instruments.

Fingering

A knowledge of how the instrument is fingered makes it possible to write passages that are not only playable but *easily* playable. Example 2-2a gives a fingering chart that can be used for this purpose. Each stepwise series represents notes playable on a given string. *After the first note, each note stands for itself and the same note flatted or sharped;* for example, the third note on the top staff stands for G, G-flat, and G-sharp. (The exception to this is F, the second note on that staff, which cannot stand for F-flat, since that is the same as E, the open string.)

Example 2-2   Fingering chart for the violin

a. Numbers are for fingers in each position.

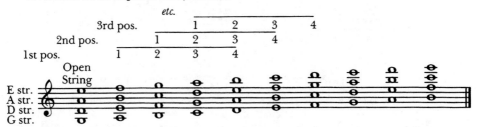

b. Examples of applying the fingering chart.

1. To finger

find two columns having these notes on ADJACENT strings.

They are

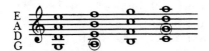

Since these notes lie on adjacent strings and within a four-column group, they are playable as a double stop. The lower note can only be played by the first finger in first position on the G string. The upper note, being TWO columns to the right, can be played by the finger that is TWO more than the first finger—the third finger.

2. To finger

These notes can be found on the chart in three different columns:

Since they form a DIMINISHED fifth, they cannot be played by the same finger. One respelling is

which involves these columns:

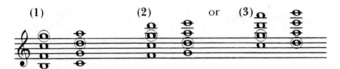

Thus, the fingering could be $\frac{1}{2}$, $\frac{2}{3}$, or $\frac{3}{4}$ in (2) and (3), but only $\frac{1}{2}$ or $\frac{2}{3}$ in (1).

The choice between (1), (2), and (3) determines which position and which strings will be employed. The easiest of these, and the best-sounding, is (1), which is in the LOWEST position. The easiest fingering is $\frac{1}{2}$, since the lowest-numbered fingers are the strongest.

The first column of notes shows the open strings. The remaining columns show all the notes that are playable by a given finger on each string. (For example, the second column indicates that the same finger can play f^2, $f\sharp^2$, bb^1, $b\natural^1$, $b\sharp^1$, eb^1, $e\natural^1$, and so on.) A "position" is defined by the notes playable by the first (the index) finger: When the hand is in *first* position, the notes on the *second* column are played by the first finger, the notes in the third column are played by the second finger, and so on for the next two columns. Thus, in first position, the range of the *fingered* notes is ab on the G string through $b\sharp^1$ on the E string. The *available* notes include all the notes on the first five columns (which includes the open strings) and the alterations of the notes on the second through the fifth columns.

When the hand is in *second* position, the first finger plays the notes on the *third* column, the second finger the notes on the fourth column, and so on; the range of fingered notes is now $bb-c\sharp^3$, in addition to the open strings. The fingering for every note in every position can therefore be determined by the chart, as well as all notes available in that position. The range of fingered notes in a position extends from the lowest note on its left-most column (not including the open-string line) to the highest note on the third column to the right. Each position encompasses four columns on the chart—one for each finger. Thus, for example, in first position, the notes a, $f\sharp^1$, and d^2 are normally played by the first finger on the G string, the second finger on the D string, and the third finger on the A string, respectively. Accomplished players can shift from position to position very quickly.

Double Stops.   To play double stops is to play two strings at the same time. When bowing, this is possible only for adjacent strings (with normal bowing; see Chapter 11 for another possibility). Nonadjacent strings can be plucked at the same time by using more than one finger on the right hand. The fingering chart tells us which notes can be bowed as double stops: any two notes within a four-column group, plus open strings, for two adjacent strings. A single finger can stop both strings to produce a perfect fifth (but not a diminished fifth). The notes b^1 and f^2 in first position cannot both be played by the first finger because the interval between them is a diminished fifth, but the notes b^1 and $f\sharp^2$ can.

To play such notes that are in the same column, one can respell one of them, thereby "placing" it in a different column. In the case of b^1 and f^2, we can respell b^1 as $c\flat^2$, which moves it on the chart to the next column to the right (which has c^2 in it). That makes it playable by the second finger. We could not alternatively respell f^1, as $e\sharp^1$ because that would place the note in the first column, which represents only open strings, not fingered notes that are adjustable up and down. In the case of b and f^1, there are alternative respellings, and thus two possible fingerings: $c\flat^1$–f^1 in second position and b–$e\sharp^1$ in first position.

For examples showing how to apply the chart to the fingering of double stops, see Example 2-2b.

How difficult a double stop is depends on how many fingers are used and on the interval between the notes. The following list gives categories of double stops in order of their difficulty, beginning with the easiest.

1. Both strings open.
2. One string open.
3. One finger used for both strings (perfect fifth only—this interval is not easy to play in tune, however).
4. Two fingers used, with an interval of a sixth or a seventh.
5. Two fingers used, with an interval other than a sixth or a seventh.

(Unisons are practical only if one note is an open string.)

An independent variable is position—the higher the hand position, the more difficult a double stop is.

Triple and Quadruple Stops.   Bowed multiple stops are executed in one of two ways: (1) broken into double stops (see Example 2-3 for some possibilities) or (2) with all the notes played at the same time. The second of these is practical only for the duration of about a half-second.

It is not advisable to write a multiple stop that has notes in the same column *unless such notes are on adjacent strings and produce a perfect fifth.* Thus, the chords

Example 2-3

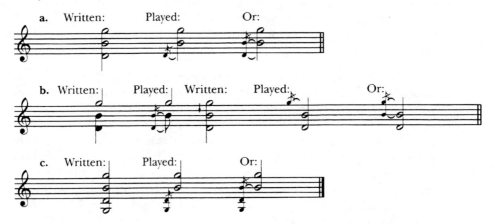

Example 2-4

shown in Example 2-4 are not practical: The chord at a requires the same finger for a and b^1 on the G and A strings, respectively, which are not adjacent (see the second column on the chart). (This chord is playable, with respelling, but is difficult.) The chord at b requires the same finger for *three* notes—c^1, g^1, and a^2. The notes c^1 and g^1 *can* be played by the same finger, since the notes are on adjacent strings—the G and the D—but a^2 is on the E string, a nonadjacent string. It is not practical to stop three or four strings at the same time with one finger.

All the fingered notes in a chord must lie within four adjacent columns. Multiple stops, listed from the easiest to the most difficult, will have

1. A maximum of open strings
2. One fewer than the maximum of open strings
3. Open strings only below or above fingered strings
4. One or two open strings between fingered strings
5. All strings stopped with intervals only of a perfect fifth, a sixth, or both
6. A perfect fifth or a sixth and smaller intervals, or an octave
7. All strings stopped and no interval larger than a tritone

The first five of these are the most practical.

Again, the higher the position, the more difficult the stoppings are. For professionals, the lower note of a double stop should not be higher than about a^2, the lowest note of a triple stop not higher than about b^1, and the lowest note of a quadruple stop not higher than about e^1.

Example 2-5

By fingering notes as if they were multiple stops, a player can easily slur between notes on adjacent strings, as in Example 2-5.

Multiple stops and double stops are useful for forceful, short, accented notes. It is actually easier to play such notes as a part of multiple, rather than single, stops, because forceful action of the bow on single notes might cause strings to sound that are not desired. Playing on more than one string, the player has more confidence, not having to avoid the unwanted strings.

Free movement from position to position is possible, and even large shifts can be accomplished with great speed. If the bow is moving while a shift is made, and the player does not disguise or minimize the sound of the shift, there will be a portamento or glissando. Accomplished players minimize this effect, but if it is desired, that should be indicated.

The orchestrator can construct complicated passages that are playable if he or she is aware of how the notes lie in positions, taking into account the limitations of slurring with and without changes of position. Some guidelines are given in the list called "Factors That Make String Passages Relatively Easy."

Glissando. Glissando *(gliss.)* is the deliberate sliding of a finger along the string, producing a continuous change of pitch upward or downward. The range of a true glissando is that of the practical range for the string on which it is played—between the open string and about an octave and a fifth higher. Example 2-6 shows a gliss on the G string, with its usual notation. (The "port.," or *portamento*, in Example 7-60 is another term for *glissando.*) Glisses that cannot be played entirely on one string must be faked by glissing to some point on the first string and continuing on other strings, which means that there will be gaps. Fake glisses are common (there are many in Mahler symphonies).

Example 2-6

Glissandos are sometimes played tremolo or with a change of bow at the end of the gliss (see Example 7-52). They can also be done immediately after a plucked note. Plucked glisses die out quickly—especially when the gliss is downward.

Tremolo. A *tremolo (trem.)* is a fast repetition of a note or an alternation between two notes. A *fingered tremolo* is a rapid alternation between two *slurred*

Example 2-7

notes, written as in Example 2-7. Obviously, the notes must be fingerable in the same position. If they are played on different (necessarily adjacent) strings, the *bow* must move back and forth between strings while the fingers act as a double stop. This form of "fingered" tremolo is not as smooth as when the notes are on the same string. *Bowed tremolo* is discussed under "Bowing Styles."

Vibrato.   On most notes lasting at least as long as half a beat in moderate tempo, string players ordinarily use *vibrato,* which is a fast oscillation of the pitch up and down, from about five to seven oscillations per second. To some extent, both the speed and the width of the vibrato can be controlled, and it can be suppressed altogether. Since the normal mode of playing is *with* vibrato, "non vibrato" and "senza vibrato" are ways of indicating that it is not used. "Vibrato" or "con vibrato" indicates that it be resumed. Without vibrato, the tone is thinner and less rich or "alive." It is possible to ask for vibratos that vary in speed, width, or both; this is usually shown graphically with undulating lines over the notes and a verbal explanation. The greater the speed or width, the greater the intensity of the effect.

Bowing

Notation.   A string player bows successive notes in alternate directions unless they are under slurs—all notes under a slur are bowed with the bow moving continuously in the same direction. Example 2-8a begins with four notes that have no slurs. As indicated (by the conventional signs above the notes), the first note is downbow (drawn toward the right side of the player), the second note is upbow (drawn toward the left), and so forth, until the second measure, where the four notes under the slur are all downbow. If alternating strokes are desired, as in the first measure, it is necessary to indicate the direction of the *first* stroke only.

Bowing influences phrasing, since change of bow gives the effect of articulation; thus, slurs have the effect of phrasings. It is possible, however, to show phras-

Example 2-8

ings that are longer than bow strokes, as in Example 2-8b: Note that each two-beat group has its own slur under the long slur. If the bowing were marked as in Example 2-8c, the player would probably be confused, because the bow marks contradict the only slur that is present; therefore, the notation in 2-8b is preferred.

Bowing Dynamics.   Bowing is a complex affair. The bow is not heavy, but because its weight increases sharply at the frog end (the end of the bow that is held) and because two kinds of motion are involved (*across* strings and *between* strings), a set of variables is created that interact in complicated ways.

All other things being equal, the faster the bow moves across a string, the louder the tone. The speed of the bow can be measured by how long a complete stroke lasts. Assuming the player maintains a constant speed over a stroke, a duration of twelve seconds will yield a dynamic level of about *pianissimo.* The following is a guide for various dynamic levels.

12 secs.	*pp*
6 secs.	*p*
3 secs.	*mf*
1 sec.	*f*
.5 sec.	*ff*

This can easily be used to show that six beats at quarter note = 60 or twelve beats at quarter note = 120 will produce a dynamic level of about *piano,* for example. It is unreasonable, therefore, to expect a note or a group of notes in one bow stroke that lasts four seconds to sound *forte,* as in Example 2-9a. Using the preceding guide, the orchestrator can accomplish what a concertmaster would do to achieve the desired dynamic level—break up the four-second slur into one-second bow strokes, as in Example 2-9b. In Example 7-51, the second violins are slurred in one-beat groups so they can play *ff,* while the flutes and clarinets, playing the same thing, are slurred over more than three beats. This is typical of such cases.

Example 2-9

The fact that the bow is much heavier at the frog end than at the tip end helps to determine the natural character of the downbow and the upbow stroke. Another factor is that the effective weight of the bow on the string depends on how much of the bow extends to the left of the string. When the bow is placed on the string near the frog, nearly all of the bow's length is to the left of the string, and its weight is maximal. When the bow is drawn downward (to the right), the effective weight decreases, as the amount of the bow that is above the string decreases; when it is drawn upward, the weight increases. Thus, there are two important properties regarding bow direction:

1. Downbows are more natural for accented beginnings and diminuendos.
2. Upbows are more natural for soft beginnings and crescendos.

If downbeats are to be stronger than the preceding notes, a downbow there will be effective; therefore, the upbow–downbow sequence is natural for such a case as ♩ | ♩. It follows that onbeat notes are more naturally played downbow and offbeat notes upbow.

Equalization.   If the orchestrator wishes to arrange the bowing so that a passage will most naturally have an *unchanging dynamic level,* the most effective device is equalization of bow strokes. Equalization is accomplished by arranging the bow strokes so that their durations are as nearly equal as they can be (with one exception, which will be explained). In Example 2-9b, each bow stroke has two beats' duration; this passage is therefore equalized, and it will be easy to maintain a steady *forte* throughout. If, on the other hand, the first measure were all under one slur, that measure would tend to sound softer than the following one, since the first bow stroke would last four beats, whereas the bow strokes in the second measure would last two beats each.

There is an exception to this rule: *If an even number of short durations fall between two long ones,* the bowing will be equalized. Example 2-10 shows two such cases: (1) The first note is four eighth notes in length and the fourth note is six eighth notes in length, whereas the two eighth notes that come between them are each relatively short. (2) The last note is also four eighth notes' duration, and there are four eighth notes between it and the previous long note in the second measure. The whole passage is equalized because in both cases there is an even number of short durations between the long ones. A player would have no trouble playing at an even dynamic level.

Example 2-10

When the desired bow strokes are not of equal duration and do not fit the exception, the way to equalize the bowing while maintaining the desired articulation is by *hooking.* Hooking is articulating two or more notes in the same bow direction, assuming that the player either stops the bow at the end of the first note and starts the next from that point on the bow, or articulates with bow pressure and then continues. (The alternative is "retaking" the bow—lifting it and moving back to start over—but that is not hooking.) Example 2-11a illustrates the technique of hooking and the recommended way of notating it. The two notes in the first mea-

Example 2-11

sure are articulated downbow and those in the second measure upbow. This makes a total of four beats on each stroke (the two downbows and the two upbows each constitute one stroke), whereas without hooking (downbow, upbow, downbow, upbow), it would be very difficult not to play the quarter notes louder than the dotted halves.

Hooking provides a slightly softer articulation than change of bow does. The advantages of equalization usually offset the slight loss of definition. Dotted rhythms such as those in the example are very often hooked in this way.

Hooking has other limitations: It is not effective downbow if there are more than two fast notes involved, and it may not be effective if it ends on an accented or a long note. Example 2-11c is more difficult to accomplish than 2-11b because the fast hooking is downbow (the notation here is preferred when several notes are involved). Example 2-11d is less effective than 2-11e because the hooking ends on a long note, whereas it does not in 2-11e.

Hooking can affect phrasing or metrical definition. Examples 2-12a and 2-12b are both equalized by hooking. (In 2-12b, the first two downbows equal four eighth notes, which is close to the three-eighth-note duration of the last notes. The two upbow–downbow single eighths between the longer strokes make an even number.) But the nature of the hooking is such that the two versions have different metrical implications: Because hooked notes tend to group together, the bowing in Example 2-12a will sound like three groups of three eighth notes' duration, which could be 3/8, 6/8, or 9/8, and so on. The bowing in Example 2-12b, on the other hand, suggests groups of four, one, one, and three eighth notes. The four-group implies two quarter-note beats, and 3/4 is the likely effect here.

Example 2-12

Of course, we usually do not want every passage to have an even dynamic level. When crescendos or diminuendos are desired, *unequal* lengths of bow stroke are useful. Suppose we want a crescendo at the end of the first measure of Example 2-9b. That would almost be guaranteed if those notes had a bow stroke that was shorter than the ones before and, furthermore, if the direction of the stroke was *up*. A bowing solution that satisfies both conditions is shown in Example 2-13.

Example 2-13

Changing Strings.   When the player draws the bow across one string, then another, the plane of the bow changes, regardless of whether the bow is moving up or down. Although string changes can be accomplished very quickly, certain bowing sequences associated with them are easier than others and can make complicated, fast-moving or repetitive passages more playable than they would otherwise be. For example, when a note is played on one string and a second note is played on a higher string *after a change of bow,* the sequence down–up is better than the reverse. This makes Example 2-14a easier than 2-14b. Conversely, the sequence up–down is better when moving from a higher to a lower string, as is also shown in those examples. Following the same principles, slurring notes while moving to higher strings is easier downbow, and slurring while moving to lower strings is easier upbow (see Example 2-14c for the recommended bowing).

Example 2-14

Bowing Styles.   String players can articulate notes in a wide variety of ways. Some of these have been given traditional names and are described here.

Détaché ("detached"): *Détaché* generally does not imply a separation between notes but, rather, an articulation at the beginning of each note, caused by the change of bow direction. Distinct from staccato, this is the normal way notes are played with separate strokes for each note. No special notation is required. There is no limitation of speed, beyond a reasonable one of about sixteenth notes at quarter note = 160. Orchestrators not familiar with stringed instruments tend to use too much détaché (that is, too many notes unslurred). Unless the notes are intended to have some definite articulation, they should be slurred, at least in groups. An examination of orchestral string parts will give the student a good idea of the typical distribution of détaché and slurred notes.

Staccato (played on the string): This generally implies a certain attack and a clean (usually somewhat abrupt) release. It cannot be expected to be executed faster than about four notes per beat at quarter = 110. The most forceful version of staccato is called *martelé.* A succession of staccato notes, upbow, can be effective, up to a speed of about four notes per beat at quarter = 120, but a series of downbow staccatos is less natural.

Spiccato (*spicc.*; played off the string): This is a brilliant, somewhat noisy type of stroke made by bouncing the bow off the string. Normal spiccato can be executed at maximum speed, but the clarity of the sound is likely to be sacrificed at anything beyond about four notes to the beat at quarter = 132. At fast tempos, it cannot be as loud as staccato, although Examples 7-15 and 7-54 call for loud spiccato at a fast tempo. The sound of spiccato differs from that of staccato in that the former's attack is somewhat noisier but not as loud, and as the bow rebounds, the string resonates; whereas, at the end of a staccato stroke, the resonance of the string is inhibited, with a drier, more stifled effect.

If the tempo is not fast, a variety of note lengths can be called for in spiccato; otherwise, the note lengths should be the same throughout. "Brush stroke" gives a softer attack and relatively long note lengths. At the other extreme, "very spiccato" or "sec" implies very short notes with a relatively noisy, brittle attack. A series of repeated upbows played spiccato is a good effect at a moderate tempo.

To summarize: Staccato is heavier, slower, stronger, more defined, and less resonant than spiccato, which is lighter and more brilliant.

There are other styles of bowing that are played "off the string": *Pesante* calls for a heavy stroke near the frog, and *sec* is generally produced near the tip. At fairly fast tempos, the mixed figures shown in Example 2-15 can be executed by accomplished players. A series of downbows near the frog is good for a series of heavy, evenly accented notes. In this case, the bowing is not hooked: The bow is moved back to the frog each time. (See Example 2-16.)

Example 2-15

Example 2-16   Tchaikovsky, Symphony No. 5, mvt. 4, mm. 58–60

Jeté, Ricochet: These terms are synonymous. They require the bow to be thrown against the string and allowed to rebound two or more times during a single stroke. Usually, *jeté* is used when the pitches change, as in Example 2-17a, and *ricochet* or *saltando* when they do not, as in Example 2-17b. This style is easier and more effective when the figure begins downbow, which gives it an accented beginning. As many as about eight fast notes can be played in this way. It is best if all the time values in the stroke are of the same kind (for example, all sixteenth notes) and a single upbow, also bounced, follows.

Example 2-17

Louré, Portato: This is a form of hooked bowing, usually notated with a slur and lines, dots, or both lines and dots over the notes (see Examples 2-18 and 7-14). The effect is a soft, even pulsation that is not possible with alternations of down and up strokes, partly because downbow articulation is slightly different from upbow articulation, and partly because a change of bow reverses the vibrational pattern of the string, causing a more distinct articulation than pulsation of the bow in one direction does.

Example 2-18

Bowed tremolo: This is a rapid, unmeasured succession of strokes. The most accepted notation shows three beams through the note stem when the quarter note or the eighth note is the beat and two beams when the half note is the beat, as in Examples 2-19a and 2-19b, respectively. Unmeasured tremolo has several advantages:

1. It can give a feeling of mystery or excitement at low dynamic levels. Tremolo on the cellos and the basses produces an unusually eerie timbre, particularly when played ponticello.
2. It allows the effect of legato connections between notes and long sustained tones without the problems of bow changes or bow direction. See Example 7-40.
3. Any dynamic level and any changes of dynamic level are easily produced, such as swells or sharp accents.
4. It allows a tone to be sustained indefinitely; however, constant tremolo at high dynamic levels is fatiguing and should be avoided.
5. Tremolo is the means by which strings can play at their very loudest.

Example 2-19

The speed of the tremolo can be varied. Players usually play faster tremolo in loud passages and slower tremolo in softer ones, but the orchestrator can specify relative speed by "slow tremolo," and the like, or ask that the speed fluctuate in some desired manner.

Most often, tremolo is played with very short strokes near the tip, where it is most comfortable. For that reason, *unless an accent at the beginning of the tremolo is desired*, it is good to arrange for the bow stroke preceding the tremolo to be a downbow. Otherwise, to get quickly to the tip, the player will begin the tremolo with a fast stroke—an accent. For the same reason, any tone immediately following tremolo is best played upbow if a good connection is desired.

If the notation in Examples 2-19a and 2-19b is used as shorthand for *measured* repetitions, it is advisable to write out the individual notes for the first beat, as in Examples 2-19c and 7-32, or to give the number of notes desired above the note, as in Example 2-19d. A third method is to indicate "non-trem."

Sul ponticello (sul pont., pont., s.p.; "near the bridge"): Although this term literally means "on the little bridge," the player actually draws the bow near, rather than on, the bridge. This causes the tone to become very nasal, pinched, and somewhat penetrating. It is often combined with bowed tremolo.

Sul tasto (tasto, s.t.; "on the fingerboard"): The player draws the bow farther away from the bridge than normal. The result is a weaker, less rich, and somewhat bland sound that is often called for when the orchestrator wants the strings to serve as a background, or to create a hazy, filmy effect.

It is not customary to ask for just a single note in a passage to be played either sul ponticello or sul tasto, although that is entirely possible. It would be most feasible in slow passages.

Col legno (c. l.; "with the wood"): The player uses the wood of the bow instead of the hair either to strike the string (*battuto*) or to draw it across the string (*tratto*). The context of the passage usually makes it obvious which form is intended: Staccato notes imply *battuto,* and slurred or détaché notes imply tratto. In either style, the tone produced is very faint; *battuto* (the more usual) gives a percussive, clicking sound, and *tratto* gives a ghostly whisper. Players are usually not happy to play col legno, because it tends to scratch the finish of the bow; therefore, extensive use of this device, especially at loud levels (which is anyway somewhat unrealistic), is to be discouraged.

For any unusual uses of the bow, a return to the usual style *must* be indicated where it takes place. The common indications are "naturale," "normale," "normal," "ordinario," or "ordinary." If "sul ponticello" is called for in a passage that ends with a long rest, after which the normal style is to be resumed, "normale" should be indicated at the point where playing is resumed—not *before* the rests.

Con sordino (con sord., sord., c.s.; "with mute"): This directs the player to place a mute on the bridge. The mute reduces the brilliance and power of the instrument, giving a muffled or distant character to the tone. To indicate that the mute is to be removed, "senza sordino" or "mutes off" should be used. If there is a long rest before the mute is to go on or to come off, the indication should appear *before* the rest in the *part* and *after* the rest in the *score*. (The needs of the player and the conductor differ.)

If the mute is to be put on or taken off *within* a passage, a few seconds should be allowed for the change. It is possible to put on or take off the mute while playing an open string, since the left hand is not occupied at that time.

The problem of going from muted sound to nonmuted, or vice versa, without breaking the melodic line can be solved by indicating "remove [or place] mutes one at a time" or the same "stand by stand." In this way, the sound will change gradually from one to the other with no break.

A quick change from nonmuted to muted, or vice versa, will be easier for the player if the change is preceded by an upbow, which moves the right hand toward the bridge, and followed by a downbow.

Pizzicato (pizz.): The strings are plucked—usually with the first or second finger of the right hand. This makes a rather explosive, but not necessarily loud, attack. The decay is relatively quick or slow depending on the length of the string and the tuning of the string (high or low). The shorter the string length (that is, the higher the position of the left hand) and the higher the string is tuned, the quicker is its decay. Above e^3, the decay is so quick that most of what is heard is the attack, which is not well defined in pitch.

Plucked notes should not go faster than about four notes to a beat at quarter = 96, although faster passages are encountered in the literature. Long passages of fast pizzicato are fatiguing and are best broken up by periodic rests, which can be very brief. Other string sections can fill in the gaps, if desired.

The player can be instructed to pluck either farther away from the bridge, or "sul tasto" (for a more hollow sound), or closer to the bridge (for a more banjo-like sound). This is a routine part of guitar playing and is more effective on the cello and the bass than on the upper strings.

Double stops and chords in pizzicato can be quite effective. It is possible to arpeggiate them, but it is not easy to time the arpeggiations precisely. Upward arpeggiations are more natural than downward ones. A guitarlike strumming, with an alternation of downward and upward motions, is possible and is best with chords. This can be indicated by downbow and upbow signs. The player can be directed to hold the instrument under the arm in guitar fashion, which makes it easy to use the thumb for a fuller sound. At least four seconds should be allowed to move to or from normal playing posture.

If, after a passage of pizzicato, there is a return to bowing, "arco" (bow) must be indicated where it is desired (both in the score and in the part). If there is a change from one to the other within a passage, it is best to allow at least a second for the change. Many passages do not allow "any" time; this is possible at a speed of about half a second per note, which means, for example, that a passage of eighth notes in quarter = 60 can be played with changes to and from pizzicato. In such cases, the pizzicato should be approached upbow and left downbow. (See the contrabass parts in Example 7-52.)

It is possible to play pizzicato with a left-hand finger. When this is done, there is no need for a time lapse between pizzicato and arco—in fact, arco or right-hand pizzicato can be played on one string and left-hand pizzicato on another string at the same time, preferably if the latter is on an open string. The usual indication for left-hand pizzicato is "l.h." or "+" over the notes. Left-hand pizzicato is brighter, but somewhat weaker, than right-hand pizzicato; thus, a pas-

Example 2-20

sage using both types of pizzicato can exploit the variety of color, as well as help to lessen the fatigue of constant right-hand pizzicato. A succession of left-hand pizzicatos is feasible only if the notes descend within the range of a third, unless the lowest note in the group is an open string. See Example 2-20 for some examples of left-hand pizzicato. These can be, and usually are, played rather quickly. The sound approaches that of the guitar.

Harmonics

When a string vibrates freely, it does so in sections, each division vibrating a whole number of times (or very nearly so) as fast as the string as a whole: The division into two halves creates sections that vibrate twice as fast as the whole string; divisions in thirds vibrate three times as fast; and so on. At any given moment, all these divisions vibrate at the same time and at different rates, creating a complex tone consisting of fundamental and harmonics (or overtones). If a finger stops the string lightly at a dividing point of one of these sections (a node), the string will tend to produce the pitch that results from the vibration of that portion of the string. For example, if the finger is at a point one-third of the length of the string, the pitch will tend to reflect the vibration of that one-third length—three times as fast as that of the whole string. Tones produced in this way are called *natural harmonics*. The quality of a harmonic is different from that of a fully stopped tone—it is less rich, but clearer and more ringing. Perhaps most important, since the location of the finger must be precise and constant, vibrato is not feasible, which adds to the "whiteness" of the tone.

Tones produced as natural harmonics are members of the harmonic (or overtone) series of the string. Example 2-21a shows the first four natural harmon-

Example 2-21

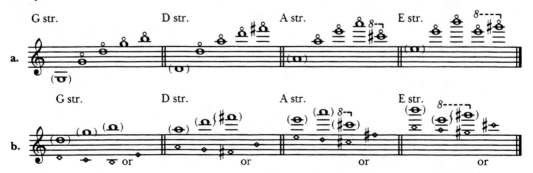

ics playable on each of the violin's strings. These harmonics should be indicated by a small circle placed near the notehead. The division of the string into two halves has only one node—at the middle, which produces the lowest harmonic (in acoustical terminology, this is called the *second* harmonic or the first overtone, the first harmonic being the same as the fundamental, or open string). As divisions get smaller, there are more and more nodes. For them, the same pitch can be produced as a harmonic with more than one finger placement. Example 2-21b shows alternative fingering for the notes of 2-21a, after the lowest harmonic. It is best, for these fingerings, to indicate not only the string, but also the sounding pitch, in parentheses. Diamond-shaped notes are best used for harmonics that do not sound the note that is fingered.

It is easy to see that alternative fingerings can be advantageous in certain situations. For example, imagine a passage calling for all four harmonics on some string in quick succession. The fingering in Example 2-21b would require no shift, whereas the same notes fingered as in 2-21a would require two shifts into high positions. By the same token, a player can remain in the same position and play both stopped notes and alternatively fingered harmonics, thereby executing wide skips without changing position—see Examples 2-22 and 7-39. Example 2-22a shows Rimsky-Korsakov's notation; and 2-22b shows the recommended notation, which gives the fingered notes, as well as the sounding pitches.

Example 2-22   Rimsky-Korsakov, *Scheherazade*, mvt. 3, m. 122

A common, effective use of the natural harmonic is after an upward glissando. The harmonic may be sustained or short. If short, the tone will ring, somewhat like a resonating bell. It is often played with an accent, preceded by a crescendo; thus, uphow on the gliss is characteristic. Long glisses to high harmonics are occasionally found, as in Example 2-23. It is also possible to slide the finger lightly along a string while drawing the bow and produce the natural harmonics in order, up and down the harmonic series. Intervening notes will not be heard. Another interesting effect is plucked harmonics (rarely used, however)—only the first overtone (one octave above the open string) is effective on the violin and the viola.

Example 2-23

A word of caution about natural harmonics, especially higher ones—they can be noticeably flat, and there is no good way of adjusting the intonation. An example is found at the end of "Petit Poucet" in Ravel's *Mother Goose* Suite, with a rather charming effect.

Artificial Harmonics.   If the string is stopped by a finger, it acts like an open string: A second finger can produce a harmonic by lightly stopping the same string at a nodal point of the vibrating length. This is called an *artificial harmonic.* The most usual artificial harmonic spans a perfect fourth between the stopped note and the lightly stopped one. The result is a pitch that is two octaves above the "note" stopped by the first finger. Example 2-24 shows the notation that is recommended. It gives both the location of the fingers and the resulting pitch. Artificial harmonics have the advantages that they are not limited to the overtones of the open string and vibrato is possible, since the two fingers can oscillate together. A series of artificial harmonics is possible, not faster than about four to a beat at quarter = 60. A pure legato (with slurring) is not possible without the sound of shifting (portamento) or the lifting of fingers (in the case of slurring from string to string unless the same fingers are used on adjacent strings). Natural harmonics can be slurred with each other or with artificial harmonics. Example 2-25 gives some possibilities.

Example 2-24

Example 2-25

Advanced players can play artificial harmonics whose interval between the notes is a perfect fifth. The resulting pitch is an octave higher than the upper "note." (See Example 2-26.) This harmonic is easier in higher positions.

Artificial harmonics are not always easy to produce. The usual type (that shown in Example 2-24) loses clarity when the lower note is higher than a^2.

A table of all the harmonics playable by the string section is given in Example 2-38.

Example 2-26

THE VIOLA

Most of the playing characteristics of the violin hold for the other stringed instruments, with allowances for their greater sizes.

The tuning of the viola strings is given in Example 2-27. High positions are more difficult to manage than on the violin, owing to the viola's greater size, but the range of each string can still be considered to be about an octave and a fifth. The instrument in general has a more nasal sound than the violin, especially on the A string. The C string does not have a fullness and power comparable to that of the violin G (since the air resonance is not in the same relative location), and its sound is somewhat rough and hoarse, but composers have used this quality very effectively.

Example 2-27   Open strings of the viola

Fingering charts for all the stringed instruments are given in Appendix A. Fingering considerations are, by and large, the same as for the violin.

Violists are accustomed to reading both the alto and the treble clefs. The choice of clef should depend on two things: how many ledger lines are needed in a given passage and how often clef changes occur. The most satisfactory choices will minimize both of these factors. (The same is true for any player who reads more than one clef.)

Viola bowing is similar to violin bowing, although the bow and the strings are heavier, which makes for a slower response. This ordinarily calls for a slightly more percussive attack. Added to the slower response is the fact that the bow is a little shorter than that of the violin; thus, the durations of bow stroke given for the violin for each dynamic level on page 19 should be reduced by a second or so for the viola.

THE CELLO

The full name of this instrument, *violoncello,* has the stem *viola.* The Italian suffix *-one* means "large," and the suffix *-cello* means "small"; thus, *violoncello* literally means "small large viola." The *violone,* or "large viola," was the bass member of the viol (viola) family of the sixteenth and seventeenth centuries. *Violin (violino)* literally means "small viola."

The cello strings sound an octave lower, respectively, than those of the viola—see Example 2-28.

The cellist reads mostly from the bass and tenor clefs and occasionally from the treble. In the eighteenth century and some of the nineteenth, cello parts in treble clef were often meant to sound an octave lower than written, but no longer.

Example 2-28   Open strings of the cello

The character of the cello strings is rather like that of the comparable violin strings, the outer strings being rather stronger than the inner ones. The most typical pitch area for important melodies—those that are to be heard clearly—is about g–g^1 where the instrument is at its brightest and fullest, although the tone is also somewhat nasal (see Examples 7-19 and 7-24).

Because the instrument rests on the floor and is not held in the air by the left hand, as the violin and the viola are, there is more freedom to play in upper positions, although distances from position to position are greater. Since the instrument rests on the floor (by means of an endpin), a whole section of instruments playing on the lowest string can create a rumbling sensation that is felt as well as heard.

In lower positions, the range of fingered notes is a third, rather than a fourth as for the violin and the viola. This means that on the fingering chart, *three* adjacent columns define the range of a position. However, the left-hand thumb may be used to play the note just below the first finger's note. It is not ordinarily used except for the positions beginning an octave above the open string. In "thumb position," four columns encompass the range of the position. The cellist anchors the hand with the thumb on the string, rather than around the neck (as for lower positions); therefore, vibrato is not as successful with the thumb as with a finger. See the fingering chart in Appendix A.

From this it can be concluded that fingered double stops on the cello should not exceed a seventh, at least not in lower positions (although octaves are not uncommon in chamber and solo literature, with the thumb playing the lower note). Otherwise, double and multiple stoppings are much like those for the violin and the viola.

The cello bow is shorter and heavier than that of the viola, with similar implications—the attack is more percussive and there is less sustaining power.

Whereas the violin's highest string is on the player's right, the cello's *lowest* string is on the right. For this reason, when changing strings, it is easier to move to a higher string on or from an upbow and to a lower string on or from a downbow than the reverse. This is the opposite of the case for the violin and the viola. See Example 2-29 for an illustration of the more natural bowing.

Artificial harmonics require the use of the thumb. They have been called for occasionally in twentieth-century scores, even in low positions, which require the greatest stretches.

Example 2-29

THE BASS (CONTRABASS, DOUBLE BASS, BASS VIOL)

The bass is played while the player either stands or sits on a stool. Even more than the cello, its vibrations can make the floor shake when the section is playing low notes. The modern bass has four strings, tuned in perfect fourths (see Example 2-30). Some instruments have an extension built on to the scroll of the instrument that allows the E string to be played down to *C* (written). Most orchestras have at least one or two basses with an extension. Notes below E should be approached, played, and left slowly. Players not having the extension play those notes an octave higher.

Example 2-30   Open strings of the bass
                    (sounding one octave lower)

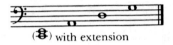

(𝅘) with extension

Bass players should be able to read bass, tenor, and treble clef. In each of these, *the part is written an octave higher than it sounds*, although in some recent scores the *sounding* pitch is given (as it is for all instruments in such scores).

For the most part, the range of one position on one string is a second (two columns on the fingering chart), which means that the largest feasible double stop is a fifth. Since the strings are tuned a perfect fourth apart, the same finger placed on adjacent strings will produce a perfect fourth. However, because of fingering limitations and the lowness of pitch, which causes notes close together to sound indistinct when played together, double or multiple stops are rarely employed in orchestral writing, except where one or more open strings can be used.

Artificial harmonics are possible with limitations. For the most part, they are not used in the orchestra.

The instrument can be surprisingly agile, although the response is slow. Any fast low notes will tend to rumble and be indistinct. Bow attacks tend to be percussive, especially on lower strings. As on the cello, the upper register has a singing quality, but in no register is the instrument particularly brilliant. A section of basses playing heavily on the E string, however, is imposing. Among the strings, the basses have the least sustaining power, requiring more frequent bow changes than the higher instruments. Also, for that reason, bass parts are often doubled by other instruments. Since the dimensions of the instrument are so large, vibrato sounds more constricted than on the upper instruments, giving a somewhat "flatter" or "whiter" quality than that of the cello, a difference that should be remembered when the two sections have parts that are joined. On the other hand, this difference could be effectively exploited as a contrast.

Pizzicatos can be gentle, booming, and resonant. Whereas bowed notes can be stronger than pizzicato on the upper instruments, it is the reverse with the bass and possibly also the cello. The orchestrator should consider the exact length of tone desired for bass pizzicatos: For short tones, it may be advisable to indicate "dampen."

FACTORS THAT MAKE STRING PASSAGES RELATIVELY EASY

1. String crossings are minimized and confined to adjacent strings.
2. Consecutive string crossings are in one direction (e.g., upward, then upward again) or alternating between adjacent strings.
3. Bowing patterns or styles are consistent: Example 2-31a shows an inconsistent bowing pattern and 2-31b a consistent one. Example 2-32a mixes bowing styles—spiccato and legato—whereas 2-32b maintains a consistent style—legato.
4. Shifts are minimized (no more than one at a time). Successive shifts are in the same direction.
5. Finger changes are in one direction (from lower to higher, or vice versa).
6. Patterns are diatonic (following a scale line).
7. Pitch patterns are consistent (see Examples 7-27 and 7-50, both of which break up string lines into simple patterns moving in one direction).
8. Rhythmic patterns are consistent.
9. Like accidentals are used in succession, where possible (a sharp followed by a sharp or a flat followed by a flat); e.g., E♭ to A♭, rather than E♭ to G♯.
10. Double or multiple stops are isolated rather than consecutive.

Example 2-31

Example 2-32

When writing for advanced players, you need not be concerned with these guidelines except when a part is very fast or repetitious. Observe them, however, when writing for less advanced players. For all types of players, they offer more comfortable and better-sounding parts and are more easily sight-read.

Any passage that has extended repetition, no matter how difficult or easy, is fatiguing, both physically and mentally. Even a momentary respite can be refreshing. It is also helpful to make every part, even a simple accompaniment, as interesting as possible under the circumstances. Examples of how to avoid monotony will be seen later in this chapter and in Chapter 7.

THE STRING SECTION

Any of the sections of the string family can be divided into parts as small as individual players. There are three ways of notating this:

1. On one staff, with the word *divisi (div.)*. See Example 2-33a.
2. On one staff, with stems going up for outside players and down for inside players ("div." is not needed, although it is helpful—see Example 2-33b).
3. On two (or more) staves, with "div." between them. See Example 2-33c.

Example 2-33

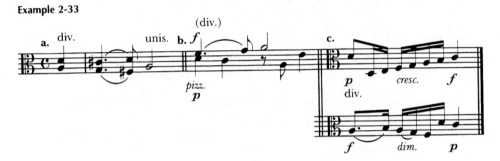

If "div." is used, the return to unison playing must be marked "unisoni" ("unis.") where it occurs, both in the score and in the parts.

The choice of notation method should be dictated by the complexity of the parts. Notation 1 is practical only when the parts move in the same rhythm (it is assumed that outside players take the upper notes). Notation 2 is needed if the parts are not in the same rhythm. It is also better than 1 if there are alternations of divisi and non divisi, since "div." and "unis." would not need to appear many times. Notation 3 is recommended if the parts interact in so complex a manner that they would be difficult to follow individually on one staff. Notice in Example 2-33b that all articulation, dynamics, and the like, are marked *above* the staff for the outside players and *below* the staff for inside players. For divisi in three or more parts, very simple dispositions of the parts may use 1 or 2; otherwise, 3 is recommended, with the indication "div. a 3" (which should be used for 1 as well). It is possible to divide a section unequally—for example, by the indication "two thirds" [of the section] and "one third," or "two players" and "the rest," or "two stands," and so on.

The leader of the section or the conductor usually decides how divisi is to be played. For example, division in two parts might be executed with the players on the first few stands of the section playing the upper notes and the remaining players the lower notes, rather than the traditional inside–outside method. The orchestrator can indicate any disposition of the parts he or she likes, such as "divide by player," "divide by stand," or "second and third stand."

Dividing a section with the divisions alternately playing the same thing is one means of avoiding monotony and fatigue on the part of individual players.

Example 2-34

Example 2-34 shows how a repeated figure can be shared in this way. Similarly, very long tones or tones too long to be played at a given dynamic level on one bow can be rendered with overlapping bow changes. For this, divisi notation is not needed: The direction "free bowing" or "change bow" will suffice.

Divisi bowing can also solve problems of phrasing. For example, if one wants the whole line in Example 2-35 to be phrased as one, notation 1 can be used with overlapping slurs, as shown. Problems with fast changes between arco and pizzicato or between muted and nonmuted, and so on, can be avoided by giving divided groups rests at different times, allowing one group to make the change while the other is playing.

Example 2-35

One should be aware that *the use of divisi reduces the strength of the part in proportion to the number of divided parts.* Thus, for example, if there are just three melodic lines of equal importance in the music and one is given to a full section of strings and the other two are given to two divisions of another section, the one given to the full section will undoubtedly sound stronger than the others.

This consideration bears also on the question of whether to use double or multiple stops or divisi for notes played simultaneously by one section. The decision is not always clear-cut, as Example 2-36 demonstrates. In both a and b, all the simultaneous notes can be played as double or multiple stops. If that is desired, the recommended notation for the pertinent notes is shown in c. (For a series of double or multiple stops, the indication "non div." is more efficient.) If divisi is preferred, one of the methods listed earlier can be used.

Example 2-36

The differences between divisi and non divisi are as follows:

1. Divisi reduces the strength of the individual notes, whereas non divisi does not.
2. In many cases, divisi promotes a smoother rendering of the divided parts in both line and tone quality.
3. With divisi, the individual parts tend to be more secure and in tune.
4. Non divisi multiple stops tend to be accented.

Thus, in Example 2-36a, the chord would provide more power if played non divisi than if played divisi. Divisi would cause each note in the chord to be the weakest notes in the passage, but the chord would probably be more legato in character, with better melodic connection between tones. In Example 2-36b, divisi would balance the parts well and bring out their independence, whereas played as a succession of double stops, the passage would be stronger but perhaps less clear in quality and intonation. A compromise between the two methods, often employed, is to divide the section and ask only one of the divisions to play double or multiple stops.

Soloists may be drawn from string sections. They are usually the first player(s) of the section but can be other players so designated (for example, "the last player"). Although one player is not as strong as a whole section, he or she is somewhat stronger than a small fraction of the section: The difference between a solo and the whole section is more importantly one of *volume*—the solo player sounds thinner and smaller but at the same time more expressive than a section; therefore, solo passages offer interesting contrasts to section passages.

Many examples of string solos are found in the works of Wagner, Strauss, Mahler, and Schoenberg. They are often combined with section parts. At times, the string family is reduced to a group of soloists, such as a string quartet. In that case, ensemble can be a problem, because the players are more distant from each other than from their section colleagues. If possible, it is best to call for soloists who sit close to each other, such as four first violinists instead of two violinists and two violists, assuming that range is not a problem.

Solo parts must be marked "solo," "two solos," and so on, as needed, and when the solo players are to return to playing with the section, the part must be marked "tutti." If the rest of the section plays with the soloist(s), the part they play should be marked "the others" or "the rest." See Example 2-37. Solo parts are often written on a separate staff.

The string family as a whole can serve many functions, as you will see in Chapters 7 and 8. As other families are studied, it would be well for you to form an impression of how comparable members of the families relate: For example, how does the range of the flute compare with that of the violin, and what are their respective strengths and limitations?

Example 2-37

Example 2-38 gives an overview of all harmonics available from the string family as a whole. This assumes normal tuning. With scordatura, others are possible.

Example 2-38a   Natural harmonics (first four)

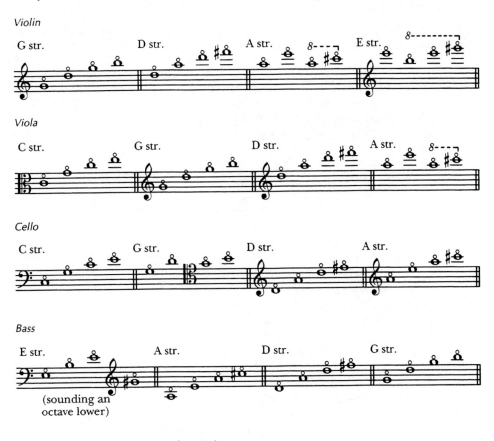

Example 2-38b.   Composite (sounding pitch)

Example 2-38c.   Range of artificial harmonics (sounding)—perfect fourth only

The ranges of the viola and the violin can be extended downward by a perfect fourth if the interval between the fingers is a perfect fifth.

Example 2-38d.   Composite

EXCERPTS FOR LISTENING AND STUDY

Strings alone

Mendelssohn, Symphonies for Strings
Tchaikovsky, Serenade for Strings
Dvořák, Serenade for Strings
Elgar, Serenade for Strings
Mahler, Symphony No. 5, Adagietto
Britten, Variations on a Theme by Frank Bridge
Penderecki, *Threnody to the Victims of Hiroshima*

Strings in the orchestra

Rimsky-Korsakov, *Scheherazade*, mvt. 2, mvt. 3
Mahler, Symphony No. 2, mvt. 2, mvt. 3; Symphony No. 4, mvt. 2, mvt. 3
Stravinsky, *The Firebird* Suite, mvt. 1 (glissandos over natural harmonics)
Shostakovich, Symphony No. 5, mvt. 1, mvt. 3
Prokofiev, *Peter and the Wolf* (various bowing and pizzicato effects)
Tchaikovsky, Symphony No. 4, mvt. 3 (pizzicato)

Violas

Tchaikovsky, Symphony No. 6, mvt. 1 (no. 8)
Shostakovich, Symphony No. 5, mvt. 1 (no. 15)
Elgar, *"Enigma" Variations* (no. 19, solo; and no. 39)
Strauss, *Don Quixote* (solo)

Cellos

Brahms, Symphony No. 2, mvt. 2
Dvořák, Symphony No. 9, mvt. 4 (eighteen measures after no. 9)

Rossini, *William Tell* Overture, beginning (solos)
Saint-Saëns, *Carnival of the Animals*, mvt. 13 (solo)

Basses

Saint-Saëns, *Carnival of the Animals*, mvt. 5
Mahler, Symphony No. 1, mvt. 3 (solo)
Prokofiev, *Lieutenant Kije*, mvt. 2 (solo)

Violin solos

Rimsky-Korsakov, *Scheherazade*, every movement; *Capriccio espagnole,* mvt. 3, mvt. 4, mvt. 5
Shostakovich, Symphony No. 5, mvt 2 (no. 57)
Strauss, *Ein Heldenleben* (no. 22)

Studies

Orchestral Studies, International Music Co.

CHAPTER 3

The Woodwinds

The term *woodwinds* is no longer literally descriptive of all the instruments in this family. The flute, originally made of wood, is now often made of some kind of metal, and the body of the saxophone is actually made of brass.

The basic members of the woodwind family are the flute, the oboe, the clarinet, and the bassoon. Other woodwind instruments can be considered smaller or larger forms of one of these. The saxophones will be discussed separately.

ACOUSTICAL CONSIDERATIONS

Just as the basic vibrating medium of a stringed instrument is a string that is stretched between two boundary points, that of a woodwind instrument is the air within the tube, stretching from the blowing end to an opening at the other end. The partly confined air is at a different pressure from the air outside the tube; thus, some of the energy that is imparted by the blowing bounces off the ambient air at the open end and is reflected back toward its source.

The sound wave is initiated either by directing the breath against an edge, as in the case of the flute, or by blowing against one or two reeds, as in the case of the other instruments. Blowing against an edge creates small eddies, or whirls, of air, and blowing around a reed or reeds causes the reed(s) to move sideways, also creating turbulence. In all cases, the air in the tube is disturbed much like the water in a still pond when a stone is dropped into it, except that in a tube, the energy wave is directed down a narrow channel rather than spreading in all directions, as in a pond.

The pitch produced depends most of all on the distance the wave travels before it is reflected and the speed at which it moves. The latter is a function of the temperature of the air—the warmer the air, the faster the wave will move. The rate of vibration directly affects pitch—the faster the vibration, the higher the pitch. Thus, *shorter wavelengths and higher temperatures produce higher pitches.* One practical result of this is that an instrument will play sharper when it is warmer.

The production of pitch, however, is not as simple as it may seem. The conditions of the blowing have important consequences for the pitch that is produced. The dimensions and structure of the tube predispose it to "want to vibrate" at some rates more than at others; these are called the "resonances" of the tube. If the vibrations of the blowing do not correspond in some way to those resonances, a clear pitch will not result—the two have to be "in harmony." The critical factors in the blowing are the speed, direction, and force of the air current, the distance to the edge (in the flute), and the vibrating characteristics of the reeds (that is, *their* resonances). An important influence on these factors is the *embouchure*—the control of the lips.

The shape and dimensions of the tube influence resonances—in particular, whether the tube is *cylindrical* (the diameter is the same throughout its length) or *conical* (the diameter increases toward the open end), the general ratio between the diameter and the tube length (the bore size), and whether the ends of the tube are closed (stopped) or open.

By and large, the flute and the clarinet are cylindrical tubes, and the oboe and the bassoon are conical. All but the clarinet act, in effect, as if they are open at both ends. The pitch of the lowest note of open conical tubes is determined by twice the length of the tube, whereas the pitch of the lowest note of a cylindrical pipe that is closed at one end, such as the clarinet, is determined by four times the length of the tube. This makes the lowest note of the clarinet much lower than that of the flute, even though the two instruments have the same tube length.

Quality

The double reeds of the oboe, the English horn, and the bassoon, and the conical shapes of the instruments, contribute to the relatively brilliant and nasal character of those instruments, setting them apart from the flutes and the clarinets in tone quality and articulation. (In Chapter 7, the double-reed instruments will be referred to as the "sharp" instruments, and the flutes and the clarinets as the "soft" instruments.) Generally speaking, in their usual playing registers, the double reeds have a more focused, penetrating sound than the flutes and the clarinets, whereas the flutes and the clarinets are less projecting and more blending. The clarinet's tone quality and fingering are affected by the fact that its tube acts as a pipe closed at one end—its sound spectrum emphasizes different harmonics from the ones in the other instruments, specifically, the odd-numbered harmonics, whereas the double reeds, especially, have strong even- *and* odd-numbered harmonics.[1]

Pitch Production

Tone-holes are drilled into the walls of the instruments to create various *effective* lengths of tube. They can be closed or opened by means of key pads directly or

---

[1] *Harmonics* and *overtones* are two names for the same thing but have different numbers—the first overtone is the second harmonic, and so on. See Chapter 2.

indirectly operated by the player's fingers. If all holes are closed, the lowest tone is produced, since the wavelength is its maximum length—that of the whole tube. As holes are opened, beginning at the lower end of the tube, the wavelength is shortened and the pitch is raised.

Fingering.   Fingering in woodwinds requires the use of both hands (not just the left hand, as in the strings). The bassoon uses all fingers of both hands, including the thumbs, and the other woodwinds use all but the right-hand thumb, which is used to hold the instrument. The fingering system of each instrument is based on the major scale spanning one octave—the flute and the oboe on the D major scale beginning on d^1, and the clarinet and the bassoon on the G major scale, beginning on g and G, respectively. (This will become clearer with an examination of the fingering charts in Appendix B.)

In all but the clarinet, these basic tones can be played an octave higher with the same basic fingering by a change in embouchure, called "overblowing," or by the aid of a vent hole, a register key, or a speaker key. These keys or holes open a small hole in the tube where the sound wave has a node. (A node is a point of minimum vibration, or air pressure: Since the air is traveling in two directions at once—the blown air moving opposite the reflected air—the interaction of the two streams creates a pattern of air pressure that does not change while a given tone is being sounded. This is called a "standing wave," whose pattern consists of gradations of pressure from maximum to minimum.) The open vent hole makes the tube more likely to vibrate two, three, or four times as fast as it would otherwise—in other words, to vibrate as a string does (in sections) when harmonics are being played, at higher pitches.

When the lowest tone of a woodwind instrument is played, all holes are closed and the sound energy that escapes the tube does so through the open end. As holes are opened for higher tones, the sound energy is radiated mostly through these holes, which face in the same direction as does the player; thus, when the player faces the audience, most of the energy for most notes is directed that way. But higher notes are radiated differently. For the oboe and the clarinet, they are directed somewhat downward, for the flute off to the right, and for the bassoon upward. (These differences relate to how the instruments are held: The open end of the oboe and the clarinet aim downward, that of the flute to stage left, and that of the bassoon upward.)

One way of producing tones other than those in the scales of D and G major is by "fork-fingering"—closing one or more (usually one) holes between open holes. Another is by using holes that have been added to the original ones. A third is by "half-holing"—allowing a hole to be partly opened. These various devices are often combined in an attempt to achieve either the most convenient sequence of fingering, the desired pitch, or the desired quality of tone. At times, one consideration is sacrificed for the sake of another. Because of the variables of the player's technique, the construction of the instrument, and the characteristics of any reeds that may be used, fingering preferences can vary among individual players.

Looked at from the positive side, the availability of several different fingerings for a note allows the player to select the one that best fits a given musical situation—that is, the choice can be a musical, as well as a technical, one. Appendix B gives basic fingering charts for flute, oboe, clarinet, bassoon, and saxophone, but does not include the many alternative fingerings.

Registers

The term *register* can refer to some general part of an instrument's range, such as "the high register." In the case of woodwinds, a register can also be determined by the way the notes in it are fingered and how the embouchure is set. Thus, the lowest register consists of notes that are not overblown; the next register consists of notes played with the same fingering plus a speaker key, and the notes are overblown to sound an octave higher (in all but the clarinet); and so forth for higher registers. Register is a vital consideration in performance because moving from register to register can involve embouchure changes, changes in tone quality, and changes in tonal strength. These factors interact; for example, the tighter embouchure and increased wind flow needed for overblowing may contribute to an undesired quality or an undesired loudness in higher notes. Generally, wind instruments sound most "normal" in their middle register. Except on the clarinet, it is in this register that the player is most comfortable, having greater security in the control of intonation, dynamics, and fingering. *At the greatest extremes of the range, most instruments are more limited in those things, and should be handled with care.* The highest notes are generally the most difficult to produce and the most tiring to sustain. The lowest notes require the most breath and are the most difficult to articulate well and fast.

Each of the woodwinds has not only a distinctive set of timbres but also a distinctive set of attack and release characteristics. Characteristically, the tone begins with a slightly explosive "puh" that we are so used to hearing that we rarely are aware of it. The higher the notes are in the range of the instrument, the more pronounced this attack will be. Since there must be a certain level of intensity of blowing to maintain a tone, it is very difficult to end a tone by fading away gradually to silence—the tone tends to be lost below a certain level The clarinet is the least affected by these problems.

Another problem is the crossing of registers, meaning the switching from nonoverblowing to overblowing, or from one mode of overblowing to another. Just as an unintended (or intended) portamento can occur when a string player changes position during a slur, a blurring of the tone can occur when a woodwind player slurs across a register boundary. This blurring can take the form of an unsteadiness of pitch or quality that is so fleeting that it may not be noticed. Such "impurities" are accepted as part of the sound of the instrument; still, it is well for the orchestrator to be aware of them, since they could become a problem if they are emphasized (for example, by being repeated) or if they occur at a particularly important point in a solo melody. A good example occurs at numbers 110 and 112 in Stravinsky's *Orpheus*, where the oboe is asked to slur from $c\sharp^3$ to b^2 several times. See Example 3-1. (Apparently, the composer was aware of the effect and wanted it.) On the other hand, when the player slurs *upward* while moving to a higher register *without changing fingers*, the connection can be extremely smooth: There is hardly anything more legato than an oboe slurring an octave upward by this means.

Example 3-1   Stravinsky, *Orpheus*, no. 110

It is a little harder to slur large leaps (a fifth or more) downward over register boundaries than upward. The reason for this is that the embouchure can be tightened (for a higher register) more accurately than it can be relaxed (for a lower one). Slurring up to a high note can present problems.

For all instruments, as the tone becomes louder, it also becomes brighter, and, conversely, as it becomes softer, it darkens. Register affects loudness differently for two groups of the woodwinds: The double reeds are strongest in their lowest register and generally become weaker as pitch rises. The flute and the clarinet, on the other hand, are strongest in their highest register. The clarinet is weakest in its middle register, and the flute is weakest in its lowest. *Register is one of the most important aspects of writing for woodwinds.*

Articulation

As mentioned earlier, each instrument has its own distinctive way of beginning a tone. In order of clarity or sharpness of attack, the instruments might be ranked as follows: the oboe (the clearest or most articulate), the bassoon, the flute, and the clarinet. In all wind instruments, clarity of attack can be associated with brilliance or projecting character of tone: With allowances for variations from register to register, the instruments follow the same order in the ranking of brilliance.

Articulation is accomplished mostly with interruption or modification of the airstream by the tongue. A great variety of attacks is possible for all the instruments, and it is difficult to notate precisely each variation. The two extremes of articulation are legato (which is indicated by a slur and executed with no tonguing after the first note) and a very dry staccato (indicated by short notes with dots over them). Between these extremes, the degree of tonguing (how hard or soft it is) can be indicated in one of two general ways: with a slur or without a slur. A slur requires an airstream that is not completely interrupted, whereas no slur requires an interruption of the air between tones. Within these intermediate groups, variations can be indicated by lines (least articulated), lines with dots, or dots (legato tonguing) over the notes. Notes with no slur or other mark over them are articulated "normally," a little more than notes under a slur. From here to most staccato, the order is lines (implying some stress and perhaps also some length), lines with dots, and finally dots. Example 7-41 illustrates a moderate, soft style of tonguing. If the orchestrator is particularly concerned with how a passage is articulated, it is advisable to add some descriptive word such as *leggiero, pesante,* or *legato.* A good musician will probably respond better to these than to the traditional signs alone, since the latter have been used very differently by composers.

The last note under a slur is usually a little clipped so that the next note or group can be articulated. Articulation of slurred notes is somewhat different for winds and strings: Winds tend to attack the first note and clip the last note more than strings do.

Agility

All the instruments are quite agile. As in other families of the orchestra, the smaller instruments speak more readily than the larger ones do. In a rough order of agility, the flute is probably first, followed by the clarinet, the oboe, and the bassoon. (As with all such comparisons, "the flute" includes the piccolo and the larger flutes; "the oboe" includes the English horn; and so forth.) Since more breath is required for lower notes, instruments are not as agile in the lowest registers as in the higher ones, especially when it comes to articulated passages.

Fast staccato notes can be accomplished by "single-tonguing" (single strokes of the tongue), "double-tonguing," or "triple-tonguing." Players think of these techniques in terms of syllables such as *du, tu,* or *ku* (the last of these is an interruption of the air by the throat, not the tongue). Double- and triple-tonguing involve alternations of tongue and throat "syllables." Because of this alternation, some precision and control may be lost, in comparison with the more controllable single-tonguing. Fast tonguing is easier on the flute and the clarinet than on the oboe and the bassoon. For the double reeds, single-tonguing is preferred, although some bassoonists have developed an effective double-tonguing technique.

The decision as to which type of tonguing is to be used is better left to the player, but if desired, double- and triple-tonguing can be indicated by and , respectively, or by specifying the syllables just mentioned.

A special tonguing effect is "flutter-tonguing." This is done by fluttering the tongue against the tube opening or the reed(s), or by making the throat vibrate, like gargling. It resembles string tremolo somewhat but is much rougher-sounding. It has the effect of sustaining the tone, but with the activity and energy provided by the rapid repetitions. Pitch movement is possible, but the effect is best confined to middle registers. The flute is the most adept at this technique. In other instruments, the ability to flutter-tongue varies from player to player, and it would be well to check with the intended player, if possible.

Example 7-60 shows two flutes flutter-tonguing a half step apart. This has the effect of a half-step trill, because the interval creates a rapid pulsation (beats), which is added to the pulsation of the flutter-tongue. It reinforces the actual trill played by the clarinets on the same notes. (Bartók did a similar thing in the first movement of his Second Violin Concerto at m. 114, where two trombones, sustaining the notes F and G-flat, imitate the three half-step trills on higher F's heard just before on other instruments—the clash of these low, intense notes sets up an almost violent pulsation, making it sound as if a single trombone is trilling!) The notation used for flutter-tonguing is the same as for bowed tremolo. Often, the word *flutter-tongue* or an abbreviation is added.

Vibrato

All the instruments but the clarinet ordinarily play with vibrato. This is produced by some means of regularly varying the air flow. It tends to be most noticeable in low registers, especially in the flute, and least of all in the bassoon. In upper registers, it becomes faster and more intense. American clarinetists, at least in "classical music," do not ordinarily use much vibrato. David Pino speculates that since the clarinet tone has a "sparse harmonic series," any change in intensity (and vibrato involves fluctuations of both pitch and intensity) would be noticeable and would blur the normal tone.[2] Although we are used to the relative lack of vibrato in the clarinet, it is a factor to be remembered when a group of woodwinds are to sustain—especially if flutes are low (emphasizing the contrast in tone) or when the clarinet plays in unison with another woodwind. Woodwind players do learn to adjust in such circumstances.

On the other hand, many clarinetists use a moderate amount of vibrato in solo lines. Even without it, clarinet tone need not be bland—sustained tones are played by good clarinetists with discreet variations in color and pitch that give them a subtle and unique beauty. The smoothness of the clarinet tone blends admirably with most other instruments when it is not in its highest register.

Glissando

The somewhat limited ability of woodwinds to make glissandos is related to vibrato technique. By variations in embouchure or by manipulating the instrument (in and out of the mouth), a gliss of up to a major second is possible, and by fingering a chromatic or even a diatonic scale while making such movements, the player can approximate a longer gliss. This is more easily done upward than downward.

[2]David Pino, *The Clarinet and Clarinet Playing* (New York: Scribner's, 1980), p. 112.

Harmonics

Harmonics on woodwinds resemble string harmonics in that they produce a paler version of notes that are produced "normally," but they are less, rather than more, resonant. They are played by unusual fingerings—generally involving forking and overblowing, without the use of vent holes (or, in the case of the oboe, by using a vent hole that is different from the usual one). Since they must be overblown, they lie in upper registers: on the flute, from g^2 up, and on the oboe from about f^2 up. It is mostly on those instruments, particularly the flute, that they are called for. They tend to be flat in pitch. (Harmonics are sometimes used in normal playing for a better fingering or intonation.)

Muting

A woodwind instrument can be muted by placing a cloth in the open end. Only the lowest tones radiate energy through that end; therefore, the effect is limited to them (see the discussion of muting in the oboe). The flute is never muted, and the bassoon is rarely muted.

Doubling

One or more woodwind players may be asked to alternate, or "double," on two or more instruments. Usually, the "last" player does this—for example, the third flutist, if there are three flutes. The third flutist may be asked to double on the piccolo or the alto flute as needed during a composition. The second oboist may double on the English horn, the oboe d'amore, or the Heckelphone; the second clarinetist on the piccolo or the bass clarinet; and the second bassoonist on the contrabassoon.

Since an instrument being played is warmer than one that is not, it is well to leave time for the player to warm up the second instrument by breathing into it before its entrance. It is then advisable, if possible, to bring in the new instrument on a part that is not exposed—an inner part of a chord or an accompaniment. In both the score and the part, the indication to change instruments should come immediately after the first instrument stops playing. Usually, "take piccolo" or "change to piccolo" is used. The name of the new instrument should also appear where it begins to play.

Notating More than One Part on a Staff

In the wind families, one player is assigned to a part. If two instruments are written on one staff—for example, two clarinets—and only the first player is supposed to play, the part should be marked "1." ("first"; see Example 3-2a), or, for the second player alone, "2." (The word *solo* should be restricted to passages that are especially prominent. It does not substitute for "1." or "2.") Another way of notating the same thing is shown in Example 3-2b. The upward stems and the rests below show the first clarinet and the second clarinet parts, respectively, and labels are unnecessary. If the two players are to play the same part, either "a 2" (in Italian, *a due*, "with two") should be used, as in Example 3-2c, or stems should go in *both* directions, as in Example 3-2d, in which case, "a 2" is not used.

Example 3-2

2 Cl. Bb

As with string divisi, the choice of notational style is best suited to the context: If either a single player or unison playing is used for several measures at a time, the "1." and "a 2" forms, respectively, are practical. If, on the other hand, there are fairly frequent changes between one and two players or *between* the players, the double-stem format is more efficient. *If the double-stem format is not used, remember that every change requires a label.* It is not appropriate to use "div." or "unis." in orchestral wind parts (and, unless only two players are desired, "a 2" is not appropriate for string parts).

Of course, if the parts would interfere with each other on one staff, it is better to put them on separate staves. Several parts can be placed on one staff as long as there is no problem in distinguishing among them, as in Example 3-3.

Example 3-3

5 Fls.

Another element of notation is ledger lines. Woodwind players associate lines and spaces very closely with fingering, and most of them seem to prefer to read ledger lines for very high or very low notes, as opposed to octave signs (*8va*, and so on). (On the other hand, octave signs are often welcome in string parts using the treble clef.) They can be used in the *score* to save space but should never be used to indicate *lower* octaves (for any instrument other than the piano or the harp), unless there is a space problem.

THE FLUTE

The flute (called *grande flûte* in French and *flute in C* in English to distinguish it from the other flutes) has a practical range of about three octaves (see Example 3-4). (Woodwind ranges for elementary, high school, and professional players are given in Appendix E.) The instrument is made in three sections: the head joint (the blowing end), the body joint, and the foot joint (the open end). A bb or even

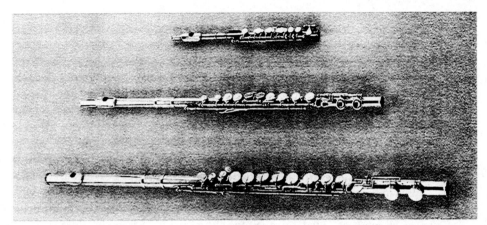

Ed Brown Studio

FLUTES
Piccolo
Flute (in C)
Alto (in G)

a *bb* can be played if the instrument has a longer-than-normal foot joint. The longer foot joint darkens the tone of the instrument slightly, but it also makes the fingering of higher notes a little easier. (Not all flutes have the longer foot joint.) The notes above b^3 are the most difficult to produce and control. Beethoven and Mendelssohn kept their flute parts from going beyond a^3, but Berlioz called for a c^4 at least once (the French were, and may still be, superior woodwind players). Most works avoided going above b^3 until late in the nineteenth century.

Example 3-4 Range of the flute

As has been mentioned, the lowest register is the weakest from the standpoint of projection. The flute's second octave (c^2–c^3) is brighter and stronger, and the strongest part of its range lies above c^3. The low register has been used for its breathy, exotic character and its unobtrusive presence as a filler between or below more important parts (see Example 3-5). In this register, it can also take on a vaguely trumpetlike quality, as in Example 8-14b, where it plays an accompanying rhythm that is later given to the trumpet (Example 8-14c). Notice that the composer gave the lower part to the first player, perhaps because he considered it more difficult. The difference in register of the two flutes almost causes them to sound like different instruments.

Example 3-5   Franck, Symphony in D Minor, mvt. 1, m. 167

Most leading lines in the flute are written in the area of about c^2–g^3. Example 7-48 shows off the brilliance of the upper part of this area. The leaps to higher notes and the accents contribute to the sparkle of this passage, which is not interfered with by the accompanying, softer-sounding clarinets and horns that are lower in pitch and dynamics. Note that in m. 11, when the flute drops to a relatively weak d^1 for its sixteenth-note figure, it is reinforced by the second flute, two bassoons, and the harp.

If a leading line is written below c^2 or so, it is especially important to keep the accompaniment light and below the flute line.

Many authors point out that the dynamic range of the flute is relatively small. The careful orchestrator will, therefore, pay close attention to breathing (as for all wind instruments). The flute requires much breath, particularly in the extreme registers and for loud playing; thus, long, uninterrupted, high passages are not kind to the player. A soft note in the middle register can be held for about a minute but without a tone of much substance: The minimum for the sustaining of a more substantial tone is about 30 seconds. At *ff*, it is more like 10 seconds. If a leading line is in a middle register and at a medium loudness, a phrase lasting 10–20 seconds can be comfortably played in one breath, as in the beginning of Debussy's *Prelude to The Afternoon of a Faun*. See Example 3-6.

Example 3-6   Debussy, *Prelude to The Afternoon of a Faun*, opening

For the sake of security, very high notes should be approached by notes just below them to prepare the embouchure (composers are not always careful to do this). Upward scale lines and arpeggios are typical approaches. Soft notes are almost impossible above b^3, but one still finds many composers who ask for *piano*s and *pianissimo*s in that region.

Double-tonguing is needed if tongued notes are faster than about four to a beat at quarter note = 168. Fast tonguing is fatiguing. Fast or frequent changes in register and dynamics can also be tiring. Although Stravinsky is famous for brilliant woodwind writing, most of his very fast and high passages are brief ones, and they are often shared by other instruments, as in the early movements of his *Firebird* and *Rite of Spring.*

Fingering

When the lowest note is played, all the fingers are down. Generally speaking, as the chromatic scale is played from c^1 (or b) through $c\#^2$, the fingers are lifted one by one. The process is then repeated for d^2 to c^2. From this point, the sequence again repeats but in a much less straightforward manner. The most striking thing about the fingering is that between $c\#^1$ and d^2 and between $c\#^2$ and d^3, there are sudden changes from many to few fingers when ascending scalewise, and the opposite when descending (see Appendix B). These sudden changes make for relatively difficult or awkward fingering progressions. They are precisely the register breaks that were referred to earlier as being potentially troublesome. In addition, there are awkward finger changes within the third octave. Up to $c\#^2$, notes an octave apart can be fingered almost the same; thus, octave leaps are easily managed. It follows that if intervals lying *across* the break are *not greatly different from an octave* (sixths, sevenths, ninths, and tenths), they will require only few movements of fingers and thus also be relatively easy. The same is true for intervals no larger than a fourth or so when a break is *not* crossed (that is, *within* a register). These facts have implications for fast alternations of notes, as in tremolos, and suggest that such passages involving larger intervals, or crossing breaks, can present problems. (One conductor has remarked that $c\#^2$ is difficult to get in tune for the woodwinds in general.)

In general, the more sharps or flats there are in a passage, the more difficult is the fingering.

Until recently, orchestration books gave sometimes extensive lists of trills that are either unplayable or ineffective on the flute. With the addition of trill keys and special fingerings, many problems with trills have been solved, and now only the trills in Example 3-7 are generally considered impossible or impractical. (Berg calls for the third of these in *Wozzeck.*) Very high trills are difficult.

The trill problems mostly involve the keys that were added for notes below the original d^1. They are played by the weak fourth finger: In the worst cases, the trill can be played only by moving that finger from one key to another. For that reason, a tremolo between c^1 and eb^1 is not possible. Elsewhere, tremolos should be no larger than a fifth in the lowest octave and a third in higher registers.

Example 3-7

THE PICCOLO

The full name of this instrument is *flauto piccolo* (Ital., "small flute"). Its written range is very close to that of the C flute (see Example 3-8), and it is ordinarily written an octave *lower* than it sounds. Its basic D major scale was not extended downward below written d^1, as on the flute, probably because the low register of the piccolo is not considered its most desirable feature, and because the notes below d^2 (the lowest *sounding* note) can easily be taken by the flute. Piccolos, like flutes, are made in both wood and silver. Professionals tend to prefer the wooden type for its greater warmth. It is conical in shape, whereas the silver piccolo is made in both conical and cylindrical versions.

Example 3-8   Range of the piccolo
(sounds one octave higher)

Several authors have remarked that the sound of the piccolo is cold and life-less (a few have said this about the flute as well). Having heard some fine players on the instrument, this author cannot agree. Several passages can be found that suggest that the composer expected a warm sound from the piccolo. Listen, for example, to the piccolo solos in Examples 3-9 and 3-10. The marking "tres doux" ("very sweet") is indicative of the desired character.

Example 3-9   Debussy, *La Mer*, mvt. 1, two before no. 26

Example 3-10   Debussy, *La Mer*, mvt. 2, m. 140

Orchestration texts often discount the registers of "nonstandard" wood-winds whose notes are weaker or less projecting than the same notes in the cor-responding "standard" instruments—that is, the lowest registers of the piccolo (flute) and the piccolo clarinets, and the highest registers of the alto flute, the English horn, the bass clarinet, and the contrabassoon. Nevertheless, there are

many examples of these registers used very effectively. A composer or an orchestrator would be unduly restricted not to look on *all* instrumental sounds as legit-
imate and potentially useful elements of music (this is a major point to be
elaborated in Chapter 8). The sound of each instrument is unique and can have
its own type of warmth—the warmth of a wind instrument, for example, is quite
different from that of a stringed instrument. By the same token, any instrument
can be *made* to sound cold.

The extreme registers of the piccolo are like those of the flute, only more
so—the highest notes are very strong and penetrating, and the lowest ones thin
and weak (some writers say "hollow"). Very fast passages are clear and brilliant.
Trills are not the problem they are on the flute, because there are no "added" keys.

The piccolo is seen in a typical role in Example 7-52, where it joins the flutes
as they reach the top of their range, extending the line upward. In Example 7-60,
the piccolo ("ott."—"ottavino") is added to make a brilliant highlight of the trills
in the other woodwinds.

THE ALTO FLUTE IN G

The alto flute in G is larger than the C flute. It has the same *written* range but must
be written a perfect fourth higher than it sounds. It is not as powerful or as brilliant as the C flute in upper registers. Its most-used register is the lowest one,
which is dark and rich but not strong. Much breath is needed, both for short passages and over a longer stretch of time, and articulation is slower than on the C
flute. Example 7-47 illustrates the use of the low notes ("fl. in sol"). In Example
7-52, the alto supplements the other flutes (much as the English horn, the piccolo
clarinet, and the bass clarinet supplement their related instruments).

THE OBOE

The oboe's practical playing range is shown in Example 3-11. Like the flute, it is
made in three sections. Whereas the flutist blows against the edge of the blowing
hole, the oboist holds a folded-over reed between the lips and forces air between
the two pieces, causing them to vibrate against each other.

The lowest few notes are the strongest on the instrument, but it is difficult to
control their loudness, response, and quality. One should be hesitant to call for
delicate articulation or soft playing here. On *bb*, it is difficult to match the quality
of the upper notes (which, however, is not to say that it has no musical quality

Example 3-11 Range of the oboe

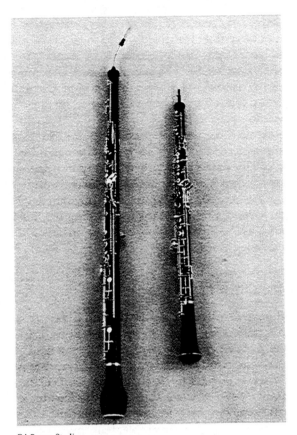

Ed Brown Studio

OBOE AND ENGLISH HORN
English Horn   Oboe

whatsoever).[3] The middle register projects well but is weaker. The notes from about f^1 to c^3 are probably the most used. Above c^3, they become increasingly thinner and difficult to produce but still have projecting power.

The upper notes can have a plaintive quality—many writers refer to the oboe's sound in general as somewhat melancholy. This may be simply because the oboe so often is assigned slow, lyrical melodies. The upper tones are more secure if approached stepwise than by leap. Before Wagner, the upper limit was about e^3, but Ravel, for example, calls for a^3 in his *Rapsodie espagnole*. Good examples of the "singing register" can be seen in Examples 7-28 and 7-49. In Example 7-25, the sound becomes noticeably thinner as the part ascends above the staff, which may be why the flute is called on to double it.

---

[3]The earlier oboe did not have the problem of playing softly on low notes, because it had a larger bore and a resulting darker sound. This older instrument is still in use in Europe.

Oboe reeds are lighter now than they were in the past and have a correspondingly lighter, smoother sound. Since the choice and preparation of the reed
(cutting, shaping, and soaking) is the responsibility of the player, there can be
variations in sound or response from player to player and even from moment to
moment with the same player.

Tone production involves a slow but intense airstream through the small air-
space between the reeds, which is both tiring for the embouchure and taxing on
the lungs. For those reasons, oboe parts should have even more rests than other
woodwind parts. On the other hand, long breaths can be more readily managed
than on other instruments.

Articulation is incisive, and soft tonguing is not as idiomatic as it is for the
flute or the clarinet. (That may be why Brahms left the oboes out of the soft, pulsating offbeats in Example 7-33). Single-tonguing can go as fast as about four notes
per beat at quarter = 120, but not for long. The interspersion of some slurred
notes is very helpful in avoiding fatigue at fast tempos, as in Example 3-12. (See
Chapter 7, under "Weber and Mendelssohn," for discussion of the oboe in fast
repeated-note passages.)

Example 3-12

Double- and triple-tonguing are not as effective as on other instruments, nor
is flutter-tonguing. (In Variation II of *Don Quixote*, which imitates the bleating of
sheep, Strauss used flutter-tonguing in the brass, the clarinet, and the bass clarinet, but not the oboes. The oboes are used instead to play low notes a half step
apart, which, with the pungency of the low register, achieves somewhat the same
effect. Schoenberg, on the other hand, called for flutter-tonguing in both the
oboe and the bassoon in his Five Pieces for Orchestra.)

Fingering

The fingering system for the oboe is similar to that for the flute. Register changes
occur at c^2 and around c^3, and some of the guidelines for fingering given for the
flute hold, although there are many alternative possibilities for individual notes.
Legato passages are a little more articulate than on other instruments, and slurs
over register breaks can be noticeable (see the reference to Stravinsky's *Orpheus* on
page 44). The most troublesome trill is between $b\natural$ and bb, for which the fourth
finger of the left hand must slide back and forth between adjacent keys. Tremolos
are best limited to a fourth in lower registers and are not effective above the staff.
As with the flute, a high density of sharps, flats, or both makes a passage more difficult than it would otherwise be.

In his First and Fourth Symphonies, Mahler tells the oboe and clarinet players to hold the "bells in the air" ("Schalltrichter auf")—that is, to point the open end of the instrument directly at the audience. He obviously wanted those passages to penetrate, and presumably the tendency of some of the pitches to radiate downward in the normal playing position causes them to radiate horizontally (at the audience) when the instrument is held in that direction. (This device is more often used with brass than with woodwinds, however.)

Muting of the oboe is possible, as with all woodwinds but the flute, but not with the lowest notes, $b\natural$ and bb.

THE ENGLISH HORN

The English horn resembles the oboe but is larger and differs from the oboe in its bulging, bulblike bottom joint and its bocal, or curved tube, onto which the reed is fitted. The name of the instrument does not seem indicative either of its place of origin or of its family membership. As with several instruments, the modern name is usually explained as a corruption of an obsolete name, a misunderstanding of a term, or a misspelling. There does not seem to be a definitive explanation at present.

The instrument is in F, which means that its part is written a perfect fifth higher than it sounds. The written range is close to that of the oboe, but most instruments do not have the written bb, and the uppermost register is more restricted. The usual range is from b to $c\#^3$. The lowest notes, rather than being troublesome and of doubtful quality like those of the oboe, are generally considered *characteristic*. The highest register is almost universally condemned as ineffective or useless; yet, imaginative composers, such as Ravel (for example, in the second movement of his Piano Concerto in G), have found good use for it. It should be handled carefully, since it has its difficulties.

The sound of the English horn is almost universally declared to be melancholy—again, perhaps because of its association with slow melodies. The tone is reedy, but not as dominating or as piercing as the oboe's can be. Its strength is in its lowest register, and as the pitch rises, the color changes considerably and the tone becomes thinner. One can hear this difference in the second movement of Franck's Symphony in D Minor, where the English horn plays the theme near the beginning (m. 16) and later returns to it an octave lower (m. 86).

The instrument has become increasingly popular since the end of the nineteenth century and, like the piccolo and the bass clarinet, is now practically a "standard" instrument. An extended, unaccompanied solo is found near the beginning of the first scene of the third act of Wagner's *Tristan und Isolde*. Most of the notes of this long melody are on the treble clef, a pitch area of a–bb^1 (sounding), which is a typical tessitura.

If an oboist is expected to double on the English horn, it is best to allow about ten measures for the change to be made, mostly to warm up the instrument.

THE CLARINET

Clarinets have been built in various sizes, or "keys," but since Beethoven, most orchestral scores use only the B-flat or A clarinets. There is some controversy over how much difference there is between these two instruments. Generally, the A clarinet, which plays a half step lower than the B-flat, is considered to have a slightly darker sound. Fingering is an important difference; this will be discussed a little later on.

The written range of the clarinets is shown in Example 3-13. The B-flat and A clarinets are written exclusively in the treble clef, even though the lowest tones require several ledger lines. Parts for the B-flat must be written a major second higher than sounding, and the A must be written a minor third higher.

Example 3-13   Range of the clarinets

Acoustical properties unique to the clarinet cause its range to fall into fairly distinct registers. Alone among the standard woodwinds, the clarinet acts as a stopped, cylindrical pipe. Such a sound medium emphasizes odd-numbered harmonics in its lower notes—that is, the first harmonic, which is the same as the fundamental; the third harmonic, which is a perfect twelfth above the fundamental; the fifth harmonic, which is two octaves and a major third above; and so on. Since the other standard woodwinds have strong odd- *and* even-numbered harmonics, they overblow readily at the octave (second harmonic), but the clarinet does not: It overblows at the *perfect twelfth*. Its lowest note is a written *e* (some clarinets also have an *eb*); thus, the lowest overblown note is *b¹*.

The fingering system is based on the G major scale. Just as the oboe's system adds notes lower than its basic "tonic" of D, the clarinet has "added" keys that take it down to *e*, and the basic scale of G ends with *f♯¹*. The notes bounded by *e* and *f♯¹* are referred to as the *chalumeau* register (named for a predecessor of the clarinet). This register is full and resonant, but dark and not penetrating. The notes between *f♯¹* and the first overblown tone, *b♮¹*, are called the "throat register"; they are made possible by added keys, making this the weakest, the least resonant, and the palest part of the range. To cross the break between *bb¹* and *b♮¹* presents the usual fingering problem of having to move many fingers at once. The skilled player uses fingerings that alleviate some of these problems.

Next comes the *clarion* register—*b♮¹* to *c²*—which is an overblowing of the notes *e–f♯¹*. This could also be called the "money" register, since it is here that many of the most prominent leading lines are written. The notes above this make

Ed Brown Studio

CLARINETS

E-flat Clarinet
B-flat Clarinet

| E-flat Alto Clarinet | Basset Horn | Bass Clarinet | E-flat Contra-alto Clarinet | B-flat Contra-bass Clarinet |

up the *altissimo* register, which is powerful and strident. The highest notes cannot be played quietly and are difficult to control otherwise.

There are few serious fingering problems: Fast alternations around the breaks can be difficult.

Example 7-32 shows a passage in which strength of tone is important. Either the oboe or the clarinet could be chosen to double the flutes in the highest octave, but the clarinet is chosen, probably because here (in its clarion and altissimo registers) it is stronger than the oboe. Example 7-19 shows the clarinets in the chalumeau register, playing an inner line among the low strings. In Example 7-53, this register is used to imitate the low bassoons with a somewhat eerie effect.

Example 7-28 shows that, to some extent, the clarinet and the oboe sing well in the same general area—the upper treble clef and a little above.

The clarinet is perhaps the most versatile of all the woodwinds. It offers a wide variety of colors through its various registers and its broad range of dynamic and articulation control. It can begin and end a tone almost inaudibly and swell to a *fortissimo*. In the chalumeau register, a very soft, mysterious quality, called "subtone" or "echo tone," can be produced by lightly dampening the reed with the tongue, reducing resonance. The normal, non vibrato tone can be made paler by calling for "white tone."

The clarinet rivals the flute in agility. Its glissando is the truest of the woodwinds if it begins no higher than $b\natural^1$ and moves upward. It excels in both leading lines and accompaniment figures, blending well at pitches below about b^3. Slurred arpeggios appear very often in the parts, probably because the soft texture of the tone prevents them from becoming obtrusive in accompaniments.

The best tonguing style is single-tonguing, in which a reasonable limit is about four notes per beat at quarter = 124.

For music that is tonal (in a key), the choice of which instrument to use is often based on fingering: The fewer accidentals in the key signature, the easier the fingering. To some extent, following this guideline, concert keys with flats in their key signature are more easily played on the B-flat clarinet, and concert keys with sharps are easier on the A clarinet.

To illustrate, if the concert key (that used by nontransposing instruments) is E-flat major, the B-flat clarinet will be written in F major, which has only one accidental. If the A clarinet were to be used, its key would be G-flat major (six flats) or F-sharp major (six sharps). On the other hand, a concert key of D major is easier on the A clarinet, which would be written in F major (one flat), than on the B-flat, which would be in E major (four sharps). Still, some professional clarinetists play most or all A clarinet parts on the B-flat clarinet because this avoids the problem of changing from a warm to a cold instrument during a piece (even though the same mouthpiece and reed can be used for the two instruments), and the B-flat seems to be the preferred instrument. Improved fingering systems have reduced many of the problems with accidentals, and some B-flat clarinets are equipped with a low *eb* key to produce the concert *c♯* of the A clarinet (a tone otherwise unreachable by the B-flat).

THE PICCOLO CLARINET IN E-FLAT

The piccolo clarinet in E-flat has the same written range as the B-flat and A clarinets and is notated a minor third *lower* than it sounds. Authors point out that the chalumeau register is not as rich as that of the larger instruments, and its tone has been referred to generally as hard and inelastic. It is often used in its very bright upper register, where it can reinforce higher notes in the flutes and the violins or more securely play notes that are difficult on the larger clarinets. The high notes are strong and can be shrill. Although textbook writers tend to disregard the lower notes, composers have written passages for the instrument that lie *below* the B-flat and A clarinet parts, an indication both of the desire for a special tonal combination and of some confidence in them.

For a while, the piccolo clarinet in D was considered obsolete, but it may be making a comeback. Parts for it are usually played on the E-flat instrument.

THE BASS CLARINET (IN B-FLAT)

This larger clarinet has a written range that is nearly the same as that of the other clarinets (see Example 3-14). Instruments are being made with keys that allow it to go down to a written *C*. When written in treble clef ("French notation"), its notes are a major ninth higher than they sound. In bass clef ("German notation"), the notes are written a major second higher than sounding. The French notation allows the player to associate the placement of notes on the staff with the fingering of the B-flat clarinet; thus, it is the more popular method. A bass clarinet in A is still used in Germany, but not in America.

Example 3-14 Range of the bass clarinet

(Sounding a
M9 Lower)

The instrument is noted for its dark chalumeau register, which has come to be associated with mysterious or somber moods. In *fortissimo* and in upper registers, it can sound harsh, but it can also furnish a smooth, resonant, and blending bass for the woodwinds. Most writers on orchestration disdain the highest register.

THE BASSOON

The bassoon is a double-reed instrument made in four parts: the wing, or tenor, joint; the butt, or boot, or double, joint; the long, or bass, joint; and the bell joint. The reed fits around the end of a bocal, which extends from the beginning of the

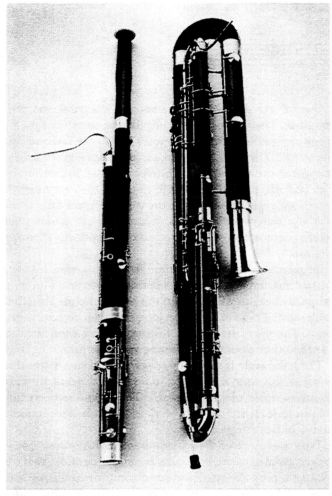

BASSOON AND CONTRABASSOON
Bassoon   Contrabassoon

tube. Since the butt joint is folded upward, the bell joint also faces upward, which tends to make the sound radiate well in that direction. The instrument is usually supported by a seat strap.

The professional range is shown in Example 3-15. The notes above a^1 are better avoided for less advanced players. Some instruments have an attachment that allows *AA* to be sounded. Otherwise, an extension in the form of a cardboard tube, or the like, can be inserted to produce that tone; this temporarily eliminates *BB♭*, however, and makes intonation somewhat insecure. Bassoonists are used to reading bass, tenor, and, occasionally, treble clef.

Example 3-15   Range of the bassoon

Overall, the sound of the bassoon is less nasal and more resonant than that of the oboe. Nasality occurs mostly in the area of *d* to *f*. As in the oboe, the strongest register is in the lowest notes (up to the bassoon's *G*), where it is difficult to play softly.[4] The most secure notes are from *F* to about *d¹*. The tone diminishes in strength more or less as the pitch rises, but the weakest tones are between *c♯* and *a¹*, and the most troublesome note on the instrument is *f♯*: It is difficult to play softly with quality. Above *d¹*, the tone becomes thin and increasingly insecure. As with the other double reeds, it can take on a somewhat plaintive sound, as Stravinsky demonstrated at three after no. 49 in *Petroushka,* where he marks "lamentoso."

In general, the bassoon's tone is not powerful. Above *g*, it blends very well with other instruments. There is a considerable variation in quality throughout the range, partly because the holes in the wing joint are drilled diagonally (for fingering purposes). These holes are so long that their resonant characteristics influence the tone. The resonances of the instrument as a whole are more pronounced than they are in other woodwinds, causing variation in quality from note to note.

The basic scale is the G major scale, an octave below that of the clarinet. The notes below this scale are "added" ones, and, as usual, they present some fingering problems (see the next paragraph). The break between fundamental tones and overblown tones is at *f–f♯*. The break at *d¹–d♯¹* is less pronounced, with fewer complications in fingering changes.

Trills are more of a problem than on the other woodwinds. Those below *E* are better avoided, although some are more playable than others. From *D♭* to *E♭*, for example, both the left-hand thumb and the left-hand fourth finger must move from key to key. Trills on notes above *a¹* are also difficult. Orchestration books do not agree on which specific trills are not playable, which is probably a reflection of differences among players consulted by the writers. Thus, the orchestrator is advised to check any desired trills, tremolos, or other intricate note patterns with an accomplished player.

The bassoon can be quite active, as long as the usual cautions are observed (avoid extensive use of extremes and prolonged tonguing or loud playing, and so on). Single-tonguing can go rather fast for short passages, and double-tonguing (for those who do it well) can go faster than four notes per beat at quarter = 126.

---

[4]This is well illustrated in m. 160 of the first movement of Tchaikovsky's Sixth Symphony. Here the composer called for a series of low notes to be played by the bassoon at the extreme marking of *ppppp.* Today this passage is usually played by the bass clarinet, which reveals an important relationship between the lowest registers of these instruments.

Large, nonslurred leaps can be accomplished readily: It is not uncommon to see leaps from notes below the bass staff to notes above it. Slurred leaps are easier ascending than they are descending, but not when they move to notes at the top of the bass staff.

Sustaining should not persist for more than about 8 seconds at a time, but it is possible to hold a tone in *piano* for about 12–30 seconds, depending upon the register.

THE CONTRABASSOON

The contrabassoon can play lower than the usual orchestral instruments—down to *BBBb* sounding. It is written an octave higher than it sounds. The usual range is shown in Example 3-16. Authors generally consider the low notes more useful than the high ones. The size of the instrument dictates careful handling, especially in the extremes. No note, phrase, or passage should be very long. (The almost continuous playing demanded of this instrument in the finale of Beethoven's Ninth Symphony has led some to suspect that the part was intended for a smaller instrument or for a different instrument, or that the player was not expected to play all the notes.) The lowest notes contain a large component of noise, the individual vibrations of the reed being noticeable. Fast passages are not effective.

Example 3-16   Range of the contrabassoon
                   (sounding one octave lower)

One writer considers the quality throughout the range to be coarse; yet, Ravel used the instrument as a lyrical soloist at the beginning of his Concerto for the Left Hand and in his *Mother Goose* Suite ("Beauty and the Beast"). Although the contra often is used to double the contrabasses at the unison, it can also effectively double them an octave lower. Brahms used it as a resonant bass for the winds (see the beginning of his *Haydn Variations* and the choralelike passage in the introduction to the fourth movement of Symphony No. 1).

LESS COMMONLY USED INSTRUMENTS

The Bass Flute

The bass flute is written an octave higher than it sounds. Sometimes confused with the alto flute, it is larger than that instrument, and major problems in playing it are breathing and endurance. It has about the same written range as the C flute. An instrument known as a Contra Bass in FF was made in England in 1922, and a contrabass was made in Italy in 1925. More recently, there exists a Contra Alto flute and a Japanese contrabass that plays an octave below the *bass* flute—it is so large that it has to stand on the floor like a contrabassoon. These unusual instruments are used in flute ensembles.

The Oboe d'Amore

The oboe d'amore was used in the Baroque period and is known mainly for its use by J. S. Bach. It has made a modest comeback in works by Strauss and others. Built in A, it is written a minor third higher than sounding, with a written range similar to that of the oboe. The lowest written note is $b\natural$. It is somewhere between the oboe and the English horn in size, range, and mobility. It has a less aggressive sound than those instruments, and it is easier to control in the lowest notes.

The Baritone Oboe

Sometimes called "the bass oboe," the baritone oboe has a written range similar to that of the oboe d'amore, and is written an octave higher than it sounds. Its quality resembles that of the Heckelphone.

The Heckelphone

The Heckelphone was invented in 1904 and soon afterward was used in operas by Strauss. It has a full, reedy sound. Written an octave higher than it sounds, its written range is similar to that of the oboe, but it can go down to *a* (sounding *A*).

The E-flat Alto Clarinet

The range of the E-flat alto clarinet is e–e^3, written a major sixth higher than it sounds. It has been described as versatile and beautiful, with a sound somewhere between that of the B-flat/A clarinets and the bass clarinet, but it is also said to lack the resonance and brilliance of the former; this impression may have come from hearing poor instruments played by nonprofessionals.

The Basset Horn (in F)

Used by Mozart in some of his works, the clarinetlike basset horn is also undergoing something of a revival. Its written range is *c* to g^3, and it is written a perfect fifth higher than it sounds. Its sound is very much like a lower B-flat clarinet but without that instrument's dark chalumeau register.

The E-flat Contralto Clarinet

This large clarinet is usually made of wood. Its written range is *e* to a^3, and it is written an octave and a major sixth higher than sounding; thus, its lowest note sounds

GG. It is easier to play than the B-flat contrabass, and it is sometimes referred to as a contrabass.

The B-flat Contrabass Clarinet

Usually made of metal, the B-flat contrabass clarinet has a written range of c to d^2, and is written in the treble clef two octaves and a major second higher than sounding; thus, its lowest sounding tone is $BBBb$, which ranks it with the contrabassoon as the lowest sounding of wind or string instruments. It has a very dark and rich sound, with clear pitch and a great dynamic range.

The Saxophones

A whole family of saxophones was invented by Adolphe Sax in the 1840s. It consists of these instruments:

Sopranino in E-flat (written a minor third *lower* than sounding)
Soprano in B-flat (written a major second higher than sounding)
Alto in E-flat (written a major sixth higher than sounding)
Tenor in B-flat (written a major ninth higher than sounding)
Baritone in E-flat (written an octave and a major sixth higher than sounding)
Bass in B-flat (written two octaves and a major second higher than sounding)

Ed Brown Studio

SAXOPHONES

B-flat Soprano   E-flat Alto   B-flat Tenor   E-flat Baritone

The written range of all the instruments is $bb-f^3$ (to $f\sharp^3$ if an extra key is provided). Some baritones have a low *a*, and some players can go higher than $f\sharp^3$. Only the treble clef is used. Since the instruments have a mouthpiece with an attached single reed like the clarinet, most saxophonists also play the clarinet. The tube of the instrument is made of brass.

The alto and tenor instruments are probably the most used in general, and in orchestral music in particular. The sopranino and bass are rare. The French occasionally used the saxophone in the orchestra in the nineteenth century. Under the influence of popular music in this country, the style of playing changed toward a freer, less controlled tone, heavy with vibrato and other inflections. In addition to the assertiveness of the sound, this seems to have kept the instrument from being used with much frequency in the orchestra. The instrument tends to be used only for special effects, especially where popular music is suggested.

The saxophone does not blend readily with other instruments in some instances. This is possibly due to the rich sound of the vibrato and the brassy edge to the tone at higher dynamic levels. If the clarinet were to be played with a similar vibrato, it also might not blend as well as it does; however, the saxophone is acoustically different from the clarinet—it acts as a stopped *conical* pipe, whereas the clarinet acts as a stopped cylindrical pipe, and the saxophone's tone emphasizes both even and odd harmonics, which allows it to overblow at the octave. Players today have learned to play in a plainer, more orchestral style, as well as in the jazz style. For more about the blending qualities of the instrument, see Chapter 9, under "Scoring Considerations."

The extremes of range must be handled carefully. As in the oboe and the bassoons, the lowest notes are difficult to play softly. The tone is in general somewhat intrusive and powerful, but it can be produced very softly in all but the extreme registers. Its "presence" allows it to be combined successfully with the brass in some contexts. It speaks readily, and low tones can be richly resonant.

The saxophone is very agile, as we know from hearing jazz artists. Single-tonguing is not as easy as on the clarinet, but double-tonguing is becoming a normal part of the technique.

Prokofiev used the saxophone in at least two works—*Lieutenant Kije* and *Alexander Nevsky*. In the latter, the tenor saxophone is used as another member of the woodwind family—in ensembles and doubling other winds. In *Lieutenant Kije*, the instrument is used more for special solos than as a regular member of the family. In Ravel's orchestration of *Pictures at an Exhibition* ("Il Vecchio Castello"), the alto is used only as a solo instrument.

FACTORS THAT MAKE WOODWIND PASSAGES RELATIVELY EASY

1. Most notes are not in extreme registers.
2. Loud playing is not prolonged.
3. Fast tonguing is not prolonged, and fast staccato passages include some slurs.

4. Complex or fast passages are in middle registers (except for the clarinet around $bb^1-b\natural^1$.

5. Dynamic changes do not come in fast succession.

6. Phrases are not excessively long (not over 20 seconds), and rests are provided between them.

7. High notes are approached stepwise.

8. Notes in extreme registers are no softer than *mf* (except for the low register of the clarinet).

9. Accidentals are few.

10. An important solo is preceded by at least one passage that is not exposed.

11. Slurred leaps ascend.

12. Fast alternations of notes do not cross register breaks.

COMPARISONS OF RANGES
WITH STRINGED INSTRUMENTS

Example 3-17 shows comparable ranges of woodwind and stringed instruments. All the notes are as they sound. This comparison reveals combinations of instruments that are likely to be made when parts are doubled between the two families.

Example 3-17   Comparison of woodwind and string ranges (sounding)

EXCERPTS FOR LISTENING AND STUDY

Woodwinds

Frank, Symphony in D Minor

Tchaikovsky, Symphony No. 4, mvt. 2, mvt. 3

Bartók, Concerto for Orchestra, mvt. 1 (nos. 155–220, 272–313, 396–476), mvt. 2, mvt. 4

Piccolo

Tchaikovsky, Symphony No. 4, mvt. 3 (m. 194)

Ravel, Piano Concerto in G, mvt. 1 (beginning); *Mother Goose* Suite, mvt. 3 (no. 1); *Daphnis et Chloé No. 2* (no. 156 and no. 182)

Debussy, *La Mer,* mvt. 1 (no. 41 to end)

Shostakovich, Symphony No. 5, mvt. 1 (no. 41–46)

Flute

Brahms, Symphony No. 4, mvt. 4 (m. 97)

Rimsky-Korsakov, *Capriccio espagnole,* mvt. 4

Ravel, *Daphnis et Chloé No. 2* (no. 176–188); *Bolero* (m. 5)

Debussy, *Prelude to The Afternoon of a Faun,* beginning

Shostakovich, Symphony No. 1, mvt. 1 (no. 13)

Prokofiev, *Peter and the Wolf* (no. 2); *Lieutenant Kije,* mvt. 2 (no. 24)

Hindemith, *Symphonic Metamorphosis,* mvt. 2 (four before C)

Orchestral Excerpts (Wummer), International Music Co.

Alto flute

Ravel, *Daphnis et Chloé No. 2* (no. 188)

Stravinsky, *The Rite of Spring* (no. 27, five after no. 93, nos. 130 and 131)

Bass flute

Chihara, *Willow, Willow*

Crumb, *Lux Aeterna*

Oboe

Rossini, Overture to *La Scala di seta* (mm. 37, 201)

Beethoven, Symphony No. 5, mvt. 2 (beginning)

Brahms, Violin Concerto, mvt. 2 (beginning); Symphony No. 2, mvt. 3 (beginning)

Tchaikovsky, Symphony No. 4, mvt. 2 (beginning)

Prokofiev, *Peter and the Wolf* (no. 6)

Bartók, Concerto for Orchestra, mvt. 4 (m. 4)

Tower, *Silver Ladders* (m. 379)

Vade Mecum of the Oboist (and English horn), (Albert Andraud) Southern Music Co.

Orchestral Studies: Difficult Passages (Evelyn Rothwell), Boosey & Hawkes (also oboe d'amore and oboe da caccia)

English horn

Rossini, *William Tell* Overture

Berlioz, *Roman Carnival* Overture (m. 21)

Dvořák, Symphony No. 9, mvt. 2

Wagner, *Tristan und Isolde* (beginning, act 3)

Franck, Symphony in D Minor, mvt. 2 (mm. 16, 86)

Sibelius, *The Swan of Tuonela*

Debussy, *Nocturnes*, mvt. 1
Ravel, Piano Concerto in G, mvt. 2 (m. 6)

Heckelphone

Chávez, *Sinfonia de Antigona*
Copland, Symphony No. 2

Oboe d'amore

Ravel, *Bolero* (no. 4)

Piccolo clarinet

Berlioz, *Symphonie fantastique*, mvt. 5 (no. 63)
Strauss, *Till Eulenspiegels lustige Streiche* (mm. 591–631)
Ravel, Piano Concerto in G, mvt. 3 (no. 1); *Bolero* (no. 3)
Stravinsky, *The Rite of Spring* (nos. 4 and 56)

Clarinet

Weber, Overture to *Oberon* (D)
Mendelssohn, *Hebrides* Overture (m. 202); Symphony No. 3, mvt. 2 (m. 9)
Brahms, Symphony No. 1, mvt. 3; Symphony No. 4, mvt. 2 (m. 5)
Tchaikovsky, Symphony No. 5, mvt. 1 (m. 4—chalumeau register); mvt. 3 (mm.19, 169);
    Symphony No. 6, mvt. 1 (m. 153)
Rachmaninoff, Symphony No. 2, Adagio (m. 6); Piano Concerto No. 2, mvt. 2 (m. 12)
Rimsky-Korsakov, *Capriccio espagnole*, mvt. 4
Stravinsky, *Petroushka* (No. 100—clarion register)
Shostakovich, Symphony No. 1, mvt. 1 (no. 8), mvt. 2 (no. 1), mvt. 4 (no. 6)
Prokofiev, *Peter and the Wolf* (no. 11)
Ravel, *Bolero* (no. 1)
Orchestral Excerpts (McGinnis and Drucker), International Music Co.

Alto clarinet

Henze, *The Raft of the Medusa*
Stravinsky, *Elegy for J.F.K.*

Bass clarinet

Tchaikovsky, *The Nutcracker*, "Dance of the Sugar Plum Fairy"
Wagner, *Siegfried's Rhine Journey*, m. 8 (Introduction to act 1 of *Die Götterdämmerung*);
    Tristan und Isolde, act 2, scene 3 (m. 59)
Dukas, *The Sorcerer's Apprentice* (fourteen after no. 42)
Dvořák, *Scherzo cappricioso*
Strauss, *Don Quixote* (no. 14)
Stravinsky, *The Rite of Spring* (nos. 48–52, 140)
Schoenberg, *Pierrot lunaire*
Schuman, Symphony No. 3

Contralto clarinet

Penderecki, *Pittsburgh Overture*

Contrabass clarinet

Xenakis, *Akrata*
Donald Martino, Triple Concerto

Saxophone

Sopranino: Ravel, *Bolero* (no. 7)
Soprano: Copland, Piano Concerto
Alto: Bizet, *L'Arlésienne* Suite No. 1; Ravel, *Pictures at an Exhibition*, mvt. 2
Tenor: Ravel, *Bolero* (no. 6); Prokofiev, *Lieutenant Kije*, mvt. 2 (no. 18), mvt. 3 (no. 30)
Bass: Schoenberg, *Von Heute auf Morgen*

Bassoon

Beethoven, Symphony No. 4, mvt. 4 (m. 185)
Bizet, *Carmen*, Entr'acte between acts 1 and 2
Tchaikovsky, Symphony No. 5, mvt. 3 (D)
Rimsky-Korsakov, *Scheherazade*, mvt. 2
Dukas, *The Sorcerer's Apprentice* (no. 7)
Ravel, Piano Concerto in G, mvt. 1 (no. 9), mvt. 3 (no. 14); *Rapsodie espagnole,* mvt. 1 (no. 8)
Shostakovich, Symphony No. 1, mvt. 2 (nos. 5 and 15)
Prokofiev, *Peter and the Wolf* (no. 15)
Stravinsky, *The Firebird* Suite, Berceuse; *The Rite of Spring*, beginning
Stadio passi difficile a "a solo," Ricordi
Bassoon Excerpts, Belwin Mills

Contrabassoon

Dukas, *The Sorcerer's Apprentice* (no. 42)
Ravel, *Mother Goose* Suite, mvt. 4 (no. 2); Piano Concerto for the Left Hand, mvt. 1

CHAPTER 4

The Brass

ACOUSTICAL CONSIDERATIONS

The acoustics of brass instruments are similar to those of the woodwinds: The player forces air into a tube, and the effective length of the tube is a critical factor in the pitch that is produced. Vibration is initiated by forcing air between the lips, which are framed by a mouthpiece; this is somewhat comparable to the action of double reeds in the woodwinds, but the brass player has more control because the lips are part of the body. The instruments do not have tone-holes, and pitch changes are effected by changes of tube length, by changes in embouchure, or by both. All of the energy of the sound wave is directed through the bell of the instrument; thus, the sound is more focused and directional than it is in the woodwinds. The bell is proportionately much wider than in the woodwinds, and the bore much smaller; this causes a brighter tone and allows for greater ease in playing high notes.

There are seven basic tube lengths, producing fundamental pitches that span a tritone. With each of these, notes of the overtone series can be produced by changing the embouchure, the airspeed, or both. For example, if the tube length produces a fundamental of C, the overtone series shown in Example 4-1 comprises the notes that can be gotten from this tube length. Some instruments have extra tubing to help the fingering or to extend the range. On all but the trombone, tube lengths are changed by depression or release of valves (although some trombones also use one or two valves for limited purposes.)

Example 4-1 The overtone series

♭ and ♯ indicate deviations from usual tuning

The trombonist changes tube lengths primarily by moving the slide from one to another of seven positions. Differences in the size and shape of the mouthpiece, the bore, and the bell cause differences among the instruments in attack, timbre, and responsiveness. The trumpet and the trombone have relatively shallow mouthpieces and bells in comparison with the horn and the tuba, and, for the most part, a cylindrical bore. This gives them a relatively pointed attack and a brilliant, penetrating timbre. (In Chapter 7, the trumpets and the trombones are referred to as "the sharp brass.") The other brass, including the less-used cornet, baritone horn, and others, have a softer attack and timbre.

The horn and the trumpet have relatively small bore diameters, which makes it somewhat difficult for them to produce the fundamentals appropriate to their tube lengths, called *pedal tones*. Professionals generally overcome this difficulty, although pedal tones are not often called for or required.

Whereas the bells of the trumpets and the trombones are normally pointed more or less toward the audience, those of the horn and the tuba are not. This, in addition to their structure, causes the horn and the tuba to have a somewhat more diffused tone than the trumpet and the trombone: The bells of the horns are normally pointed to one side and toward the rear, and the bell of the tuba points upward. The horns can be asked to play with "bells up," which increases the brilliance of the tone because it aims the bell more forward, but it also makes it more difficult to produce a good quality. The trumpets and the trombones can also be asked to aim their bells more directly toward the audience or, for *less* brilliance, into the stands.

ARTICULATION

There are many similarities between brass and woodwind articulation, especially as regards notation. A variety of tonguing styles is available, from the hardest to the softest, and sensitive writing will indicate one or another. In Example 7-47 at m. 11, lines over the notes in the brass are used to indicate more weight. The speed and loudness of the horns' eighth notes make these notes very marcato in performance, even before the word *marcato* appears.

It is difficult to begin a note on a brass instrument without a slight explosion of air; this is so much a part of the brass sound that in most situations we hardly notice it. Fast tonguing is expected of all the instruments, but it is less effective in the lowest instruments and in the lowest registers. Double-, triple-, and flutter-tonguing are effective in middle registers.

A smooth legato comparable to that on woodwinds can be achieved, especially on the valved brass. As on woodwinds, there are fingered legatos, lip slurs (between notes in the overtone series), and combinations of the two. The trombone has a true legato only with the lip type. If the slide is moved while the player is blowing, there is a change of pitch like the change that occurs when a string player slides a finger along the string while drawing the bow—a glissando—but accomplished players can make it practically unheard by interrupting the air flow just long enough to move the slide to the next note (see further discussion under "The Tenor Trombone"). Not all trombonists can match the legato of the other brass when doing this.

FINGERING

For the valved instruments, three tube lengths (sometimes more) are controlled by either piston or rotary mechanisms. If the first valve alone is depressed, the open pitch of the instrument (the pitch that sounds when no valves are depressed) is lowered by a whole tone. If the second valve alone is depressed, the pitch is lowered a semitone. The first and second valves together lower the pitch a minor third, as does the third valve by itself. The second and third together lower the pitch a major third; the first and third lower it a perfect fourth; and all three together lower it a tritone. A thumb valve on the horn puts that instrument into B-flat, transposing the pitch produced by the other valves a perfect fourth higher. As with woodwinds, the more awkward pitch changes are those that require the movement of more than one finger at a time. Fingering charts for the brass are provided in Appendix C.

TRILLS

Trills can be accomplished either by use of valves or by lipping between upper overtones that are a second apart. The trombone can use only the second method, except for some trills on the tenor-bass or bass trombone that can be executed by the use of a valve. Brass trills tend to call attention to themselves: In the horn, they can be raucous. (A good example is six after C in the last movement of Dvořák's Eighth Symphony.) Trills that use more than one valve at the same time are the most difficult (see the fingering charts in Appendix C). Tremolos are possible on intervals of moderate size, and are best on the trumpet, but one should still beware of awkward fingerings.

VIBRATO

In American orchestras, brass vibrato is usually reserved for solo passages, and then it is used in moderation.

GLISSANDO

The trombone is the only one of the brass that can execute a true gliss for more than a semitone. All the instruments can raise or lower the pitch a small amount with embouchure change. With further change, the pitch jumps to the next overtone. Since the horn can play easily on the upper overtones and since these notes lie close to each other, a horn player can produce the effect of an extended gliss by lipping upward through them, as in Example 4-2. This lip gliss is naturally accompanied by a crescendo and an accent at the end.

Example 4-2   Stravinsky, *The Rite of Spring,* two before no. 107

Other glisses can be faked by all the brass (as by the woodwinds) by lipping a note as far as possible, then fingering the next note, or by moving the valves in and out rapidly before doing so. Another gliss technique is "half-valving" (or "smear")—done by slowly depressing or releasing the valves while moving from one note to the other. On the trumpet, this can give smooth glisses through most of the range either upward or downward. It is more effective in the upper register. On the horn, tone quality during the gliss is not as good as that before and after. If this type of gliss is desired, the indication is "half-valve" or "smear," with a diagonal line between the tones.

MUTES

The standard brass mute is the *straight mute.* Like the string mute, it cuts down on the volume (fullness) of the tone, but unlike the string mute, it can make the tone edgy, nasal, and penetrating, particularly at louder levels. Whereas the string mute reduces the energy of upper overtones, the brass mute largely reduces the energy of *lower* overtones. In Example 7-47, note that the first trumpet is muted and marked *mf* while all other instruments are marked louder. The composer must have expected the first trumpet to at least hold its own. On the other hand, the soft, muted brasses in Example 7-59 sound truncated and pinched (in keeping with the fragmentation of the melody, which, one could say, makes it truncated and pinched, also).

Other mutes, used primarily in popular music, have occasionally been called for in the orchestra. They are made for the B-flat or C trumpet and the trombone and vary in their material, in their shape, and in the amount of air they allow to flow around them.

The cup mute gives a rather neutral, muffled sound. Some cup mutes can be adjusted for a relatively brighter or darker effect. A cloth can be inserted into the mute for a very pure sound.

The mica mute, used more on the trumpet than on the other brass, gives a somewhat thinner sound.

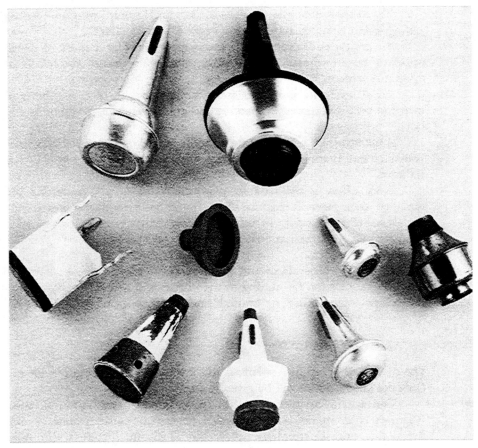

Ed Brown Studio

BRASS MUTES

Straight (trombone)	Cup (trombone)		
Bucket (trumpet)	Plunger	Straight (pic. trumpet)	Harmon
Wispa	Cup	Straight	

The Harmon mute has a stem that can be extended or removed, each position yielding a different color. With the stem all the way in, the sound is very pointed and nasal. As the stem is pulled out, the sound becomes more gentle and distant. With the stem in any position, the hand can be moved toward and away from the mute to create a wa-wa effect (which can be notated "wawa," "wa-wa," or "+ o"). The most usual position of the stem is all the way in, but other colors (and a limited range of wa-wa) are available with the stem removed. The stem usually *is* left out.

(The wa-wa also can be made by using other objects in front of the open bell, including the hand or other mutes.)

The *Solotone mute* (Mel-O-Wah) is like the Harmon, with an even more projecting, even irritating, tone. It can produce a wa-wa effect.

The *whispa mute* reduces the sound greatly, giving a sense of distance. It is ordinarily used for practicing, since the sound can be hardly audible. Intonation is a serious problem.

The *plunger mute* is derived from the rubber end of a plumber's tool, held near the bell. It can produce sounds that are like speech vowels or like a stopped horn.

A *hat mute* can be held in the hand or placed on the stand to be played into. Brilliance and loudness are reduced, with little other change in the character of the tone.

Extra effort is required to play with most mutes, since the air flow is impeded; thus, passages that use them should be in middle or upper registers and not especially demanding in other respects. Balance is difficult to gauge when brass are muted. Combinations of muted and unmuted brass are unusual but offer special colors.

At least 10 seconds should be allowed for players to insert or withdraw a mute. The indication for muting in the brasses is much the same as for muting in the strings: "con sordino" or "muted" and "senza sordino" or "mute off."

HISTORICAL BACKGROUND

The history of brass instruments is too involved to be recounted here in detail. Only the salient points will be given.

The system of valves did not come into general use until the time of Wagner's later operas (some of which he called "music dramas"), about 1870. Before that, only the trombones could play all chromatic tones within their ranges, whereas the other instruments (the "natural" horns and trumpets) were limited mostly to the overtones of the single tube lengths with which they were provided. From the time of Mozart on, horn players developed a hand-stopping technique that allowed other notes to be used, but with uneven quality. The trombones were excluded from symphonic music until Beethoven's Fifth Symphony and became standard members of the orchestra only gradually.

The horns and the trumpets supplemented their tubing with crooks of various sizes, which changed the total tube length and, thus, the overtone series available. Composers from about Haydn through Brahms called for horns and trumpets in various "keys," so that although the part was always written in C major, the tones produced were the overtones of the instrument's "key" note; thus, a horn in D would be used when the orchestra played in D major, and so on. To reach tones not in the overtone series, instruments in other keys might be used at the same time. For example, in the first movement of Schumann's First Symphony, there are two horns in F and two in B-flat, making most of the notes in both the tonic key (B-flat major) and the dominant key (F major) available from one or the other pair at any moment.

The traditions of writing for natural instruments was so strong that the practice of writing the parts "in C major"—that is, with no key signature—persists today. Some scores do use key signatures, but most do not. Players on modern instruments have to learn to transpose many of the old brass parts into the keys in which they are now built.

The tuba is the youngest of the standard brass. It was invented in the early nineteenth century and was accepted generally only in the later part of that century. It did not begin, as the trumpets and the horns did, as a valveless instrument and, thus, is not a transposing instrument, even though it is built in various "keys."

Today's instruments are different from those used a hundred years ago and earlier. The trumpets are smaller and much brighter-sounding. The trombones are more powerful, but as the oldest of the group, they have changed the least since they were known as sackbuts as early as the fifteenth century.

A large number of instruments invented in the nineteenth century are now used mostly in bands. Many of these are discussed at the end of the chapter. Some were invented by composers, such as Wagner and Rimsky-Korsakov. New instruments, such as the piccolo trumpets, have been built recently to play high parts in Baroque music that were written for obsolete instruments; the instruments that took their place were not designed to go that high with ease.

THE HORN

In Norman del Mar's *Anatomy of an Orchestra*, the horn is discussed in a section by itself, rather than in the section on the brass.[1] Although the instrument is certainly a brass instrument from the standpoint of construction and playing characteristics, it is often considered almost a woodwind because it blends so well with those instruments; indeed, it plays with them so often that there are few purely woodwind passages. The fact that it appears in most scores just below the woodwinds, rather than below the trumpets, seems to reflect that association (some early scores place the horns above the bassoons—for example, Wagner's *Tannhäuser* and Berlioz's *Harold in Italy*). Furthermore, the horn is a bona fide member of both the woodwind and the brass quintets.

The tubing of the horn begins by extending from a tapering mouthpiece and continues in angles and coils in a long, expanding bore, until it opens in a wide bell. The player holds the instrument with the right hand partly inside the bell, and the left hand manipulates the rotary valves that change tube lengths. The instrument is called "horn in F" or simply "horn" these days. No one seems to be able to explain the origin of the former name, "French horn."

Most professionals today use a double horn. This instrument has an extra set of tubes that are in B-flat, a perfect fourth higher than the F tubes. A thumb valve acts as a switch that transfers the air flow from one "horn" to the other. The part

[1]Norman del Mar, *The Anatomy of an Orchestra* (Berkeley and Los Angeles: University of California Press, 1981), p. 215.

HORN AND WAGNER TUBA

B-flat/F Descant Horn   B-flat Wagner Tuba
F Horn

is written entirely in F, a perfect fifth higher than sounding. The normal range is shown in Example 4-3. (Brass ranges for elementary, high school, and professional players are given in Appendix E.) Since the B-flat side of the horn has shorter tubes, it is helpful in playing the higher notes in the parts, as well as offering alternate fingerings for notes playable by both sides. Notes written from g^1 up are usually played on this side, as are notes below written F♯ (pedal tones). (See the fingering chart.)

Example 4-3   Range of the horn
                 (sounding a perfect fifth lower)

The horn is written mostly in the treble clef, even though several ledger lines may be needed below the staff at times. In scores written before the early twentieth century (and in some written since), notes in the bass clef were meant to sound *higher* (by a perfect fourth) than written, as in Example 4-4. Since then, most scores (and now probably *all*) assume that the transposition is the same as in the treble clef.

Example 4-4   Shostakovich, Symphony No. 5, mvt. 1, three after no. 17
                 (sounding a perfect fourth higher)

Hns.

The most-used notes for the horn are those on the treble staff (a sounding pitch area of *ab* to *b¹*—like the English horn). In this register, it has a lovely yet solid substance. In lyrical passages, the relatively diffuse sound lends an enchanting character to the melody. Example 7-25 shows the horn in this vein. Notes written above the treble clef place great stress on the embouchure, which must find just the right note among the many high overtones that are very close in pitch. Such notes are easily missed unless they are approached from notes a short distance below. They have a bright, piercing quality and cannot be produced quietly with ease. *Any exposed entrance will be more securely produced if the player has just been playing in that pitch area.*

As the horn descends from about written *c¹*, the embouchure must slacken, and the tone becomes progressively more difficult to control. The lowest register is usually used for quiet, sustained tones, often doubled at the unison or the octave for security or fullness or both. In this role, the horn is very effective. To get a *forte* horn sound in this register, Shostakovich wrote the very striking passage shown in Example 4-4 with four horns in unison. The sound is rather coarse and unhornlike, but obviously just what the composer wanted and very effective. One horn alone would not have been strong enough. In Example 7-50, the low horn *C* (sounding *F*) by one horn is a rather discreet "growl," hardly noticeable, even though it is the lowest note in the score. At the higher end of the range, the horn tone becomes quite penetrating, although not with an edge (like the trumpet or the trombone), and even irritating. Because of their generally diffuse character, *when horns are combined at forte and above with other brass, they are usually doubled or tripled to balance the others.*

In the area of about *c♯–b* (written), any leading lines are better doubled and not very active, loud, or staccato. Pedal tones are difficult on the F side, and more manageable on the B-flat side of the instrument. The pedal tones of all brass instruments are those that are an octave below each of the lowest seven notes of the usual range. The pedal tones of the B-flat side are the lower octave, respectively, of the lowest seven notes of the B-flat side, which are *B, c, c♯*, and so on—thus, the pedal tones are *BB, C, C♯*, and so on.

The horn is most agile in the most-used area. Fast leaps, slurred or not, are easier upward than downward. In the low and middle registers and at a soft level, long notes can be sustained for 30 seconds or more.

Flutter-tonguing is possible, but it is difficult to do softly. A mute is actually helpful here, because the player can use more force with less sound. Low notes are not advisable with muting.

Stopped Horn

The position of the right hand in the bell affects both the quality and the pitch of the tone, since it can alter the air flow in subtle ways. Pushed in further than normal, it acts as a kind of soft mute. When the direction to the player is "stopped," or when there is a "+" over the note, the hand is forced partway into the bore opening to the extent that the airstream is much more compressed, or stifled. The sound becomes muffled and distant, but also rather nasal. (The pitch is affected, too, causing the player to transpose the written pitch, but the part does not have to be further transposed.) To indicate a return to the normal, open sound, write "open" or "o"'s over the notes.

It is very common to call for an accent with stopped horn, which increases the nasality and pungency of the tone. It is also common to indicate "cuivré" or "brassy" when a forced, raucous sound is desired, and this can also be done when the horn is *not* stopped. For an unforced and more covered sound, "half-stopping" can be called for. Stopping is not effective below about a written *g*. If it is called for, the player will usually use a mute instead, perhaps a special stopping mute.

Muting

Muting is similar to the effect of stopping, but a bit more nasal and less muffled-sounding. Although stopping can be applied or withdrawn almost immediately, a few seconds should be allowed to insert or withdraw a mute. Both muting and stopping increase breathing demands on the player; extreme registers or prolonged loud playing is fatiguing.

Notation of Four Horns

When four horns are used, which is very often, they are usually written on two staves, with the first and second parts on the upper staff and the third and fourth on the lower. The odd-numbered players by tradition play higher parts than do the even-numbered players, and this arrangement spreads out the notes on each staff more legibly than if parts with similar tessituras were on the same staff. Players tend to specialize in either high or low registers, although professionals can be expected to deal with any note with assurance. Fourth horn players may use a larger mouthpiece to aid the playing of very low notes. In spite of Example 4-4, it is not advisable to write horns "a 4" in extreme registers.

There are many scores with the first and third horns on the upper staff. (Mahler used the two methods in the same piece!) This arrangement is more efficient when there are extended passages of unison playing.

Gunther Schuller cites several difficult horn passages.[2] One, shown in Example 4-5, is difficult because it is relatively soft, it is in unison with the clarinet, which is playing in its troublesome middle register (which creates intonation problems), and it is in a "strange key." Another is at m. 108 in the third movement of Schumann's Third Symphony; here, the third horn goes to two c^3's, then to an e^3—an exhausting and risky passage.

Example 4-5   Franck, Symphony in D Minor, mvt. 2, m. 33

THE TRUMPET

In recent decades, two sizes of trumpet have become standard—the B-flat and the C. There is some disagreement among authors as to which of them is more popular in American orchestras. The B-flat instrument was formerly the preferred instrument, and the C was standard in France. After players in the Boston Symphony began using the C, its use spread to other orchestras. Delbert Dale estimates that first trumpet players use it about 80 percent of the time.[3] However, the trend seems to be moving away from the C. Although that instrument is brighter and more comfortable to play, the B-flat is liked for its greater warmth and for solo playing. As with the B-flat and A clarinets, trumpet players are likely to use whichever instrument they prefer in general or for a given part. The differences between them are not great. The C may be used for parts that go very high.[4]

---

[2]Gunther Schuller, *Horn Technique* (London: Oxford University Press, 1962), p. 87.

[3]Delbert Dale, *Trumpet Technique*, 2nd ed. (Oxford: Oxford University Press, 1985), p. 74.

[4]The author checked eighty-five twentieth-century scores, none of them by French composers, and found that fifty of them use the C and thirty-five the B-flat trumpet. Many composers used both instruments, but not in the same score.

Ed Brown Studio

TRUMPET AND FLUGELHORN

Bass Trumpet

B-flat Trumpet

D Trumpet

Rotary Trumpet

Flugelhorn   Piccolo A/B-flat Trumpet

The written range of the trumpets is shown in Example 4-6. The usual playing range is a rather limited one—like that of the horn, the notes of the treble staff. Above this, the sound becomes very piercing, but also less reliable because the overtones are close and more easily missed. It is difficult to play the highest three or so notes softly. Notes above d^3 are possible for those who have developed the lip for it (mostly, players of popular music), but such a technique does not usually allow the normal notes to be played with good quality.

Example 4-6   Range of the trumpet (written)

Below the treble staff, intonation and quality become a problem as the tone becomes shaky and rough, although this register has been effectively used for sombre, funereal music. Shostakovich followed the low horn passage quoted in Example 4-4 with a comparable one for two trumpets (see Example 4-7). The sound could be described as "pleasantly nasty" and uncharacteristic of the instrument. Notes below the written range can be reached by special fingering, by a tuning slide (for written *f*), or by pedal tones, which are achieved mostly by the lips (rather than the valves). These tones are rarely used, because their quality does not match that of the normal notes. They are occasionally needed for parts written for the older F trumpet that go below the range of the modern instruments.

The response of the instrument is very quick, which makes fast passagework—tongued or slurred—brilliant and crystal-clear. Single-tonguing can reach four notes per beat at quarter note = 132, and with double-tonguing this increases to about quarter = 180–200. As usual, the extreme registers impose limitations.

Example 4-7   Shostakovich, Symphony No. 5, mvt. 1, no. 18

Since the instrument is naturally powerful, it takes special effort to play softly, and continuous soft playing is taxing. By placing a cloth over the bell, it is possible to cut down the power of the trumpet without affecting the air flow. This can also give the effect of distance without requiring the player to leave the stage for that purpose. Several compositions call for an offstage trumpet, which can be a very effective device; however, because the temperature offstage is usually lower than onstage, the pitch of the instrument may be noticeably lowered, and if the player has difficulty hearing the onstage instruments, which is often the case, he or she may not be aware of intonation discrepancies.

The Rotary Trumpet

In German-speaking countries, a rotary-valve trumpet is used. This instrument has a bore that is much more conical than that of the piston-valved instrument, which results in a darker sound and a slower response. It is occasionally used in the United States for older music, such as that of Mozart and Haydn, whose brass parts are difficult to keep in balance when played on modern instruments. Apparently, no score has called for it specifically.

THE TENOR TROMBONE

In the nineteenth century, three sizes of trombone were commonly used: alto, tenor, and bass. The alto has fallen out of the ranks of the standard instruments, although it is useful for playing not only parts originally written for it but also high notes in some parts intended for the tenor (see the section on the alto trombone). The basic tenor is in B-flat but is nontransposing, as are all its fellow trombones. The range is shown in Example 4-8. Pedal tones are more easily produced than on the trumpet and the horn, but only the first three of these—*BBb*, *AA*, and *AAb*— are the most used. Their quality is rough, and they should not be required of less accomplished players.

Example 4-8   Range of the tenor trombone

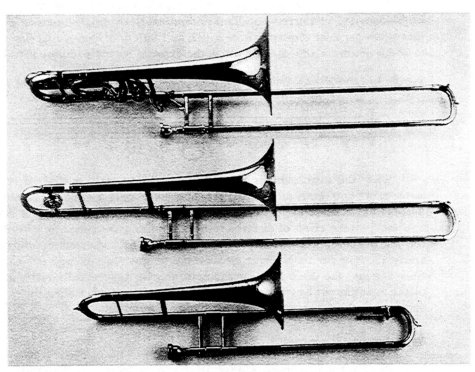

Ed Brown Studio

TROMBONES
Bass Trombone
Tenor Trombone
Alto Trumbone

The tenor trombonist most often encounters tenor and bass clefs but must learn alto clef to play old parts. Treble clef is also coming into use.

The lowest register should be treated with some care: It is not as responsive as the upper notes, the quality is not as good, and a fast-moving part could present difficulties if excessive slide motion is required. The reason for the last is that each of the lowest notes, *E* to *Bb*, can be played in only one slide position; thus, a quick movement between *E* and *Bb* means a cumbersome movement of the slide as far as it will go—between seventh and first positions. *B♮* must be played in seventh position and *Bb* in first position; thus, the same problem prevents a fast movement between those two notes.

Intonation can be precisely controlled by the position of the slide. If the player moves the slide to a higher-numbered position and the pitch goes down, or vice versa, a gliss results.[5] As mentioned earlier, when legato is desired under these conditions, the slide must be moved quickly while the air flow is interrupted by the tongue. The difference between this type of "tongued slur" and others is noticeable. The tongued slur is illustrated in Example 4-9a (roman numerals indicate slide positions). Here, the position change is to a *lower*-numbered one while the pitch rises, which requires the tongued slur (see the fingering chart). Any other slur involves a change of embouchure with or without slide movement. These slurs result in a slight clicking sound like that of the valve movement on other brass instruments. Example 4-9b is a lip slur between two notes played in fourth position. Example 4-9c is a "partial crossing" (motion to a lower-numbered position with a pitch *drop*, or vice versa). Players are advised to use only one kind of slur during a passage to avoid inconsistencies.

Example 4-9

The usual playing range is from about *Bb* to *g¹*. When higher notes are played loudly, the tone becomes stentorian. Played softly, the sound is more blending and has a granitelike smoothness. Near the end of the second movement of his First Symphony, Schumann successfully combined three trombones with two bassoons in a five-voiced texture in *pianissimo*. He was careful, however, to make the trombones harmonically complete in themselves in case of an imbalance between the brass and the woodwind instruments.

Loud, low tones can have a snarling effect, as the beginning of Sibelius's *Finlandia* demonstrates. Staccatos can be very imposing. The true glissando is limited in range by the position in which it starts. The maximum for the tenor trom-

---

[5]Players associate slide positions with pitch movement; therefore, for them a "lower position" is one with the slide further *out*, which is actually a higher-*numbered* position, and conversely, a "higher" position for them is really a lower-numbered one.

bone is a tritone, which can be possible upward only if the gliss begins in seventh position and downward only if it begins in first position. Faked glisses can begin with a true gliss and then jump to a note that is out of the gliss range. The "fingering" chart in Appendix C can be used to determine which notes can be played in first position (for tritone glisses downward) and in seventh position (for tritone glisses upward). When the E or F attachment is used (see under "The Tenor-Bass Trombone"), the maximum gliss is a perfect fourth.

THE TENOR-BASS TROMBONE

The tenor-bass trombone is a tenor trombone to which extra tubing (an attachment) has been added, making it a double instrument. The attachment, a rotary valve, is activated by the thumb and puts the instrument into F, lowering the range by a perfect fourth. The longer tubing necessitates slide positions that are farther out than they are for the B-flat side; thus, seventh position is unreachable when the instrument is in F because the slide is too short. An extra E slide remedies the situation, acting as a "seventh position." Example 4-10 shows a chromatic descent as it could be played, first in B-flat, and then in F. Recently, D and D-flat attachments have also become available.

Example 4-10   Lower notes, tenor-bass trombone

The tenor-bass trombone is useful for parts that have notes between *BB* and *E♭*, which are not playable on the tenor. In addition, difficult passages may become more accessible with more options for choices of slide position. But the low notes do not have the darkness that is usually desired. For that purpose, the bass trombone is more suitable. Since the third trombone part is usually the lowest, the third trombonist is most likely to play a tenor-bass or a bass trombone, whereas the first trombonist normally does not play either one. Second trombone parts are normally played on a tenor-bass. Outside of the symphony, most trombonists use this instrument.

THE BASS TROMBONE

The bass trombone is the same instrument, structurally, as the tenor-bass trombone but with a wider bore, offering a darker sound and more security for the lower notes. The upper notes are more difficult than the same ones on the tenor. The bass trombonist therefore does not often get high notes and is consequently not used to reading tenor clef. The low notes, however, still present problems, since they are physically difficult to produce.

THE TUBA

The tuba is the least standardized of the brass family, there being several sizes that are in use. The most common are the bass in F and the contrabasses in BB♭ and C. Scores rarely specify the "key." The player will usually choose the instrument that is most suitable for the composition at hand. The large bore size permits the fundamental (pedal) to be produced, and all professional instruments have at least four valves that allow a complete chromatic scale within the range given in Example 4-11. All the tubas are nontransposing.

Example 4-11   Range of the tuba

The instrument is quite powerful when played loudly—somewhat like a super horn—and can make its presence felt without being irritating. It is ragged and dif-

Ed Brown Studio

TUBA, EUPHONIUM, BARITONE HORN

CC Tuba   Euphonium   Baritone Horn

ficult to manage in the lowest notes and piercing and strained above the bass staff. As an ensemble member, the tuba provides a wonderfully suave bass. It works well as such with three trombones, but if the dynamic level is loud, the brilliance of the trombones is likely to contrast noticeably with the less-focused sound of the tuba (see "The Contrabass Trombone" as an alternative).

There is no need to use any clef other than bass, although tenor and even treble have appeared in some scores. Octave signs (*8ba*) are not customarily used in parts, unless space is a consideration.

The lowest fifth or so of the range should be used with caution. A slow, step-wise descent is the most prudent one. In higher registers, the part can be rather active, as long as the player is allowed adequate time to breathe. Both fingering and tonguing complexities can be managed in middle registers.

LESS COMMONLY USED INSTRUMENTS

Most of these instruments are commonly found in bands, and some are used in jazz. Others are almost obsolete. Usage varies considerably between Europe and the United States.

The smaller versions of standard instruments generally are more capable of producing usable pedal tones than are their larger companions. They have been used mostly to play very high parts or parts written for obsolete, high instruments.

The Smaller Trumpets

Some people call all of these "piccolo trumpet," whereas others apply that term only to the smallest of them. All have a written range that is close to that of the usual B-flat trumpet, the upper limits being somewhat more constricted. *All are written lower than they sound.*

The instruments that occasionally appeared in early twentieth-century scores were the D and E-flat trumpets. Today, they are one instrument, equipped with a tube that allows a change from one key to another. As with other smaller versions of standard instruments, orchestration books almost uniformly state that the main purpose of the instrument is to extend the trumpet sound to higher pitches and that the lower notes are not needed; yet, composers more than occasionally write for a smaller instrument as if it were another standard instrument, combining it with the standard instrument(s) at the same pitch level, or even below it. The relative brightness and thinness of the tone also make it attractive for solo passages.

Several even-smaller trumpets exist. The B-flat/A instrument, like the D/E-flat, has a slide that puts the instrument in either one key or the other. The usual notation is a minor seventh or a major sixth lower than sounding, respectively, but it might be easier for both the player and the score reader if the part were written a major second or minor third *higher*, respectively, since the standard B-flat player is used to thinking of the sounding note as lower than written. This, of course, means that the part must be played an octave *higher* than written. If this is done, there should be a footnote explaining the notation.

The Bass Trumpet

The older forms of the bass trumpet, in C and B-flat, were used in late nineteenth-century large-scale works, written an octave higher and a major ninth higher, respectively, than sounding. Provided with a trombone mouthpiece, these instruments are often considered to be in essence trombones with valves and are customarily played by trombonists. An E-flat instrument, written a major sixth higher than sounding and sometimes called "alto" or "tenor" trumpet, was used effectively in Stravinsky's *Rite of Spring* at no. 132 as the lowest member of a trumpet line doubled in three octaves. (The small D trumpet is also used extensively in that work.) The instrument is not always available. It can be useful for trills and fast slurring where the trombone sound is desired.

The Cornet

The cornet was commonly used in nineteenth-century French scores as an adjunct to the trumpet. It has the same range and technique as the trumpet. The most common instrument is in B-flat. It has a smaller and more conical bore than the trumpet, giving it a mellower, less aggressive character. It has been said that the difference between the two instruments can often not be detected, and cornet parts, such as the famous solo after no. 69 in Stravinsky's *Petroushka*, are often played on the trumpet.

The Flugelhorn

The flugelhorn is considered a valved bugle and has been closely associated with the cornet. Its sound is somewhere between that of the cornet and that of the horn, owing to its relatively wide and conical bore. It is in B-flat, with a written range comparable to that of the trumpet, but its sound is considerably warmer and mellower. It blends very well.

The Triple Horn

The triple horn adds a high-F component to the double horn, which is activated by a second thumb valve. This gives further security for the playing of high notes, as well as another set of fingering possibilities for better intonation and connection of pitches.

Descant Horns

Descant horns are separate small horns in B-flat and high F. They are used for demanding high passages. Parts are not ordinarily written specifically for them.

The Alto Horn

In England, the alto horn is called the "tenor horn." Built in E-flat, its range is $f\sharp-c^3$ (written). It resembles the euphonium more than the horn, with the bell facing upward. It is said to be "brassier" than the F horn, and it is better suited to marching.

The Wagner Tuba

Wagner had a family of these instruments built to extend the tuba sound upward. The tenor is in B-flat with a range of $C-g^2$, and the bass is in F with a range of $F-g^2$. It somewhat resembles the alto horn. It is played by hornists, but few of the instruments are available.

The Alto Trombone

Used for the highest trombone parts in many eighteenth- and nineteenth-century scores (as in Example 7-16; "Pos.," which means "trombone"), the alto trombone is now rarely called for in orchestral music. The range is $A-f^3$, and the tone is lighter and less penetrating than that of the tenor. It may be difficult for the tenor trombonist to play because the slide positions are shorter than on the tenor and some adjustment is needed when switching instruments. The instrument may be making a comeback, since more players seem to be using it.

The Contrabass Trombone

In B-flat, the range of the contrabass trombone is about that of the tenor trombone, but an octave lower—$EE-bb$. Its size constitutes a considerable challenge for the performer, which is unfortunate, for it better matches the other trombones in *forte* passages than the tuba does.

The Baritone Horn and the Euphonium

The baritone horn and the euphonium are so similar that their names are often wrongly interchanged. Like the alto horn and the Wagner tuba, they look like small tubas, and have three or four valves. They have good facility and blend well with the "softer" brass, including the tuba. The euphonium, when used in the orchestra, often doubles the tuba an octave higher, as it does in wind music.

The instruments are in B-flat and are written in bass clef *at pitch*; parts in band music used to be written in treble clef, a major ninth above the sounding pitches, but that practice is no longer followed. Both have a range similar to that of the tenor trombone: $E–b^1$. The euphonium has a somewhat larger and darker tone. The pedal tones are easily produced, and with good quality.

FACTORS THAT MAKE BRASS PASSAGES RELATIVELY EASY

These factors are, for the most part, the same as those for the woodwinds.

1. Most notes are not in extreme registers.
2. Loud playing is not prolonged.
3. Soft playing is not prolonged.
4. Fast tonguing is not prolonged. Staccato passages include some slurred notes as well.
5. Complex or fast passages are in middle registers.
6. Dynamic changes do not come in fast succession.
7. Phrases are not excessively long, and rests are provided between them. As with woodwinds, professionals can usually play solo lines that have phrases of 10 to 20 seconds' duration with ease, and soft tones in favorable registers (middle to low) can be held for 30–50 seconds or more.
8. High and low notes are approached stepwise and are not the first note(s) of an entrance.
9. Notes in high registers are no softer than f.
10. Accidentals are few.
11. An important entrance is preceded by at least one passage that is not exposed and that ends near the pitch beginning the new entrance.
12. Slurred leaps ascend, are few, and are no larger than an octave.
13. Fast pitch movements require no more than one finger movement on valved instruments and no more than a short slide movement on a trombone. (The valved instruments are in general more facile than the trombone, and fast slide movements on the trombone are better when successive movements are in one direction. Chromatic movement in one direction is the easiest.)

Again, these factors are more critical for less skilled players than for professionals, but they could be helpful for the latter when other difficulties are present.

OTHER POINTS TO REMEMBER

1. The legato of the trombone is not as connected (in the case of the tongued slur) as that of the other brass.
2. When combined with other brass in loud passages, the horns should be doubled or tripled for good balance (for example, two horns for each trumpet).
3. Muting cuts down *volume*, but not necessarily the ability to penetrate, especially at higher dynamics.
4. Difficult tonguing, such as double-tonguing and flutter-tonguing, may not be effective in low registers or at soft dynamics. It may also lower the pitch.

COMPARISON OF BRASS RANGES
WITH WOODWINDS AND STRINGS

Example 4-12 shows the ranges of the standard brass with woodwinds and strings that have comparable ranges.

Example 4-12   Comparison of standard brass ranges
with woodwinds and strings (sounding)

EXCERPTS FOR LISTENING AND STUDY

Brass

Dukas, Fanfare from *La Peri*
Sibelius, *Finlandia*
Bartók, Concerto for Orchestra, mvt. 1 (nos. 323–386)
Copland, *Fanfare for the Common Man*

Horn(s)

Rossini, Overture to *Semiramide* (m. 43)
Schubert, Symphony No. 9, mvt. 1 (beginning)
Mendelssohn, *A Midsummer Night's Dream*, Notturno
Brahms, Symphony No. 3, mvt. 3 (B)
Tchaikovsky, Symphony No. 5, mvt. 2 (m. 9)
Strauss, *Till Eulenspiegels lustige Streiche* (m. 6); *Don Juan*
Mahler, Symphony No. 1, mvt. 1 (five before no. 26), mvt. 2 (no. 13—Trio)
Shostakovich, Symphony No. 1, mvt. 4 (no. 22)
Prokofiev, *Lieutenant Kije*, mvt. 5 (no. 57); *Peter and the Wolf* (nos. 19 and 44)
Orchestral Excerpts (Chambers), International Music Co.

Piccolo trumpet

Britten, *Four Sea Interludes*, mvt. 2
Respighi, *Pines of Rome*, mvt. 2
Stravinsky, *The Rite of Spring*, mvt. 1 (no. 11)

Trumpet

Ravel, *Pictures at an Exhibition*, mvt. 6 (no. 58—muted)
Prokofiev, *Lieutenant Kije*, mvt. 1, mvt. 3 (no. 32—cornet)
Shostakovich, Symphony No. 1, mvt. 3 (no. 20—muted)
Gershwin, Piano Concerto, mvt. 2 (muted)
Tower, *Silver Ladders* (m. 634)
Wagner Orchestral Studies (Hoehne), International Music Co.
Orchestral Excerpts (Bartold), International Music Co.
20th Century Orchestral Studies (Johnson), G. Schirmer

Alto trumpet (E-flat)

Stravinsky, *The Rite of Spring* (nos. 132 and 139)

Flugelhorn

Schoenberg, Theme and Variations for Band
Stravinsky, *Threni*

Bass trumpet

Ruggles, *Men and Angels*
Janáček, *Sinfonietta*

Trombone

Berlioz, *Roman Carnival* Overture (m. 315)
Schumann, Symphony No. 1, mvt. 2 (m. 112)
Wagner, Overture to *Tannhäuser* (A)
Brahms, Symphony No. 1, mvt. 4 (C); Symphony No. 4, mvt. 4 (beginning)
Ravel, *Bolero* (no. 10)
Stravinsky, *Petroushka* (no. 112)
Wagner Orchestral Studies (Hausmann), International Music Co.
Orchestral Excerpts for trombone and tuba (Brown), International Music Co.

Contrabass trombone

Ligeti, *Requiem*
Varèse, *Integrales*
Stravinsky, *Canticum sacrum*

Tuba

Mahler, Symphony No. 1, mvt. 3 (m. 15)
Stravinsky, *The Rite of Spring* (no. 64)
Prokofiev, *Lieutenant Kije*, mvt. 5 (no. 59)

CHAPTER 5

The Percussion

The word *percussion* can be a little misleading. Although its stem means "to strike," and although most of the time the instruments are struck, they can also be played by other means and some are not struck at all. Percussion instruments are capable of many different sounds, not only percussive ones!

One difference between a percussion and a nonpercussion instrument is that the sound of the former is usually a combination of two distinct sounds—the impact and the reverberation. Another is that the player does not usually control the dynamic level after the impact, other than to muffle or restrike the instrument.

Most of the standard percussion instruments are readily available. Professional orchestras are likely to own instruments that are too large to be conveniently carted around by the player: the xylophone, marimba, vibraphone, glockenspiel, timpani, bass drum, and chimes. Professional players are expected to own the other instruments, if they are the usual ones. The orchestra may borrow or rent instruments that neither they nor the player owns. In the following discussions, it is noted when an instrument is not readily available.

ACOUSTICAL CONSIDERATIONS

An understanding of the acoustics of percussion instruments requires a somewhat more basic viewpoint than that needed for stringed and wind instruments, owing to the great diversity of sounds they produce. The details of this discussion may seem rather technical, but the main points are essential to a general concept of how instruments (not just the percussion) operate and how they are heard. The main points will be summarized as needed.

Pitch

When a vibrating body has one dimension that is very much larger or smaller than all the others (and also the proper amount of flexibility), that body is likely to produce a clear pitch. The principal vibrating element of stringed instruments is the string, whose length is much greater than its thickness. The comparable dimension in wind instruments is the air column enclosed in a tube, which is far longer than the "width" or "depth" of that tube. This is an important factor in the clarity of pitch they produce. A bar, such as is found on a xylophone, does not have quite the same relationships: The length of the bar is greater than the width of the bar, which is wider than its thickness. Furthermore, the material of this bar does not have the flexibility that a string or a column of air has. Therefore, the pitch characteristics of bars are not the same as those of strings or air columns. A flat, circular vibrating body, such as a cymbal or a drumhead, has a thickness that is much smaller than its area, and the vibrating area is relatively large. All these forms of instrument are capable of emitting definable pitches to some extent.

A vibrating medium actually vibrates in many ways at the same time. These different ways, called "modes," have different rates of vibration, or pitches, and different strengths. It is generally thought that if the loudest pitches produced by these modes are members of a harmonic series (for instance, as shown in Example 4-1), a single pitch will predominate. If any pitch is not in the same harmonic series as the others, it is said to be "inharmonic," and will project a dissonant or "noisy" effect. Clarity of pitch, then, depends upon how well the modes of vibration correspond to a harmonic series. In reality, there is probably no instrument whose modes exactly conform to the series. For example, the first overtone of the piano is slightly more than one octave higher than the fundamental. But many percussion instruments have modes that are much further from this "ideal" than that, and thus do not give as clearly the impression of a pitch; rather, they give the impression of a confusion of pitches or, at the extreme, of a noise.

Another factor in the clarity of pitch is *sympathetic vibration.* If the principal vibrating element is in contact with, or close to, another that is capable of producing a clear pitch, the two may act as if they were modes of *the same body* and either reinforce or compete with each other, depending on whether their pitches are in the same harmonic series. If the pitch of one is clearer or stronger than that of the other, it may dominate, or reinforce an *overtone* of, the other. As you will see, this is the case with such diverse instruments as the marimba, the timpani, and the bass drum.

As a vibrating body flexes in various ways (modes), there are definable physical boundaries between the parts of the body that are vibrating. These are called "nodes" or "nodal lines," places where vibration tends to be minimal. Example 5-1 is a representation of two vibrating bodies—a bar (a) and a circular plate (b). In 5–1a, two modes are shown, labeled 1 and 2. The brackets show the portions of the bar that are vibrating in those modes, and the dots represent the nodal points that separate those portions. At the dots, there is minimal vibration, and at points midway between them, the vibration is maximal for those modes. If the bar is struck midway between nodal points of a given mode, the pitch produced by that mode will be emphasized. If, on the contrary, it is struck *at* a nodal point, the mode bounded by that node will be suppressed and other modes emphasized. It can be seen that if the bar is struck at the center, which is both a node of 1 and midway between the nodes of 2, the pitch produced by 1 will be *suppressed* and the pitch produced by 2 will be *emphasized*. The effect of this will be related to actual pitch in discussion of instruments like the xylophone.

Example 5-1a   **Example 5-1b**

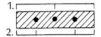

In Example 5-1b, only one of many modes is represented—the nodal lines of plates are either straight lines running diametrically across and through the center or circles running around the center, such as this one. The mode represented here is the area around the dotted line, which is the nodal line for this mode. A stroke at the center of the plate would cause this mode to predominate, but it would inhibit all the several other modes whose lines run through the center. As you will see later, this causes a drumhead or a cymbal to have a relatively "dead" sound if struck at the center.

An important consequence of this discussion is that pitch definition is affected by the shape and material of the vibrating body and by where on the body vibration is initiated.

Timbre

Acoustically, timbre can be described in terms of the relative strengths of the modes. If lower (-sounding) modes are predominant, the timbre will be relatively dark and hollow; if the higher modes are predominant, the effect will be relatively bright. (Most tones have some combination of predominant high and low modes.) The degree of pitch clarity is also a factor: Indistinct pitch is heard as relatively noisy, which can result especially when high modes are strong and are not in the harmonic series.

Timbre can be thought of as "tone quality at a given moment," whereas *tone quality* is profoundly affected by *changes in timbre*. All instruments produce sounds whose timbres change. The greatest change usually takes place over fractions of a second at the beginning of the sound. After that, change is slower. This factor enters into the discussion of several of the instruments, regarding the relationship between the attack and the decay of their tone.

There is a close relationship between loudness and tone quality: For the same vibrating body, *louder tones are usually, if not always, brighter than tones that are soft*, because a body that is struck with more energy will more readily affect *those modes that flex faster, which are the higher ones*, thus yielding a brighter tone.

The most obvious influence on timbre is the material of the instrument. Generally, the harder (and less flexible) the material, the brighter the tone will be, and the softer the material the darker. Thus, one would expect metallic instruments to have brighter qualities than those with skin drumheads, and so on.

Another influence is how much of the area of the vibrating body is initially contacted by whatever strikes it: A stick with a large head contacts more area of a drumhead than does a stick with a small head. The difference between these areas may be very small, but there is often an audible difference, because a larger area of impact includes more nodal lines or points than does a smaller one. The result is that a larger *striking surface* can cause a darker sound than a smaller striking surface (as long as other factors, especially where the instrument is struck and how hard, remain the same).

Another effect of the area and material of the striking implement is the character of the *attack*. Implements with smaller or harder striking surfaces will produce sharper, more articulated attacks than those with larger or softer ones.

Finally, when an instrument is struck, the striking implement also vibrates independently. If the sound it makes is loud enough and different enough from that of the instrument, this will add a separate and possibly undesirable element: The low notes of the marimba, for example, have a slower response and a darker sound than the higher ones; if hard mallets are used on them, two distinct sounds will be heard—the high-pitched, bright click of the mallets and the relatively low hum of the bars. A better match for the low marimba notes, therefore, is a softer mallet, whose own response is slower and timbre darker.

Decay Time

Percussion instruments can differ dramatically in decay time (the amount of time a tone remains audible): Some will decay in a fraction of a second, whereas others may ring for a half-minute or so. Most percussion instruments have either short or long decay times—few have moderately long ones. At least four factors can influence decay time: the size of the instrument, its shape, where it is struck, and the presence or absence of resonators. Generally, decay time will be *longer* if

1. The instrument is relatively large.
2. One of the instrument's dimensions is very different from all the other ones.
3. There are no resonators (resonators serve to increase *loudness*, but they decrease decay time).
4. The instrument is struck at a point that emphasizes the fundamental.
5. The striking area of the striking implement is large and of soft material.

Of course, it is obvious that the more forcefully an instrument is struck, the longer it will ring.

It is important to note the decay times of the instruments as they are discussed, since this can have important consequences for the notation and treatment of the instrument. *For instruments with short decay times, it is unrealistic to write notes that are longer than quarter notes.* Note values that are short and relatively easy to read, as in

Example 5-2

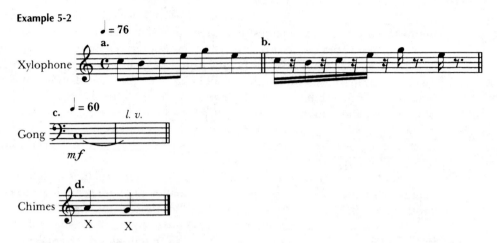

Example 5-2a, are appropriate, whereas those in 5-2b are impractically difficult to read, even if they are more representative of the actual duration.

For instruments that ring audibly for more than about 2 seconds, it is unrealistic to write notes that are shorter than quarter notes, unless they are to be damped (muffled), in which case this should be indicated, as in Example 5-2d. Notes for very reverberant instruments are better written exactly as long as they are desired to sound. To prevent a player from damping when it is not desired, the composer should write "l.v," as in Example 5-2c. *If a series of fast notes is written for a reverberant instrument, one should expect the tones to overlap, with some lack of clarity.*

At the other extreme, any long note written for an instrument with a short decay time may sound disappointingly or even humorously abrupt. Usually, rolls (fast repeated strokes) are used to give the effect of sustained notes, but the least reverberant instruments are not suitable for this effect, since the individual strokes are likely to be heard, rather than a continuous tone. (Rolls are discussed under "Notation and Sticking Techniques.")

Directionality

Generally speaking, an instrument radiates sound most strongly in any direction in which its largest surface faces. Thus, a drum or a cymbal will sound loudest to listeners who can see the most of their vibrating surfaces, or to whom the instrument appears most like a circle.

SUMMARY OF ACOUSTICAL CONSIDERATIONS

1. Instruments that have one dimension that is very different from all the others are most likely to have clear pitch.
2. The pitch that is heard can be influenced by
   a. Where the instrument is struck.
   b. Any resonators that are part of or close to the instrument.

3. Tone quality is affected by
   a. The relative strengths of the modes (prominent high modes give a brighter sound).
   b. The shape and material of the vibrating body (harder material yields a brighter sound).
   c. How loudly the instrument is played (louder tones tend to be brighter than softer ones).
   d. Where the instrument is struck (toward the center or middle can be darker than near an edge).
   e. The size and hardness of the striking surface (larger or softer striking surfaces yield darker sounds).
4. Timbre is generally not constant but changes very rapidly at first and more slowly thereafter.
5. An instrument will ring longer if
   a. It is relatively large.
   b. One of its dimensions is very different from all the others.
   c. There are no resonators.
   d. It is struck at a point that emphasizes the fundamental.
   e. The striking area of the striking implement is large and of soft material.
6. A striking implement with a smaller or harder striking surface will produce a more articulated attack than one with a larger or softer one.
7. An instrument sounds most strongly in the direction in which its largest surfaces face.

Vocal Approximations of Instrumental Sound

The various vowel sounds used in speech and singing are actually specific *timbres* of the voice, produced by the vocal cords and the way the resonating cavities of the vocal tract are shaped. We often use words to represent sounds, such as "crash," "crunch," and "bang," and quasi words, such as "ding," and "boink." (Consider some of the instrument names: "gong," "tam-tam," and "drum," for example.) We can often relate various shades of darkness and brightness to the vowels, because each vowel emphasizes certain pitch areas: Lower pitch emphasis is heard as relatively dark, and so on. The following is a list of vowels in order from the darkest to the brightest.

> *oo* as in "who"
> *aw* as in "awful"
> *uh* as in "lustre"
> *a* as in "after"
> *e* as in "pet"
> *i* as in "fit"
> *ee* as in "feet"

Consonants can approximate instrumental attacks and decays: *t* and *p* are like sharp attacks, *k* (with no sound after it) like an abrupt ending, *s* or *sh* like a high-pitched ending, *m* or *n* slower and low-pitched decays, and *n* before another consonant representing a long, steady decay, such as *ng* in "bong." Vocal sounds will occasionally be used to give the idea of an instrumental sound.

CHOICE OF STICKS OR MALLETS

Percussionists usually have at their disposal a wide variety of sticks, mallets, or beaters. In most cases, the composer can safely rely on a professional to use the sticks or mallets that are most appropriate for a given passage if the context and the character of that passage are clear. Interpretive terms are helpful in making them clear: "secco," "sostenuto," "leggiero," for example, or any number of ad hoc descriptions, such as "moderately heavy" or "caressing." It is also important to use dynamic markings at the beginning of any passage and wherever there is any change, and to include desired articulations and accents, and so on. Although the use of specific types of sticks and mallets will be discussed, the composer is advised in most cases simply to call for "soft," "medium," or "hard" varieties of implement. Common abbreviations are "s.s." for "soft stick," "m.s." for "medium stick," and "h.s." for "hard stick." These distinctions can be applied to either rubber or yarn mallets and to felt timpani sticks.

Although it will not always be mentioned, any instrument that is normally struck may also be played with the fingers or hands, for softer effects.

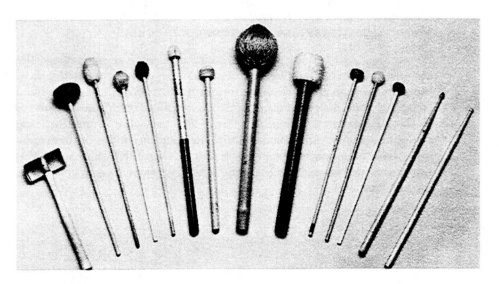

Ed Brown Studio

PERCUSSION STICKS/MALLETS

| Chimes mallet | Four yarn mallets | Two felt timpani sticks | Gong beater | Bass drum beater | Three mallets: rubber, plastic, rubber | Two wooden snare drum sticks |

PICTOGRAMS

To save space, pictograms (symbols that look like miniature versions of what they represent) may be used in the score and in parts to indicate an instrument or a stick or mallet. Some of the accepted pictograms for sticks, mallets, and beaters are given in Example 5-3. Composers sometimes invent their own (for example, Elliott Carter in his Double Concerto). Pictograms will be given for each instrument as it is presented, along with the usual sticks or mallets used for them. (It should be mentioned that some percussionists do not like pictograms and prefer simple abbreviations of the instrument's name.)

Example 5-3   Pictograms of sticks, mallets, and beaters

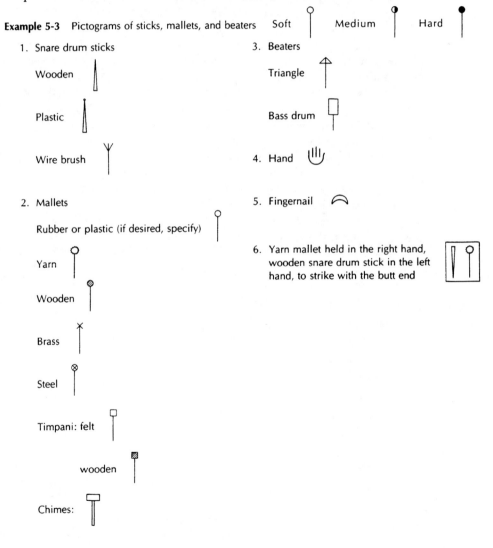

CLASSIFICATION OF PERCUSSION INSTRUMENTS

Following Curt Sachs, many writers place percussion instruments in five classifications:[1]

1. *Idiophones:* not needing additional tension (as do strings or drumheads). These instruments are either struck together, struck with some implement, or scraped, shaken, or plucked.
2. *Membranophones:* having a membrane stretched over an opening.
3. *Aerophones:* wind instruments.
4. *Chordophones:* stringed instruments.
5. *Electrophones:* having electrically generated sound sources.

Obviously, most percussion instruments fall into the categories of idiophones and membranophones. A second way of dividing them is into "pitched" and "unpitched" instruments. This is not without its problems, as the previous discussion would suggest: Under certain circumstances, a pitched instrument can have unclear pitch or an unpitched instrument can have clear pitch. Nevertheless, this is a useful subcategory. A third division is by material: skin, wood, metal, and other. A fourth is by construction.

The organization of instruments in this chapter takes into account all these methods. Following is a complete list of all the instruments discussed, in the order of their presentation. Within each group, the order is generally from the highest- to the lowest-pitched, as far as this is possible (some instruments come in various sizes, whose ranges, in toto, may overlap those of other instruments). The reason for this is that pitch area determines much of the use of percussion instruments, as you will see in Chapters 7 and 8. The main distinction between pitched and unpitched instruments is that the former are *always* given pitched notation, whereas the latter *may or may not be* given pitched notation; and, often when unpitched instruments *are* given pitches, it is without a particular octave designation.

PITCHED MEMBRANOPHONES
Roto-toms
Boobams
Timpani
Tabla

UNPITCHED MEMBRANOPHONES
Snare drum
Tom-toms
Bongos
Timbales
Congas

---

[1]Curt Sachs, *The History of Musical Instruments* (New York: W. W. Norton & Co., Inc., 1940), pp. 455 ff.

Frame drum
Field drum
Tenor drum
Tabor
Lion's roar
Bass drum

THE MALLET INSTRUMENTS

Glockenspiel
Xylophone
Marimba
Vibraphone

PITCHED METALS AND GLASSES

Crotales, Antique cymbals
Musical glasses
Handbells
Chimes
Steel drums
Gongs

UNPITCHED METALS AND GLASSES

Triangle
Finger cymbals
Cymbals
Tambourine
Wind chimes
Bell tree
Anvil
Sleigh bells
Cup bells
Brake drums
Almglocken, Cowbells
Flexatone
Musical saw
Bell plates
Tam-tam
Thunder sheet

UNPITCHED WOOD, VEGETABLE, AND SYNTHETIC IDIOPHONES

Castanets
Claves
Slapstick
Sandpaper blocks
Maracas
Cabasa

Ratchet
Vibraslap, Jawbone
Guiro
Woodblock
Temple blocks
Wind machine
Slit drum, Log drum

AEROPHONES
Police whistle
Slide whistle
Pistol shot
Popgun
Mouth siren
Auto horn, Klaxon horn
Siren

NOTATION AND STICKING TECHNIQUES

Percussion parts for unpitched instruments may be written on staves of five or fewer lines. Several such instruments may be written together on one five-line staff if the parts are not so complicated that they interfere with each other visually. For this, there are two common ways of indicating which instrument plays which notes: (1) The instruments are named in the left margin in the order of their placement on the staff, and (2) the instruments are named above the staff where they enter. A combination of the two is recommended, especially with a larger number of instruments. *One should always keep the notes for a given instrument on the same line or space throughout a piece.* Example 5-4 illustrates the use of a five-line staff. Example 5-5 shows a three-line staff for high- , medium- , and low-pitched tom-toms and a single-line staff for a tam-tam. The neutral clef clearly indicates that pitch is not specified. In some scores, each unpitched instrument is written on a separate single-line staff.

Example 5-4

Triangle
Cymbal
Bass Drum

Example 5-5

High
Tom-toms   Medium
Low

Tam-tam

Rolls. When an instrument is played with sticks or mallets, notes may be played entirely with one hand or with alternation of the hands. If the instrument and the stick or mallet have the proper flexibility, the stick or mallet may be bounced two or more times per stroke. When notes are repeated fast enough that the effect is a continuous sound, this is called a *roll.* Various ways of notating rolls have been used, especially the sign "Tr," with or without a wavy line following it. Today, most writers recommend that rolls be notated as if they were tremolos (see Example 5-6).

Example 5-6

Rolled notes followed by rests should be notated carefully, because percussionists, like other players, have the tendency to taper such a note, in effect making it shorter. If the orchestrator desires to have the note end *without* a taper, it is better to extend it to end on the next beat, as in Example 5-6a or 5-6b, rather than as in 5-6c. The eighth note in a will be played as the last of the rolled strokes, giving a gentle, unaccented ending to the roll, and the eighth note in b will sound like a detached note that ends the roll. The first of these is easier to manage. The second may be interpreted by the player as if it were written as in a, unless the context makes it clear that a separation is required.

Rolls can be played on two different instruments by alternating strokes on one and the other (see Example 5-6d). This is usually done on like instruments.

When rolling on large instruments such as the timpani, the bass drum, and the tam-tam, it is easier to make crescendos than diminuendos, owing to the inertia of the instrument. With less reverberant instruments, dynamic changes are more easily managed.

Right–Left Sticking

The mechanics of right–left sticking are an important part of technique. The most natural motion of the two hands is to play the lower notes on a keyboard with the left hand and to play the higher notes with the right hand. This is illustrated in Example 5-7a: The left-hand notes are lower than the right-hand notes. (The example shows three ways of indicating the sticking; unless the composer is knowledgeable enough about sticking technique to specify an unusual sticking, such indication is not ordinarily given. If it *is* indicated, the notation in a is recommended.)

Example 5-7

If the hands were crossed, as in Example 5-7d, the action would be less comfortable, and there would be a greater chance of missed notes; but if the crossed sticking remains *consistent*, there is no real problem. "Consistency" in this case means that neither hand moves very far from one note to the next and does not move between black and white keys.

Accuracy can be affected when there are sudden changes from one posture to another, as in Example 5-7e. The right–left alternation requires a constant crossing of one hand over the other (cross-sticking). Cross-sticking results when the right hand must play a low note and the left hand a high note. This will occur with *an odd-numbered series of notes moving in one direction,* as in Example 5-8a. Any reiterated odd-numbered pattern, such as in Example 5-8b, also creates this problem.

Example 5-8a

Example 5-8b   Berlioz, *Symphonie fantastique,* mvt. 5, twelve before 85

To avoid cross-sticking, the player can *double-stick,* as in Example 5-7f. This is mechanically easier for the arm but not for the wrist and fingers, and the result may be uneven dynamically and rhythmically. Fast double-sticking is easier when notes move by seconds and do not change from white to black keys; moving from a black to an adjacent white key is the easiest movement. Within these limits, double-sticking that is not repetitive can be accomplished at a speed of about four notes per beat at quarter note = 144; otherwise, it should be limited to 120.

If a player is expected to strike different drums in succession, the same considerations apply, but here the situation is more critical, since the distances are larger than on a xylophone. Traditionally, a set of like drums is arranged from left to right in order of ascending pitch.[2] Double-sticking, however, is easier on drums than on instruments like the xylophone because the striking areas are larger and the surfaces are more flexible, allowing the sticks to bounce more readily.

If the composer wants a fast-moving part involving a series of notes or instruments, he or she should try to visualize the motion required to execute it. If there are also irregularities in dynamics or rhythm, these will add to the difficulty of the passage; thus, the most natural pattern will be the most successful.

Multisticking (on Mallet Instruments)

At times, it is helpful to use different mallets in each hand: A marimba passage with high and low notes in alternation might benefit from a harder mallet held in the right hand and a softer one in the left, to match the different responses of those notes on the instrument. In another case, the composer might want to bring out certain notes by assigning them to the hand that holds the harder mallet, and so on.

It is possible to hold more than one stick or mallet in each hand, as is often done in solo mallet playing. In orchestral playing, no more than two in one hand is usual. The interval between notes played by one hand can be as large as an octave, and in the upper register, a tenth. Isolated chords are the most practical, but if there *is* movement from chord to chord, it is better if the motion is parallel, and black and white notes are not mixed. See Example 5-9a.

Rolls between notes are usually accomplished by alternation of hands, as in Example 5-9b, or within hands, as in 5-9c, but the *notation* should appear as it is in 5-9a. For one-handed rolls, the notes should be at least a fourth apart.

Example 5-9

---

[2]Contrary to the practice in England and America, timpanists in Continental Europe place their drums right-to-left in ascending pitch.

When the player has more than one stick in a hand, a fast, single-line passage should not come just before or just after a chordal passage unless it can be executed at least partly by arpeggiating, using different sticks in one hand. Arpeggiation should be limited to either white- or black-key notes, and the intervals between notes played by one hand should be a third or larger. Example 5-10 gives an example of such a passage.

Example 5-10

Isolated chords requiring three mallets in one or both hands are possible, and some limited chordal movement is feasible if the voice leading is strictly parallel in the white keys, as in Example 5-11.

Example 5-11

Marimba

Drums placed rim-to-rim can be played simultaneously by sticks held in one hand (the obvious limit being two), making three- or four-note chords possible.

Pictograms can be used to indicate how sticks or mallets are to be held (see Example 5-3).

Common Ornamental Patterns

Traditional figures that are used to ornament, emphasize, or give greater fullness to single notes are shown in Example 5-12. (There does not seem to be universal

Example 5-12

a. Flam   **b.** Drag   **c.** Ruff

agreement on these terms or on whether slurs should be placed over the notes.) When these figures are inserted into rhythms, they can add interest and excitement.

PITCHED MEMBRANOPHONES

Certain things are common to most of the membranophones, pitched and unpitched:

1. The normal striking point is about one-third the distance from the rim to the center of the drumhead.
2. Striking near the rim increases the brilliance and decreases the fullness of the tone.
3. Striking at the center decreases brilliance and results in a thumpy, relatively dull sound.
4. Resonance can be inhibited by
   a. Not allowing the stick to rebound ("dead-sticking").
   b. Placing the hand on the head before or after the stroke.
   c. Playing with a piece of soft material, such as a cloth, on the surface of the head ("muffled").
5. The pitch of the instrument may be altered by
   a. Striking the head at various locations.
   b. Pressing the head with the heel of the hand (which increases tension and raises the pitch).

Ed Brown Studio

MEMBRANOPHONES

Bass Drum   Three Pedal Timpani
Field Drum   Tenor Drum   Snare Drum

Ed Brown Studio

MEMBRANOPHONES

| | Two Bongos | Two Timbales | | Three Roto-Toms |
Two Congas | | | Two Tom-toms |
| | Lion's Roar | Tabla |

6. As drum size gets smaller, the decay time decreases and the sound becomes more "pingy"; as drums get larger, decay time increases and the pitch may have less clarity and stability.

7. The use of the hands alone is more idiomatic for drums without raised rims (bongos, congas, and the like). Extensive or very intricate use of the hands should be called for only if it is known that the players are capable of it and have developed protective calluses.

The Roto-Toms

Ranges.   See Example 5-13. These can be exceeded somewhat.

Example 5-13   Ranges of the roto-toms

Description.   This is a relatively new type of instrument, having one head and a raised rim. Two or three drums are usually mounted together on a stand.

Some are made with a bowl resonator, like the timpani. By rotating the drum in one direction or the other, the player can raise or lower the pitch.

Quality.   The sound is more resonant and penetrating than that of the tom-tom. The higher instruments can be used as upward extensions of the timpani, but they have clearer pitch and a more brittle sound.

Technique.   A whole set of seven drums, arranged in a semicircle, can be managed by one player. Although tuning changes can be accomplished with nearly the same speed as on the timpani, they are not possible while playing with both hands unless a second player is available, since one hand is needed to turn the drum. A second player also would make a *rolled* glissando possible.

Rim shots. The raised rim allows playing on the rim alone or playing *rim shots.* Rim shots are accomplished in one of two ways: (1) by holding one stick at the center of the head and hitting it with the other stick (a fast series of such rim shots could be played by a second player using a separate pair of sticks) or (2) by hitting the head and the rim simultaneously with one stick (sometimes called a "hoop crack"). The effect is like a pistol shot—extremely sharp and startling. If isolated rim shots are desired, they can be indicated by writing "R.S." over the notes. For more extensive use, ×'s can be used in place of the noteheads, with an explanation of their meaning. *Rim shots are associated mostly with snare-drum playing.*

Scores.   Maxwell Davies, *Eight Songs for a Mad King, Stedman Caters.*

Boobams (Bamboo Drums)

Range.   See Example 5-14.

Example 5-14   Range of the boobams

Description.   Boobams have bamboo shells 4½ inches in diameter and 9–40 inches deep. They are one-headed, with no rim. It is possible to arrange them in keyboard fashion on a rack. The main pitch comes from the length of the shell (that is, the air column within the shell) rather than from the drumhead. The instruments are not readily available.

Quality and Technique.   The quality is deep and clear, like that of a marimba. The head gives off its own pitch, most noticeably in the lower notes and in loud playing. Fast notes can be unclear, owing to confusion between the shell pitches and those of the head. Glisses are not possible from drum to drum.

Score.   Henze, *El Cimmarón.*

The Timpani (Kettledrums)[3]

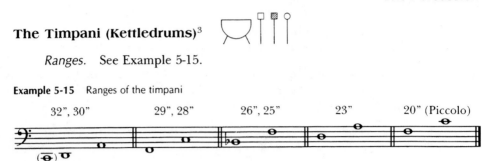

Ranges.   See Example 5-15.

Example 5-15   Ranges of the timpani

Description.   Each drum has a calfskin or plastic drumhead that is stretched across the rim of a large bowl made of copper or another material. The drumhead may be 32, 30, 29, 28, 26, 25, 23, or 20 inches in diameter. The head can be tightened or loosened by a series of screws located around the rim. The *mechanical timpano* has a master screw that acts on all the other screws at once. The *pedal timpano* has a foot pedal that tightens the head to raise the pitch and loosens it to lower the pitch. The pitch can thus be changed quickly anywhere within the range of the drum.

A professional orchestra can be expected to have two sets of timpani. Thus, two drums of the same size can be employed. This might be necessary only if a fast chromatic progression is called for.[4]

Quality.   The tone is a composite of the impact of the stick and the shimmering of the drumhead as it settles quickly down to a clear pitch. A single tone can ring for as long as 3 seconds. When the stroke is heavy, the pitch is temporarily flattened, and the quality can change almost instantly from "a" as in "after" to "oo," and resemble a crash of thunder. In a passage with a sudden rise or drop of dynamics, there might be a slight change in pitch level.

If any drum is tuned to the lowest part of its range, it loses some clarity of pitch and response; at the uppermost part, it can sound somewhat pinched and strained. The "best" quality, then, is in the midrange notes. These variations apply to all the timpani; in addition, the largest tend to rumble and the smallest to have a tight "ping."

Technique.   For most purposes, the designation "soft," "medium," or "hard" sticks will suffice. A brittle, penetrating, and articulate sound is provided by wooden timpani sticks; snare drum or metal sticks should not be used for loud playing because they can damage the head.

The initial tuning of the instruments is customarily shown at the beginning of the part in each movement. This may be given in letter names, as in Example

---

[3] *Timpani* (Ital.) is plural; one instrument is a *timpano.*

[4] For example, if the notes *d, d♯, e, f* were to be played quickly, the first two notes could be played on two 25-inch drums (tuned to *d* and *d♯*, respectively) and the last two on two 23-inch drums (tuned to *e* and *f,* respectively).

Example 5-16

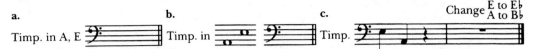

5-16a, or in musical notation, as in 5-16b. When a tuning change is needed, it should be indicated just after the last note in the old tuning. A common form of indicating this is shown in Example 5-16c. Although tuning can be changed very quickly on the mechanical and pedal timpani, the player should be given at least 10 seconds to check the new pitch.

Nevertheless, the pedal allows successive notes of different pitch to be played on the same drum. If this is intended, it is a good idea to number the drums (I for the lowest, II for the next lowest, and so on) to indicate how the notes are to be played, as in Example 5-17. When changing pitches on one drum, it is best to move by intervals of a second upward. When the pitch is raised, there will be a noticeable glissando. When it is lowered, there may not be a glissando, but the first note will be somewhat damped. An extended descending melodic line is given to the timpani after no. 65 in Copland's *Appalachian Spring*.

Example 5-17

Intended glissandos are effective. They can be rendered with a roll (Example 5-18a), without a roll (5-18b and 5-18c), with a struck note at the end (5-18a and 5-18b), or without a struck note at the end (5-18c). To make a descending gliss heard, it is best to roll it, because the lowering of the tension causes the sound to decay quickly.

Example 5-18

A timpano can act as a resonator for other instruments in two ways: An instrument can be played "into" it, or another percussion instrument can be laid on the drumhead (if it is a *pedal* timpano). In the latter case, the instrument is placed on the head with as little contact as possible, and that instrument is struck while the pedal is moved. This results in a rather eerie quasi gliss that seems to emanate from the added instrument. Cymbals and cup bells work particularly well for this, but the composer might experiment with other instruments, such as glasses, triangles, or woodblocks (played with or without rolls). Edgardo Simone in *Entrada* calls for sleigh bells to be placed on the head with the drum tuned as low as possible, and the head is slapped with the hand.

Playing a timpano with the two sticks at once gives a heavier sound than normal, which can be helpful in bringing out accents, as in Example 5-19 (indicated by the double-stemming). Some accuracy is needed for this, so it is better confined to professionals. The tone is a little duller than single-sticked notes.

Example 5-19

The flat rim does not allow the instrument to be bowed, so Crumb's *Star Child* calls for "sturdy wooden rulers with metal edges" to be used for bowing the timpani.

The Tabla

Range.   See Example 5-20.

Example 5-20   Range of the tabla

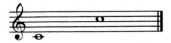

Description.   The tabla, popular in India and rarely found in the United States, is a small kettledrum having a thick, layered head of animal skins stretched over a wooden, bowl-shaped case. The center of the head has a patch made of paste that is an important factor in the pitch. The tabla is ordinarily accompanied by a larger, similar drum called the *banya, bhaya,* or *bamya.*

Quality and Technique.   The sound is like that of a small timpano. Traditional hand playing emphasizes a variety of pitches and colors; the three principal ones are called "tun," "tin," and "na." Do not expect a percussionist to even approximate the technique of a trained tabla player. Bongos can imitate the sound (as in Ravi Shankar's Concerto for Sitar).

UNPITCHED MEMBRANOPHONES

As has been said, it is difficult to decide in some cases which of these instruments sound "higher" than others. For one thing, pitch often depends partly on factors that are out of the composer's control, such as the size, material, and tension of the instrument; the sticks chosen; and temperature and humidity. For another thing, some instruments that come in sets may overlap other instruments in total range: The tom-toms, for example, overlap several instruments that are placed "lower."

The Snare Drum

Description. The snare drum came into the orchestra from the military band along with the closely related field drum, tenor drum, and bass drum. The various names for these instruments can cause confusion, partly because a given term can refer to different instruments in different countries. Basically, these instruments have a cylindrical shell made of metal or wood and drumheads on opposite sides. The tension of either head can be changed by means of screws, but not during playing. Normally, the heads are tuned to pitches that differ, creating an unpitched effect.

The top, or playing, head of the snare drum is called the "batter" head, and the bottom the "snare" head. Snares of gut or wire, stretched across the lower rim, are normally held against the batter head and vibrate against it when the instrument is struck. The snares can be held away from the head and later reengaged by means of a lever on the side of the shell. (This lever makes a snapping sound that could be heard in a quiet passage.) If the snares are to be released, "snares off" should be indicated; to reengage them, mark "snares on." No indication is needed to begin a piece with snares on.

There are various sizes of snare drum, from the piccolo snare drum, measuring 3–4 inches deep and 13–14 inches in diameter, to a large snare 10 inches deep and 14 inches in diameter. A homogeneous group can be assembled, rounded out by a field drum, to give a player an ensemble of varied pitch and color.

Quality. With snares on, the instrument is relatively high-pitched and crisp-sounding, although the snares add a bit of rattle to a basically dry attack. If the strokes are gentle enough, the snare sound may hardly be heard. With snares off, the pitch drops considerably and the sound becomes duller—more like that of a tom-tom or a bongo. It is important to note that the choice of sticks has much more effect on quality when the snares are off than when they are on, since the high pitch and the buzzing of the snares tend to override the quality of the head itself.

Playing softly near the rim can give a distant effect.

Technique. Snare-drum playing is noted for its great virtuosity. The quick response and clarity of the instrument allow very fast and intricate rhythms to be executed, along with a variety of sticking effects (see under "The Roto-toms" for a discussion of some of them; see also Example 5-12). A bewildering sequence of flams, drags, rolls, rim shots, and playing on the rim are typical of the style, although such showy playing is not often found in orchestral music. A technique not yet mentioned is the "rim click," which is a heavier version of playing on the rim: The tip of the stick is held against the drumhead, and the butt end of the stick is pivoted downward to strike the rim.

Wire brushes can be used very effectively to create a slapping sound with little resonance, a sustained swish that comes from a circular brushing, or a combination of the two.

The normal sticks can be struck together ("stick on stick" or "sticks alone"), producing a dry click with high pitch but little power.

Score.   Stick on stick: Ravel, Concerto for Piano, Left Hand.

The Tom-Toms (Tomtoms)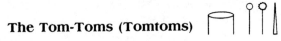

Range.   See Example 5-21.

Example 5-21   Range of the tom-toms

Description.   Tom-toms are similar in construction to the snare drum, but they are without snares and have wooden shells with raised rims. There are two-headed and one-headed versions. The diameter ranges from 10 to 18 inches and the depth from 8 to 20 inches. A set can have as many as eight drums.

Quality.   The sound is close to that of the bongos and, at the lower pitch end, that of the bass drum. The single-headed drum is more resonant and has clearer pitch than the double-headed variety, which is heavier-sounding. The decay time ranges from less than a second for the highest to about 2 seconds for the lowest drum.

Technique.   The technique is similar to that used for the snare drum. Some pitch variations, including glisses, are possible, by pressing on the head with the heel of the hand. A single player can play a full set of drums.

Scores.   Stockhausen, *Gruppen*; Joan Tower, *Silver Ladders*.

Bongos

Range.   See Example 5-22.

Example 5-22   Range of the bongos

Description. These drums are single-headed and usually have a conical shell that is rimless. The depth is about 5 inches and the width is 6–8 inches. Two drums are attached as a pair: They are of different sizes, producing different pitches. If more than two drums are to be used, they can't be arranged in an unbroken progression of lowest to highest; thus, a complicated part can be somewhat difficult for the player to learn.

Quality and Technique. The sound is rather intense. The instrument speaks very quickly and explosively and with a quick decay. Various effects can be gotten with the hands by slapping, tapping, or rubbing.

Scores. Boulez, *Le marteau sans maître;* Varèse, *Ionisation;* Copland, *Orchestral Variations.*

Timbales

Range. See Example 5-23.

Example 5-23 Range of the timbales

Description. Timbales consist of a cylindrical metal shell, ranging from 6 to 10 inches deep and from 12 to 14 inches wide, and one head. The rim is raised. Like bongos, the instruments come in attached pairs, tuned differently.

Quality. The sound is metallic and aggressive, with a very quick decay—brighter than that of the tom-tom.

Technique. The raised rim allows snare-drum-style sticking. Latin American techniques include playing with one stick on the head and the other on the shell, and using a hand to muffle the sound.

Scores. Jacob Druckman, *Prisms;* Roldan, *Ritmicas V and VI;* Hindemith, *Cardillac.*

Congas (Tumbas)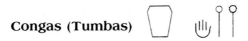

Range. See Example 5-24. Although the range of the congas is generally higher than that given for the timbales, the instrument often *sounds* lower.

Example 5-24 Range of the congas

Description. The drums are barrel-shaped and one-headed, and have a covered rim. The height can range from 18 to 30 inches and the width from 10 to 12 inches. They often come in high–low pairs.

Quality and Technique. The large size yields a resonant, hollow sound, but the head is tight, causing a very quick decay. The design favors hand playing, like the bongos; in fact, it is usually assumed that hands are to be used unless sticks are specified. Typical usage is slaps and rolls. The congas form a group with the bongos.

Scores. Druckman, *Prisms;* Copland, *Orchestral Variations;* Gershwin, *Porgy and Bess;* Boulez, *Rituel in Memoriam Maderna.*

The Frame Drum

Description. The frame drum has a head stretched across a shallow frame, resembling a large tambourine without jingles. Diameters range from 10 to 24 inches.

Quality and Technique. The sound is a brief rumble with unclear pitch. The instrument is designed primarily to be struck with the hand.

Scores. Boulez, *Le marteau sans maître;* De Falla, *El Retablo de Maese Pedro;* Orff, *Schulwerk.*

The Field Drum (Military Drum, Parade Drum, Side Drum)

Description. The field drum is a larger form of the snare drum, usually 12–16 inches deep and having a diameter of 14–16 inches. One author, at least, distinguishes between the parade drum and the field drum, calling the former a smaller version of the long drum. It is tuned by cords that run across the shell crosswise.

Quality and Technique. The field drum is more resonant and lower-sounding than the snare drum and employs the same technique.

The Tenor Drum

Description. The tenor drum is like the field drum, but without snares. In *Die Walküre,* act 3, Wagner called for the tenor drum's head to be tightened and later returned to its normal tension.

Quality and Technique. The sound is similar to that of the field drum—deep and resonant. The technique is also similar.

The Tabor and the Long Drum

Description. The tabor is a relatively long wooden drum with two heads and no snares. It is best known in France and is rarely found in the United States. The long drum, also French, resembles the tenor drum and has a few snares held against the bottom head.

Quality. The tabor is clear but rather hollow-sounding.

Scores. Tabor: Copland, *Appalachian Spring, El salón México;* Milhaud, Concerto for Percussion; Honegger, *King David.* Long Drum: Hindemith, *Mathis der Maler;* Strauss, *Till Eulenspiegels lustige Streiche.*

The Lion's Roar (Friction Drum, String Drum)

Description. The lion's roar is a single-headed drum with a long string passing through a hole in the head. It comes in various sizes. Smaller drums are suspended from a rack with the string hanging down; larger ones rest on the floor.

Quality. The sound is an animallike moan or roar, with a quick crescendo and rise in pitch ("o-*ah*-o"), which can be rather startling and unlike most other sounds in the orchestra. A "note" usually lasts about 2 seconds at the most.

Technique. The string is rubbed with a wet hand or with a rosined glove or cloth.

Scores. Varèse, *Ionisation, Hyperprism;* Stephen Rouse, *The Infernal Machine.*

The Bass Drum

Description. The bass drum is a larger tenor drum (without snares). The depth is usually 16 inches, but it can be as much as 2 feet, with a width of 24–40 inches. There are several sizes. Some have one head (*gong drum*). It may be suspended on a frame that can be fixed in any degree of uprightness or flatness. If a change of position is called for, it is best to allow some time for it.

Quality. The timbre is very dark and varies with the size of the drum, the tension of the head, and the strike point. Playing near the edge gives it some "ping." A stroke at the center produces a rather dull thump (sometimes indicated as "cannon shot"). The ring time can be as much as 5 seconds, but with a quick fall-off of energy. Soft tones can be almost subliminal, having practically no attack, but even these may shake the floor. Rolls and loud strikes can be overwhelmingly powerful.

Gong drums give a pitched effect, as do double-headed drums when the heads are tuned in unison.

A foot pedal may be used to beat the drum, freeing the player's hands, but this removes the control and variety of sound that are possible normally.

Technique.   With the drum upright, the player can beat both sides with beaters of the same kind or of different kinds. The double-headed beater offers a choice of sounds that can be produced alternately (by one hand). It can also be used for one-handed rolls if there is good reason to have the other hand free.

THE MALLET INSTRUMENTS

Construction.   The mallet instruments have bars of various length that are arranged in keyboard fashion. They are so named because they are most often played with mallets. The bars of the xylophone, the marimba, and the vibraphone are not uniformly thick, but are graduated on their underside in an arch, the thinnest point being at the midpoint of the lengthwise dimension. See Example 5-25. The purpose of this shaping is to tune the bars so that the modes are more like the harmonic series, which makes the fundamental clearer but which also brings out certain overtones, giving the instruments their unique sound.

Example 5-25

Ed Brown Studio

MARIMBA, XYLOPHONE, AND GLOCKENSPIEL.

Marimba   Glockenspiel   Xylophone

Ed Brown Studio

VIBRAPHONE

A resonator tube is placed directly below the midpoint of each bar on vibra-phones, marimbas, and most xylophones to further enhance the fundamental by resonating with it. Since the node for the fundamental is *not* at the midpoint, the normal strike point (to bring it out) *is* precisely at that point (as discussed in connection with Example 5-1a, where 1 represents the mode of the fundamental). When the bar is struck about one-half the distance between the middle and the end of the bar (*at* a node of the fundamental), an overtone is more likely to be heard than the fundamental. This effect will be enhanced if a finger is simultaneously pressed down at the midpoint. (For this, indicate "harmonic.")

Quality. Since no two bars on a mallet instrument are the same length (the higher the pitch, the shorter the bar), the physical relationship between a given mallet and the bar it strikes is never the same for any two bars (that is, the striking area of the mallet remains the same while the *proportion* of that area to the length of the bar changes); thus, *quality* will also never be exactly the same. Differences are most pronounced between the highest and lowest bars. A mallet suitable for high notes may produce an unsatisfactory sound from the low-pitched bars, and the converse is also true. For example, instead of a single-line melody from the low xylophone, a series of parallel fifths could result from a prominent overtone!

Technique. Like drumheads, mallet bars can be damped either by a hand or by the mallet itself (see the notation in Example 5-2d).

The keyboard arrangement of the notes allows some keyboard techniques to be used, especially a glissando over either the black or the white keys. Usually, the gliss is finished with a stroke by the opposite hand on the last note.

When individual strokes are used for fast passages moving in one direction, it is more difficult to play only white notes than it is to play some mixture of the two colors. Thus, Example 5-26a is more difficult than 5-26b.

Example 5-26

Xylophone

The availability of two or more mallets allows great facility of movement. (One should, as always, keep in mind the reverberance of the instrument.) Xylophone and marimba transcriptions of virtuoso violin pieces, for example, are common. As on the piano, one feature of technique is the ability to move very quickly between notes very far apart on the keyboard.

The reader should review the discussion of sticking techniques and rolls (Examples 5-6 through 5-12).

The ends of the bars, like the rims of the cymbals, the gongs, and similar instruments, can be set into vibration by a bow—usually a cello or a bass bow. The sound has no attack and is generally pure and clear (once established). The player must be given some time to play in this manner, and it must be noted that black-key notes are bowed at the back of the instrument and the white-key notes at the front; thus, although a succession of notes is feasible at moderate speed on one color, more time is needed to go between colors (unless two players share the task).

The Glockenspiel (Orchestral Bells)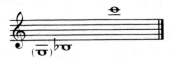

Range. The glockenspiel comes in various sizes. Ranges given in various sources generally include the notes in Example 5-27. The range *G-c* is the most common. The notation is ordinarily *two octaves lower than sounding.*

Example 5-27   Range of the glockenspiel

Description. Metal bars are arranged in keyboard fashion and attached to a portable case. Some instruments come equipped with a pedal damper. Since the early years of this century, the French have used a keyed version of the instrument, which is played like a piano (*jeu de timbres*), but its action is unreliable and it is rare in the United States. Parts written for it (for example, Ravel's *Daphnis et Chloé*) are a challenge to glockenspiel players.

Quality. The sound is highly resonant, bright, and tingly. A tone can resonate for 5 seconds. The upper tones are very clear, but the lower bars can emphasize overtones, as is curiously illustrated by the two-note passage from Copland's Third Symphony shown in Example 5-28a. In performances in which the author took part and in three commercial recordings, including one conducted by the composer, the second note, played on a much lower bar, sounded as a high F, as shown in Example 5-28b, rather than the "played" B! The F is not in the *harmonic* series of B, but it is one of the overtones for a *bar* tuned to B (as may be verified by playing the note).

Example 5-28   Copland, Symphony No. 3, mvt. 1, no. 19

© *Copyright 1947 by Aaron Copland; Copyright Renewed. Reprinted by permission of the Estate of Aaron Copland, Copyright Owner, and Boosey & Hawkes, Inc., Sole Licensees.*

Technique. One is reminded that successive tones often overlap, owing to the reverberance of the instrument. The highness of the pitches causes notes played at the same time to jangle dissonantly—such notes played loudly can be unpleasant. For that reason, the part is written on one staff, since it usually consists of single lines.

The bars can be detached from the frame and played like tuned cymbals.

The Xylophone

Range. The xylophone is also built in various sizes. Some of the ranges that have been given are shown in Example 5-29. The range *F–c* is standard. Usually, the notation is *an octave lower than sounding.*

Example 5-29   Ranges of the xylophone

Description. The bars are made of wood or synthetic material and may be reinforced by tubular resonators beneath.

Lower-pitched forms of the instrument are the *bass xylophone*, which is rare, and the *xylorimba*, which is rare in the United States but is used in Europe as an intermediary between the xylophone and the marimba, both of which it resembles.

Quality. Generally, the tone is crisp, dry, and penetrating. The lower tones can have a quality that is distinctly different from the upper ones. If marimba mallets are used on them, the sound is very marimbalike. Conversely, xylophone mallets used on the upper notes of the marimba make a xylophonelike sound.

The tonal possibilities of the instrument go beyond the usual "clatter" with which it is associated. For example, in the second movement of his *Iberia* at m. 35, Debussy doubled the xylophone with the second flute!

Technique. Very hard sticks, such as triangle beaters, should not be used, because they are damaging to the bars.

The Marimba

Ranges. Various ranges exist, two of which are shown in Example 5-30. The part is usually written *at pitch,* otherwise an octave higher or lower than sounding.

Example 5-30 Range of the marimba

Description. This instrument has wooden or synthetic bars reinforced by resonators. Bass marimbas exist, but they are rare.

Quality. In middle and lower registers, the sound is more mellow and slower-speaking than the xylophone. Low notes, played with soft mallets, can be almost attackless. When high notes are played with xylophone mallets, they sound like that instrument. In general, the tone is not penetrating and cannot be expected to cut through most textures of moderate-to-dense thickness.

Technique. The instrument is well suited to lyrical styles and fairly full textures. Within limits (as explained earlier), its parts can be somewhat like piano parts—with some three- or four-part harmony—and are often written on two staves. Constant rolling can become tiresome, however.

The Vibraphone (Vibraharp)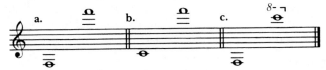

Ranges. Various ranges exist, as shown in Example 5-31. The range in c is not commonly found.

Example 5-31   Ranges of the vibraphone

Description. The vibraphone consists of aluminum bars with resonators below. Metal discs (fans) are suspended inside at the tops of the resonators. They can be rotated from a position that completely closes off the tube, to one that leaves it completely or partly open. A motor spins the fans at a desired speed (from about two to eight times per second)—the usual indication is "slow motor" or "fast motor." Dampers are normally held against the bars. A foot pedal can release them for maximum resonance. It can be held in the on position by a weight.

The bars of the vibraphone lie completely flat, unlike those of the other mallets, whose black keys are raised above the white ones, as on the piano.

Quality and Technique. The basic sound has been described as smooth, mellow, sweet, or like a tuning fork. Soft mallets can make the attack almost imperceptible. Although the tone is full and round, it is not penetrating. One of the most important features is its resonance, which can attain some 7 seconds with the damper pedal depressed. The player can manually position the fans for more or less resonance when the motor is off.

By manipulating the pedal, the player can vary the lengths of notes; thus, it is not unreasonable to write a part with a variety of articulations, such as in Example 5-32 (which shows the appropriate pedal indications). "Flutter-pedaling" can control the decay of a note by a reiterated use of the pedal, approximating a *fp* (the indication is "flutter-pedal"). With the pedal down, selected tones can be played staccato by mallet-damping them while others sustain.

Example 5-32

Vibraphone

half
pedal

When the motor is on, the fans continuously open and close the resonators, causing a periodic change of timbre, along with a slight pitch vibrato. The slowest rate yields a gentle pulsation, and the fast rates approximate the vibrato of string and wind players, although their tremulant character can be a little jarring. The motor is operated by a hand switch. It can be turned on whenever there is a free hand (while playing with one hand, or just after playing a note).

It is possible to get a very soft pitch gliss ("pitch bend") by striking a bar, then pressing a mallet against the bar while moving it toward the player. This causes a bend of about a semitone *downward*. It is more pronounced with higher notes and not very effective with the pedal off. The bend requires about a half-second to sound. The notation is "pitch bend" and a diagonal line, as for a gliss.

Hard mallets, such as plastic or glass, should not be used, because they can dent the bars.

Scores. Berg, *Lulu;* Britten, Cello Concerto, *Death in Venice.*

PITCHED METALS AND GLASSES

Like mallet bars, many of these instruments can be bowed as well as struck. Bowing is not effective on chimes or steel drums.

Although the celesta is technically a pitched metallophone, it is placed in Chapter 6, since it is often associated with the harp and the piano, and it is usually played by the pianist.

The Crotales and the Antique Cymbals

Range. Usually, the range is the upper octave in Example 5-33. The notes may be written to sound either *an octave or two octaves higher.* Example 5-33 is meant to sound two octaves higher. It is best to specify which is intended.

Example 5-33 Range of the crotales

Description. Crotales are flat, circular brass plates 3 to 5½ inches in diameter and ¼ inch thick. They may be mounted in keyboard arrangement. Individual crotales can be held and played independently, in which case they can serve as *antique cymbals,* the instruments from which they are derived. In this case, one crotale may be struck by another or by a beater.

Quality and Technique. The sound is clear and bright, with a certain high-pitched shimmer—like that of the glockenspiel. Keyboard glissandos are not practical because the plates do not form a continuous surface from one to the next. The ring time can be as much as about 15 seconds.

Ed Brown Studio

PITCHED METALS

Small Gong	Small Tam-tam	Chimes	Crotales (tilted Bell forward) Tree
Tam-tam	Gong	Tenor Steel Drum	Almglocke Almglocke
	Two Handbells		Cowbell

Scores. Debussy, *Prelude to The Afternoon of a Faun* (antique cymbals); Britten, *A War Requiem;* Adams, *Short Ride on a Fast Machine;* Davies, *Stone Litany.*

Musical Glasses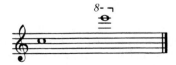

Range. See Example 5-34. This is approximate.

Example 5-34 Range of the glasses

Description.   Musical glasses are crystal drinking glasses, usually not made for musical purposes, but occasionally manufactured as such. They may be placed on a table with their bases taped down and tuned by partly filling them with water.

Quality and Technique.   The player runs a wet finger around the outside of the rim, producing a very smooth sound that seems to emerge from nowhere. The glasses may also be bowed or struck. The timbre is pure and sustained with no attack.

Scores.   Lou Harrison, *Canticle No. 1;* Orff, *Schulwerk, Der Mond;* Davies, *Stone Litany.*

Handbells

Range.   The usual range is shown in Example 5-35.

Example 5-35   Range of the handbells

Description.   Handbells are bells with handles. Movement of the bell causes a clapper to strike an inner surface. There are sets of up to sixty-one instruments.

Quality and Technique.   The tone is very pure and ringing, associated with Christmas music. The lower bells are especially smooth. They are ordinarily played in change ringing, where each player is assigned to two bells, one in each hand, and melodies can require the interaction of many players.

Scores.   Crumb, *Star-Child;* Britten, *Noye's Fludde.*

The Chimes (Tubular Chimes)

Range.   See Example 5-36. This is sometimes extended downward. The notes sound *as written.*

Example 5-36   Range of the chimes

Description.   The chimes are metal tubes from 1 to 1½ inches in diameter and from 40 to 66 inches long. They are usually hung in a rack, keyboard-fashion, with the "black" notes above and behind the "white" ones. A damper pedal can act on all the tubes at once. If only certain chimes are needed, or to arrange all of them in some other manner (for example, for a complicated passage), it is possible to remove the tubes from the rack; however, the damper pedal would then not be available.

Quality.   The sound is very reminiscent of church bells, with long decay times. The usual strike point is at the top rim. Other strike points yield somewhat different timbres but are not normally used.

As with large bells, a "hum" tone a major sixth lower than the main pitch can also be heard. Example 5-37 shows the hum tones that can accompany a melody.

Example 5-37

Chime mallets, covered with rawhide, are used for the normal sound. Uncovered metal beaters and plastic-tipped or wooden sticks give a clangorous effect, whereas yarn mallets and chime mallets covered with cloth are smooth and almost without attack.

Technique.   Involved chime parts are not usually practical because tones may overlap and the player may have difficulty keeping track of the music, the conductor, and the chime to be struck, all at the same time.

It is possible to play adjacent chimes with one mallet. It is also possible to hold two mallets in one hand, as long as the notes to be played are only white or only black notes and are not more than a third apart.

Steel Drums

Range.   Ranges are given for several sizes. Example 5-38 gives three that cover the combined range.

Example 5-38   Ranges of the steel drums

Description.   Steel drums are made from oil barrels cut down and hammered into bowl shapes. The upper surfaces are sectioned into areas that yield specific pitches when struck, and the name of each pitch is painted on its area. Since most instruments are homemade, there is no standardization of the range, pitch level, or pitch content of the drums; for example, the "A" may be something different from the orchestral 440. The highest drum, or "pan," (the ping-pong, or lead drum), has the greatest number of notes (some twenty-five, which are playable, but not physically arranged, in chromatic progression). The lower drums have fewer (the cello about ten and the bass five or fewer), and these are likely to be only "white notes." A group of drums might have six bass drums to fill in pitch gaps.

The patterns of pitches vary, but one often finds a pattern in whole tones; for example, one of a pair of tenor drums can have a whole-tone scale (with the notes arranged circularly in augmented triads) and the other drum the remaining notes—the other whole-tone scale—which makes it possible, using both drums, to play any of the notes in one octave.

Originating in the Caribbean, the instruments are not readily available.

Quality and Technique.   The sound is metallic but mellow. The pitch wavers with a fast "boing" or "boink," and the resonance is about 2 seconds. About halfway through a tone's duration, the overtone two octaves higher emerges and recedes. The other notes in the pan generally can be heard resonating; thus, all of a whole-tone scale might be faintly heard in the background. Of course, with pitch movement, those effects will be lost. The drums are usually played in complete groups, and as such can sound very much like an organ or a synthesizer. Rolls are effective.

Scores.   Henze, *El Cimarrón;* Stokes, *Captions;* Haubenstock-Ramati, *Vermutungen über ein dunkles Haus.*

Gongs

Range.   See Example 5-39.

Example 5-39   Range of the gongs

Description.   The gong is a round, flat metal disc with a bent rim and a raised dome in the center, suspended from a frame by a cord. The diameter ranges from 7 to 60 inches. Usually, the instruments are described as "very small," "small," "medium-sized," and so on. It may be possible to acquire a set of gongs and arrange them in a chromatic series, but they are very expensive. Gongs are much rarer than tam-tams; consequently, a gong part is often played on a tam-tam.

The main distinction between a gong and a tam-tam is that the gong is pitched, owing to its raised dome and bent rim. The names are often interchanged.

Quality and Technique.   The name is a good representation of the sound. It is highly resonant, with a ring that can last over a half-minute and vibrations that continue long afterward. The striking implement and the force of the stroke have great influence over the timbre. Above about *mf,* a jangling crash emerges soon after the stroke; as this subsides, the basic pitch is heard as a residual hum. A stroke near the rim brings a brighter sound, and a stroke on the crown a purer, darker one. If the vibration is damped at the crown, some clarity of pitch is lost; if the damping is done at the rim, pitch is clearer but some brilliance is lost.

For any loud tone of "good quality" on a large gong, the player must quietly set the instrument into vibration before the stroke is to occur; otherwise, the effect will be noisy. Therefore, the player who must move from another instrument to the gong should be given some time to prepare the stroke.

Bowing produces a high-pitched, sustained squeal. A few seconds are needed to prepare for it.

Metal objects, such as a coin or a triangle beater, can be scraped across the surface with a resonant "zing." Such objects also may be scraped, tremolo-fashion, giving a scratchy sound.

The "water gong" effect is achieved by lowering one of the smaller instruments into a tub of water after, or while, it is struck or rolled. This produces a drop in pitch and change of quality. Two players are needed for this. It can be notated as in Example 5-40.

Example 5-40   Water gong

Score.   WATER GONG: David Ott, *Vertical Shrines.*

UNPITCHED METALS AND GLASSES

In this group, it seems logical to include all types of wind chimes, even though some are made of glass and wood, as well as metal.

Most of the instruments are high-pitched, and it is not possible to list them definitively by pitch level. They appear, therefore, in approximate order.

The Triangle

Description.   The triangle is a metal rod bent into a triangular shape that is open at one corner. It is generally suspended from a stand or from a cord held in a clamp. Sizes range from 4 to 10 inches per side.

Quality and Technique.   The familiar sound is extremely bright and ringing, although somewhat thin. It can vary in quality and pitch over a fairly wide

Ed Brown Studio

UNPITCHED METALS

| Metal Windchimes | Large Triangle | Small Triangle | Two Suspended Cymbals |

Bamboo Windchimes

| Anvil | Brake Drum | | Crash Cymbal |
| | Crash Cymbal | Finger Cymbal | Tambourine |

range, according to how, where, and with what it is struck. High pitches are emphasized when it is struck near a closed corner. Lower pitches are produced at the center of an open side with the beater held parallel to that side.

All kinds of rhythms and rolls are possible, using one or two beaters, but the reverberation time of 5 or so seconds will make overlapping sounds indistinct. The vibrations can be damped by a hand or a cloth, or by suspending the instrument on a thicker cord, or by some similar device.

A quasi vibrato or quasi tremolo can be attained by shaking the instrument after it is struck (this varies the direction of sound radiation as it swings about).

Wooden sticks are generally not satisfactory in bringing out the full tone of the instrument—the pitch of the stick itself can be heard along with that of the instrument.

The Finger Cymbals

Description. These very small cymbals—about 2 inches in diameter—are held on the fingers with leather straps. They are also made in pairs, mounted so that they can be struck together using only one hand.

Quality and Technique. When the cymbals are struck together, strapped in the fingers, the sound is very high-pitched and trianglelike, but not strong. Repetitions can be fairly fast. If one is held free while struck by the other or by a metal beater, the pitch is clearer.

Score. Bernstein, Symphony No. 3.

The Cymbals

Description. This instrument is almost synonymous with "percussion." It has been studied from many different standpoints, especially its quality. Closely related to the gong and the tam-tam, it is a thin metal plate curving upward toward the center to form a crown, or dome. The *crash cymbals*, or two-plate cymbals, are held in the hands by means of straps. They normally range from 17 to 22 inches in diameter.

The *suspended cymbal* is hung from a hook or mounted on a stand. It comes in diameters of 10–24 inches: For most purposes, it is sufficient to call for "small," "medium," or "large" cymbals.

The *splash cymbal* is a suspended cymbal that has a diameter of 8–12 inches.

The *sizzle cymbal,* also suspended, has metal rivets loosely fixed in holes around the edge. It also comes in sizes. Its sound can be imitated by a suspended cymbal that has a small chain attached to its center and draped over the top surface.

The *hi-hat* is a pair of cymbals, one mounted on a vertical rod with its crown facing up, and the other below it with the crown down. Activated by a foot pedal, the rod brings the edges of the cymbals together by lowering the upper plate.

The *Chinese cymbal* is somewhat smaller than the usual (Turkish) cymbal and has a flatter dome. It is less available than the other cymbals.

Quality. The tonal and dynamic possibilities of the cymbals are very great. A stroke near the edge of the suspended cymbal gives a bright sound, and on the crown a relatively dull one. As with the gong and the tam-tam, the tone ordinarily begins with a relatively low pitch that is covered very soon with a "crash" as high modes take over, after which a slow decay gradually leaves a low-pitched hum that can persist as much as 15 seconds. A quick damping of the plate will cut off the pitched portion of the sound, leaving mostly a brief "tsh." A soft stroke near the edge can prevent the high modes from developing and produces a surprisingly quiet and low shimmer. A loud roll produces a sustained "tshhh," and a soft one a vibrant hum.

The crash cymbals are capable of a wider range of dynamics. These large plates are brought together at an angle and then moved forward to face the audience, directing the maximum of their energy toward them.

The splash cymbal has a splashy sound with a quick decay.

The sizzle cymbal has a sustained hiss and a longer ring than the suspended cymbal.

The hi-hat can be played softly by using the foot, producing muffled clicks, or with a stick playing on the top plate. When the plates are held together and struck with a stick, the sound is a very dry "tick"; held far apart, the upper plate rings freely; held apart closely, the plates jangle together. The symbol "+" can be used to indicate that the cymbals are to be closed, and "o" that they are to be open.

The Chinese cymbal emphasizes higher modes, yielding a good "splash." The decay is relatively short and the pitch less clear than with the other cymbals. Bowing is more successful with this instrument.

Techniques.   A wide range of sticks and mallets have been used effectively on the suspended cymbal. Timpani sticks should be avoided, because they can be damaged by the cymbal. Rolls are very common, especially on the suspended cymbal; they can also be accomplished with the crash cymbals by a scraping action, but not as satisfactorily. The fingers can tap the suspended cymbal for soft effects.

When a player has one hand occupied, the other hand can play a roll on the suspended cymbal by holding two sticks on either side of the edge of the plate or by forcing the wires of a wire brush around the edge of the cymbal.

Fast repeated notes are possible on the suspended or hi-hat cymbals, but the crash cymbals should not be asked for notes faster than about four per second.

As with the gong, a metal object scraped across the surface of the suspended cymbal gives a "zing." The crash cymbals can give a comparable effect scraped together and released, which is notated "striciato."

Crash cymbals can simulate vibrato if the player shakes the plates after the stroke.

The crash cymbals are damped by pressing the plates against the body. The suspended cymbal is damped by the fingers. Both can produce a remarkably abrupt "hand-over-the-mouth" effect.

Score.   SIZZLE CYMBAL: Foss, *Echoi.* HI-HAT: Weill, *Lost in the Stars.*

The Tambourine

Description.   A wooden hoop with slots in which pairs of small discs, or jingles, freely move on metal rods. A drumhead is stretched over one edge of the hoop, usually having a diameter of 8, 10, or 12 inches. Any movement of the instrument causes the jingles to rattle. A *jingle ring* is a headless tambourine.

Quality.   The sound of the drumhead by itself is a relatively dry pop or thud, depending on its size and tension; the jingles contribute a brief, high-pitched, metallic rustling. This has enough power to penetrate a moderately full texture, as in the excerpt shown in Example 8-14. When the instrument is shaken, the pitch of the head is still heard, but the jingles dominate.

Technique.   Single notes, moderately complex rhythms, and rolls are very common. There are various ways of using the instrument: The drumhead can be tapped with the fingertips for a softer sound, rapped with the knuckles for a harder one, or struck with sticks (with the instrument lying on a table). The instrument can also be struck alternately by the hand and against the knee. With the two hands, all sorts of combinations of shaking and striking are possible.

Rolls can be executed not only by shaking or with sticks but also by bouncing the thumb against the head. This gives a moderately soft roll that is smoother than the shaken type, but it cannot last for more than about 3 seconds. The recommended notation is "thumb roll." Shaken rolls not only can be louder but also can be immediately preceded or followed by fist strokes.

Wind Chimes

Range.   Individual pitches are usually not specified. The ensemble effect of the chimes gives a spectrum that overlaps lower-pitched instruments.

Description.   Wind chimes can consist of metal rods, rectangular sheets of glass, tubes of wood or bamboo, or shell discs. They are hung by strings from a rack and are free to swing against one another. The Mark tree is a metal form, having rods 12–18 inches in length. It comes in three sizes. Its rods are hung in a row, rather than in a circle, and can be struck individually, like miniature chimes.

Quality and Technique.   Wind chimes are usually stroked by a stick or a finger. They can also be blown by the player or an electric fan, or clutched together. The sound varies widely from material to material: As one might expect, the glass tinkles, the metal clinks, and the wood clatters. Stroking or blowing yields a low dynamic level, but clutching creates an accent. The releasing of a clutch also causes the chimes to sound. The *normal* effect is an uninterrupted jingling that dies away after 3 to 5 seconds. Typically, this is indicated by a half note with a "gliss" line extending from the notehead.

Scores.   Crumb, *Music for a Summer Evening, A Haunted Landscape;* Berio, *Circles.*

The Bell Tree

Description.   The bell tree is a set of cup-shaped bells arranged vertically on a rod in order of pitch in very small intervals.

Quality and Technique.   The sound resembles that of the wind chimes to some extent—all yield a shimmering blend of high-pitched sounds—but the bell tree produces a glissando of notes very close to each other in pitch, whereas wind chimes yield a randomly sounding collection of pitches. The notation is like that for the wind chimes.

Scores.   Stephen Paulus, Concerto for Orchestra; Crumb, *Music for a Summer Evening.*

The Anvil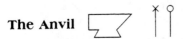

Range.   See Example 5-41.

Example 5-41   Range of the anvils

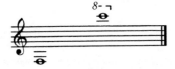

Description.   The anvil is a block of iron that may be an actual smithy's anvil or an approximation thereof. Tuned sets are made that can be used in keyboard layout. Related "instruments" are iron pipes, railroad spikes and chisels.

Quality and Technique.   The anvil produces an immediate attack followed by a short, high-pitched "cling" or "clink." It is clear and resonant. There are various striking points yielding different pitches. At *f,* the sound is very intense.

Scores.   Wagner, *Das Rheingold;* Varèse, *Hyperprism;* Copland, Symphony No. 3.

Sleigh Bells

Description and Technique.   Small, thin-walled spheres containing metal balls are mounted on a handle, which can be tapped for short notes or shaken for rolls.

Quality. The sound is the familiar jingling heard on sleigh rides. The decay is quite short, and typical passages feature repeated eighth notes.

Scores. Copland, *Billy the Kid;* Prokofiev, *Lieutenant Kije;* Mahler, Symphony No. 4.

Cup Bells (Cup Gongs, Bowl Gongs, Japanese Temple Bells, Temple Gongs)

Description. Cup bells are bowl-shaped bells of bronze, 1½–36 inches in diameter and 3½–9½ inches thick. They are made in sets of up to eight.

Quality and Technique. The sound is a gentle, resonant, and pulsating hum. As with glasses, water can be poured into the instruments, lowering the pitch.

Score. Crumb, *Ancient Voices of Children.*

Brake Drums

Range. See Example 5-42.

Example 5-42 Range of the brake drums

Description. These are brake drums taken from cars (and obtainable from junkyards). They consist of a circular piece of metal, sometimes with a raised, circular dome. They can be used in sets, generally of the same size.

Quality and Technique. The sound is very bright, ringing up to 3 seconds, and is like a lower-sounding anvil. When the drum is struck on the dome, two pitches a perfect fourth or an augmented fourth apart may be heard. There is some vibratory shimmer, a little like the steel drum. Blows to the side of the lower part give a less resonant, lower, and softer sound. Soft mallets should not be used, because they could be damaged. Scraping is feasible.

Scores. Stephen Paulus, *Concertante;* Lou Harrison, *Canticle No. 1.*

Almglocken (Swiss Cowbells) and Cowbells

Range. See Example 5-43. The notation is *an octave lower than sounding.* Pitches are often not specified.

Example 5-43   Range of the Almglocken

Description.   Almglocken ordinarily have no clappers. They range from 1½ to 12 inches in length and can be suspended or mounted in keyboard fashion. As the pictograms indicate, the (American) cowbell is less rounded in shape. Cowbells are more available in the United States than are Almglocken.

Quality and Technique.   Almglocken are rounder, less metallic-sounding than cowbells. There is a brief, low strike tone accompanied by a high-pitched ring of up to 5 seconds. When the instrument is damped by the hand, the high-pitched ring is suppressed, and a very dry "thock" is produced.

Scores.   ALMGLOCKEN: Stockhausen, *Gruppen;* Crumb, *Songs, Drones, and Refrains of Death;* Mahler, Symphonies No. 5 and 7.

The Flexatone

Range.   See Example 5-44.

Example 5-44   Range of the flexatone

Description.   The flexatone is a triangular, thin metal sheet attached to a handle. Small balls project from each side handle; these are thrown against the sheet alternately when the instrument is shaken. The top of the sheet is held by the thumb.

Quality and Technique.   The thumb can control pitch with changes of pressure on the sheet. A shaken roll produces a soft, quivering, sirenlike wail, with little glisses every time a ball strikes (a fast, continuous "doy-doy-doy"). Notated pitches can only be approximated, and melodies generally consist of glisses. It is possible, however, to play individual notes by holding one ball away from the sheet.

Scores.   Schoenberg, Variations for Orchestra; John Harbison, *Remembering Gatsby.*

The Musical Saw

Range.   See Example 5-45. This embraces the ranges of the smaller and larger instruments.

Example 5-45   Range of the musical saw

Description.   The musical saw is a saw without teeth. There are generally two sizes. The handle of the smaller saw is held between the knees, and the other end is held by a hand, which controls pitch, like the flexatone. The larger saw can be up to 6 feet in length. Its handle is held by one hand while the other end is held on the floor by a foot.

Quality and Technique.   The instrument can be bowed with a cello or bass bow or struck with some implement. The pitch wavers, much like that of the flexatone, so that melodic passages are likely to have almost continual glisses. Individual notes have an exaggerated vibrato, as well as a smooth, disembodied character. It can resemble a woodwind instrument. Percussionists are usually not very proficient in playing this instrument.

Scores.   Crumb, *Ancient Voices of Children*; Honegger, *Antigonae*; Henze, *Elegy*.

Bell Plates (Tone Plates)

Description.   Bell plates are slabs of steel, about half an inch thick, mounted on supports or suspended by ropes from a frame. They may have resonators. Several plates can be assembled to make up a keyboard of chromatic pitches.

Quality and Technique.   The plates emit a low-pitched bell sound or a higher-pitched clank, depending on their size. The pitch is sharp for about the first 3 seconds. To play a large assembly of plates has its difficulties: Their large size makes it somewhat difficult to go from one to the other; they vary quite a bit in size; they swing rather freely; and the larger plates, especially, are very difficult to damp.

Scores.   Puccini, *Tosca*; Strauss, *Also sprach Zarathustra*.

The Tam-tam

Description.   The tam-tam is a gonglike instrument with a flatter plate. Much that is said about gongs and cymbals applies to the tam-tams. There are several sizes, ranging from 6 to over 36 inches in diameter.

Quality and Technique.   The sound is like that of the gong, but less pitched. A loud stroke produces a violent "paw-*eesh*," and a very soft stroke induces a low, perhaps barely audible rumble. The loudest and most brilliant moment in a medium-loud or loud tone comes about 2 seconds after the strike. High- and low-pitched sounds compete until the waning portion of the resonance. Overtones may clash with pitched instruments: At four before no. 13 in the third movement of Mahler's First Symphony, the tam-tam is dissonant with the low G's of the harp and the timpani.

Metal beaters can be harmful.

The Thunder Sheet

Description.   The thunder sheet is a suspended, very thin sheet of iron or aluminum that can be up to 9 feet long. It is either shaken or struck.

Quality and Technique.   The effect is a sharp crack and a low rumbling, but the decay is less than a second (for one shake or stroke). It may also be bowed. Continuous shaking creates a roll.

Scores.   Harrison, *Canticle No. 1;* Barber, *Third Essay for Orchestra.*

UNPITCHED WOODEN, VEGETABLE, AND SYNTHETIC IDIOPHONES

Most of these instruments are basically high-pitched. It is not possible to put them into a definitive pitch order.

Castanets

Description and Technique.   Percussionists do not use the type of castanets that are used by Spanish dancers. Rather, they use either *paddle* or *machine* castanets. The sounding surfaces are ebonite clappers made in the keyhole shape that is seen in the pictograms.

The paddle castanet has one or two clappers attached to a handle. It is struck against something, like the knee, causing the clapper(s) to rebound against the

Ed Brown Studio

IDIOPHONES
Temple Blocks

Wind Machine	Slapstick	Two Slit Drums
	Guiro	Claves
	Maraca	Paddle	Ratchet	Two Woodblocks
Cabasa	Machine Castanets	Castanets

handle. The two clappers may have different pitches. Individual clicks and rolls may be executed.

The machine castanet consists of a small table on which two to four clappers are spring-mounted, side-by-side. They are played by the fingers, like a tiny piano, or with sticks.

Quality. Both types of instrument give high-pitched, dry, crackling clicks. The paddle type is louder, but the machine type is clearer and more precise. The typical figures are short and rhythmic.

Scores. Debussy, *Iberia;* Prokofiev, Violin Concerto No. 2; Stravinsky, *Agon.*

Claves ▭▭

Range. See Example 5-46 for an approximate range. Parts do not indicate pitches but may be "high–low."

Example 5-46   Approximate range of the claves

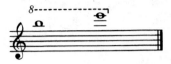

Description.   The claves are a pair of cylindrical blocks of hardwood about 1 inch in diameter and 6 inches long.

Quality and Technique.   The claves have a very bright, clicking, high-pitched, and woody sound. One stick is cradled in the hand, and the other is used to strike it. The shaping of the hand affects the pitch, quality, and resonance. If the sticks are reversed, the pitch will be different; thus, a simple, two-pitch melody is possible, if a few seconds are allowed for the exchange. A beater can be used for a softer sound.

Scores.   Roberto Gerhard, Concerto for Orchestra.

The Slapstick (Whip)

Description and Technique.   One form of the instrument is a slat attached to a handle. It is played by sudden movements that bring the boards together. The other form is two flat boards hinged together end-to-end so that they can be slapped together. Repeated notes should not be faster than about four to the beat at quarter note = 106. Usually, single notes are called for. There is a double whip that is designed for fast notes.

Quality.   The slapstick has a very sharp, startling snap.

Scores.   Ravel, Piano Concerto in G; Gershwin, Piano Concerto; Britten, *The Burning Fiery Furnace.*

Sandpaper Blocks

Description and Technique.   The sandpaper blocks are two blocks of wood covered on one surface with sandpaper. Either they are rubbed together, which requires two hands, or one is fastened down while the other is rubbed against it. The grain of the sandpaper can be specified. Accents can be made by clapping the blocks together at the beginning of a stroke or a roll.

Quality.   The sandpaper blocks give a soft, dry hiss.

Scores.   Bernstein, Symphony No. 3; Britten, *A Church Parable.*

The Maracas

Description.   A maraca is a hollow shell of gourd, wood, or plastic attached to a handle. Inside the shell are metal balls, pebbles, or seeds. Maracas are usually played in pairs.

Quality and Technique.   Single shakes of the instruments produce a sound resembling "ship," and shaking or twirling produces a continuous swish. Equal-valued repeated-note rhythms are typical. It is possible to get a two-note figure with a single shake.

Scores.   Varèse, *Ionisation;* Prokofiev, *Romeo and Juliet.*

The Cabasa

Description.   Traditionally, the cabasa is a hollow gourd on a handle enclosed with a netting that holds beads. A modern version has a metal cylinder with chains slung around it. It is turned on a handle, making the chains rub against the wall.

Quality and Technique.   A sharp rattling is produced by shaking, turning, or striking the instrument against the other hand. The metal form is more penetrating.

Scores.   Orff, *Die Bernauerin, Trionfi.*

The Ratchet

Description and Technique.   A handle turns a wooden cogwheel, against which are pressed two to four strips of wood. Rotation of the wheel makes the strips clatter against it. Short notes can be played, but it is difficult to control their length. There are various sizes.

Quality.   The ratchet produces a steady, very fast reiteration of the "atch" sound, whose pitch and loudness depend on the speed of rotation.

Scores.   Beethoven, *Wellington's Victory* Symphony; Ravel, *Pictures at an Exhibition;* Tchaikovsky, *The Nutcracker.*

The Vibraslap and the Jawbone

Description. The vibraslap consists of a V-shaped metal rod. At one end, there is a wooden ball, and at other end a wooden or metal box holding loose metal rivets. The player holds the instrument at the bend of the rod and strikes the ball against the box with the other hand, causing the rod and the box to vibrate and the rivets to rattle. The instrument is a modern substitute for the jawbone.

The jawbone is taken from a donkey or a zebra. Its teeth, or jingles, are loosely wired in the sockets. The instrument is struck against the hand or shaken. It is not commonly available.

Quality and Technique. Both produce a dry, rattling sound. The vibraslap makes a kind of *fp* roll lasting about two seconds. The metal instrument sounds relatively tinny.

Scores. William Russell, *Three Cuban Pieces;* Crumb, *Music for a Summer Evening.*

The Guiro (Rasp)

Description. The guiro is a hollow gourd about 13 inches long. It has a slit running lengthwise and notches that cross it. The player holds the instrument by two fingers in holes at the back and runs a thin wood or metal scraper back and forth over the notches. There are various sizes of instrument.

The *reco-reco* is a bamboo form of the instrument, about 16 inches long.

Quality and Technique. The sound is a soft "ricka-ricka," like a small stick being run quickly over a tiny picket fence. Downward strokes sound more emphatic than upward ones; thus, it is better if downward strokes fall on accents—one can use downbow and upbow marks as in string writing. The instrument may also be struck.

Scores. Stravinsky, *The Rite of Spring;* Villa-Lobos, *Uirapurú;* Copland, *Billy the Kid.* RECO-RECO: Villa Lobos, *Choros No. 8.*

Woodblocks

Description. Woodblocks are rectangular, partly hollow wooden boxes with a slot cut in the long dimension. There are as many as five sizes, with depths of 1–2¼ inches, widths of 3 inches, and lengths of 6½–8 inches.

Quality and Technique. The sound is high-pitched, woody, and dry. The pitch depends upon size—a set of high–medium–low is often used. Pitch also depends on strike point; except on the "piccolo" woodblock, there are two distinct pitches obtainable from two of the sides. The blocks can be placed in a row so that a gliss can be played across them. Metal beaters should be avoided.

Temple Blocks (Chinese Blocks, Korean Blocks)

Range.   See Example 5-47.

Example 5-47   Range of the temple blocks

Description.   The temple blocks are five hollow spherical or boxlike shells with holes or slits mounted on a rack. Their pitches generally span an octave and approximate a pentatonic scale.

Quality and Technique.   The sound is similar to that of the woodblocks, but hollower, fuller, and quite penetrating—something like the clucking of the tongue against the roof of the mouth. The "Chinese blocks" in Varèse's *Ionisation* are easily heard over the rest of the texture. They are often used to imitate the clip-clop of horse hooves.

Scores.   Walton, *Façade;* Gershwin, *Porgy and Bess;* Varèse, *Ionisation.*

The Wind Machine

Description.   The wind machine is a wooden barrel with slats that are evenly spaced around it. The barrel is rotated by means of a crank, causing the slats to brush against a cover of canvas or silk.

Quality and Technique.   The wind machine gives a continuous, low-pitched whistle, much like the sound of the wind. The speed of the rotation is directly related to pitch and loudness. It is difficult to stop precisely.

Scores.   Strauss, *Don Quixote;* Ravel, *Daphnis et Chloé;* Tippett, Symphony No. 4.

The Slit Drum (Split Drum) and the Log Drum

Range.   See Example 5-48.

Example 5-48   Range of the slit drums

Description.   The slit drum is a hollowed piece of tree with two slits running lengthwise. It serves as the bass of the log drum group. The log drums are hollow wooden boxes with slits on the top surface that form tongues or that divide the surface into two or more portions. There are three sizes.

Quality and Technique.   These instruments are more resonant, darker forms of the woodblock, having a hollow "thump." The decay time is about a second. Two different pitches can be obtained from most of the instruments.

Scores.   S\ufeffLIT D\ufeffRUMS: Stockhausen, *Gruppen;* Orff, *Antigonae.* L\ufeffOG D\ufeffRUMS: Berio, *Circles;* Henze, *El Cimmarón.*

AEROPHONES

The aerophones are relegated to the percussion section, probably because they are so rarely used, are so different from the usual wind instruments, and do not require special training to play. They usually appear only once or twice in a composition, with a humorous, attention-getting effect.

The Police Whistle (Referee's Whistle)

Description and Quality.   The whistle has a small ball inside a shell that bounces around within the shell when the player blows, interrupting the airstream. It emits a very shrill, high-pitched, and usually unexpected, scream.

Scores.   Ibert, *Divertissement;* Bernstein, *West Side Story.*

The Slide Whistle

Range.   See Example 5-49.

Example 5-49   Range of the slide whistle

Description.   The slide whistle is a metal or an ebony tube with a blowing end, a slotted opening, and a plunger that can slide in and out, varying the length of the air column.

Quality and Technique.   Moving the slide while blowing creates an upward or downward gliss with an accompanying quality change roughly like "oo-wee" or the reverse. Individual tones can have a wide vibrato.

Scores. Ravel, *L'enfant et les sortilèges;* Lucien Cailliet, *Pop Goes the Weasel.*

The Pistol Shot

The pistol shot is usually the type of pistol that is used to start races, firing blank cartridges. Successive shots might need more than one "instrument." The sound is, of course, very loud and sharp, and it can be modified by placing the muzzle into something that amplifies it, such as a large can, or softens it, such as a bag or a blanket.

Score. J. Strauss, *Champagne Waltz.*

The Popgun

A plunger forces a plug out of the end of a tube, making an explosive sound, much like the popping of the cork out of a bottle.

Scores. Zappa, *Dupree's Paradise;* Cailliet, *Pop Goes the Weasel.*

The Mouth Siren (Siren Whistle)

Range. See Example 5-50.

Example 5-50   Range of the mouth siren

Description. The mouth siren is a metal cylinder 2½–4 inches long, having a mouthpiece and a fan disc inside that rotates when the player blows.

Quality. The pitch of the mouth siren, like that of the mechanical sirens (see below), is always changing: As breath increases in force, the pitch and loudness increase. An abrupt cessation of breath ends the tone with a brief descent. A slowing of the breath gives a longer, gentler one. The effect is like a gentle "woo-ee!"

Scores. Hindemith, *Kammermusik* No. 1; Milhaud, *Les Cheophores;* Toch, *Bunte Suite.*

The Auto Horn and the Klaxon Horn

The auto horn consists of a flexible bulb attached to a cone. When squeezed, it produces the familiar blatting honk. Several can be mounted in a row. The Klaxon horn is operated by a plunger and makes the old-fashioned "*oo*ga" sound. Gershwin gave pitches to the auto horn.

> *Score.*   Gershwin, *An American in Paris.*

The Siren

Description.   A metal cylinder with evenly placed slots is encased in a larger cylinder which is similarly slotted. When the cylinder is turned by a crank, the slots are alternately aligned and blocked, which disturbs the air in a periodic manner, producing a pitch. It is difficult to stop the rotation precisely unless a thumb brake is provided. There are various sizes of siren. Electric versions are also made.

Quality.   The speed of rotation determines the pitch and loudness. The inertia of the cylinder creates a crescendo–diminuendo that cannot last less than about a quarter note.

> *Scores.*   Varèse, *Ionisation, Hyperprism;* Hindemith, *Kammermusik* No. 1.

THE DRUM SET (TRAP SET)

This fairly standard group of instruments, played by one seated player, comes from the dance band. A typical makeup is a 5-by-14-inch snare drum, a 9-by-13-inch tom-tom, a 16-by-16-inch tom-tom, a 14-by-22-inch pedal bass drum, three cymbals of various sizes, a hi-hat cymbal, and possibly some *traps*, which are instruments that are small enough to be attached to a drum or mounted on a nearby stand, such as the cowbell, the triangle, and the woodblock.

The drum set is usually written on a five-line staff. Rim shots are usually indicated by × noteheads.

THE PERCUSSION IN THE SCORE

Conventionally, the percussion are placed just below the brass in the score, with the timpani at the top (for more details, see Chapter 10, under "The Score"). There is no standard order for the other instruments, but they are likely to be arranged in one of these three ways:

1. High to low, exclusive of the mallets, which are separately ordered high to low (see Example 5-51a).

2. In groups of like instruments, each in high-to-low arrangement (see Example 5-51b).
3. If more than one player is needed (other than the timpanist) and if the composer wishes to assign specific instruments to specific players, the assignments are shown in the score, as in Example 5-51c.

Example 5-51a	**Example 5-51b**	**Example 5-51c**	
Triangle	Triangle		Triangle
Castanets	Cymbals	Player 1	Snare drum
Cymbals	Tam-tam		Xylophone
Snare drum	Snare drum		Cymbals
Tom-toms	Tom-toms	Player 2	Castanets
Tam-tam	Bass drum		Bass drum
Bass drum	Castanets		Tom-toms
Xylophone	Xylophone	Player 3	Tam-tam
Marimba	Marimba		Marimba

The advantage of Example 5-51a is that all instruments, exclusive of the mallets, are seen in pitch order. Example 5-51b has the advantage of organizing the score by color and pitch order *within* a given color. This is of interest to the score reader in particular. Example 5-51c is of interest to the conductor and the players, especially if there is a large number of instruments and much activity. It can then serve as a percussion score (see "Percussion Parts").

ASSIGNING INSTRUMENTS TO PLAYERS

1. Percussionists tend to be specialists. In the larger professional orchestras, there is usually one timpanist, who is rarely, if ever, asked to play another instrument, and three other players, who are the "percussionists." These three are usually specialists, one in cymbals, another in the snare drum, and the third in mallets. *If a given instrument has consistently difficult parts, it should always be given to the same player.*

2. If assignments are not based on specialties, they should be distributed in such a way that all required parts can be covered conveniently. Each player should have a chance to move from one instrument to another without undue haste: There should be enough time to change sticks or mallets or to put down an instrument without making noise.

The composer should have a mental picture of the percussion setup for each player. If the setup is elaborate, there should be diagram at the beginning of the score that shows the location of each instrument and each player.

Instruments are often put in a semicircle around the player. Those that are used only occasionally can be placed behind the player (if it is possible to play them while watching the conductor). Instruments that require much activity or great accuracy, particularly the mallets, should be the closest to the player and the most in line with the conductor. Smaller instruments, such as triangles, may be placed under larger ones like the mallets, or suspended over them, or between or behind them.

It would be well to imagine how the part would be played. Instrument changes are easiest when the player is able to reach from one to another and there is no change of stick or mallet. To avoid players crossing paths and to make individual parts more playable, it may be necessary to assign two of the same instrument to different players. On the other hand, players might share an instrument if there is no mutual interference. The players will probably decide on the setup and assignments that work best for them, especially if there are not enough players, but it is good for the scorer to plan elaborate percussion passages with an idea of how the parts might have to be assigned.

3. A factor that may be overlooked is that of *space*. Some compositions require so many large instruments that there may not be adequate room for them onstage. Percussionists may find themselves partway into the wings or at locations that make it difficult to see the conductor, or even to be heard properly!

4. If setups are to change movement to movement, they should be minimal, since they could cause uncomfortable delays. A conductor might have to wait between movements for the timpanist to prepare a new tuning, or for instruments to be moved, and so on.

An example of extravagant use of percussion is found in Crumb's *Star-Child*, which calls for a very large orchestra: woodwinds in fours, a large brass section, strings, organ, singers, a handbell choir, and four conductors! Some of these forces are placed in various parts of the auditorium. The percussion assignments are as follows:

1. Tam-tam, sus. cymb., 4 crotales, sleigh bells
2. Tam-tam, sus. cymb., 4 crotales, sleigh bells
3. Tam-tam, 3 timp., cymbal (to be put on a timp.), 2 sus. cymb., tambourine, 1 crotale, glockenspiel, chimes, claves
4. Tam-tam, log drum, chains, xylophone, 4 tom-toms, sizzle cymb., glockenspiel (with player 3), vibraphone, flexatone, bongos, wind machine
5. Tam-tam, maraca, sizzle cymb., sleigh bells, sus. cymb., tambourine (mounted), 4 tom-toms, thunder sheet, 2-octave set of crotales, chimes, flexatone, claves
6. Maraca, tam-tam, sleigh bells, sizzle cymb., tenor drum, 4 tom-toms, sus. cymb., thunder sheet (with player 5), chimes (with player 5), conga, claves
7. Log drum, chains, sizzle cymb., tam-tam, 4 tom-toms, 4 pot lids, b. drum (with player 8), tam-tam, glockenspiel, flexatone, conga, claves, tenor drum
8. 3 timp., cymbal (for timp.), b. drum, tambourine, tam-tam, low bell, 1 crotale, sn. drum, vibraphone, sus. cymb., flexatone, claves

Many of the "duplicated" instruments are of different sizes—for example, the tam-tams and the cymbals.

PERCUSSION PARTS

If more than one player is required and the parts are assigned, it might be well to give each player a percussion score. This shows all the percussion parts but the timpani. In case the music stand must be placed farther away from the player than normal, or the player has to move about, a score with larger staves and notes is recommended. The advantage of a score is that it lets each player know what his or her colleagues are doing: It provides helpful cues and it makes it easier to share duties, when needed. If the composer provides a setup diagram, the placement of the instruments in the score should correspond to the diagram—the instruments that are close to each other on the stage should also be close in the score.

Identification of Instruments

Review the discussion of Examples 5-4 and 5-5. If large numbers of nonpitched percussion are used, it might be well to identify them not by name but by a number that indicates their position in a list that is given at the beginning of the score, where the instruments are listed in pitch order; thus, instrument 1 might be the highest-sounding one, and so on. This is done in Nono's *Intolleranza* and Stockhausen's *Gruppen.* The arrangement might be:

Very small cymbal	1
Small cymbal	2
Medium cymbal	3
Large cymbal	4
Tambourine	5
Small gong	6
Medium gong	7
Large gong	8

Two of the players' parts might look like Example 5-52. (It is assumed that another player is assigned to instrument 5.) The score of Elliott Carter's Double Concerto identifies groups of like instruments in vocal categories: alto and tenor tambourine, soprano and alto triangle, and so on.

Example 5-52

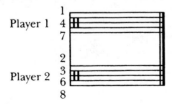

USING THE PERCUSSION AS A FAMILY GROUP

Writing for the percussion alone presents opportunities that are not much different from those offered by other families (see Chapters 7 and 8).

1. Like instruments or sounds can be combined into subgroups and played off against other subgroups, as in Example 5-53, where the first group is composed largely of drums and the second group is composed entirely of metals (except for the siren).

Example 5-53   Varèse, *Ionisation*, one before no. 9

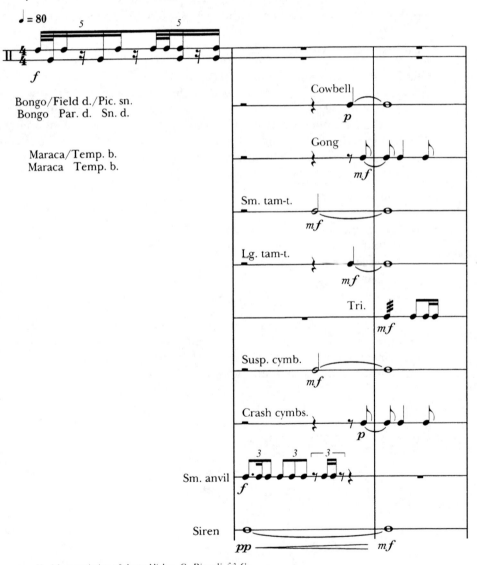

Used by permission of the publisher, G. Ricordi & Co.

2. Unpitched instruments can be combined in such a way that a "melody" is formed with distinctive shapes determined by the pitch areas of the instruments. In Example 5-54, the melodic contour of the wind instruments is imitated by that of the tom-toms and the bass drum.

Example 5-54

3. Color differences offer a second dimension for unpitched melodies along with the pitch element. See Example 5-55.

Example 5-55

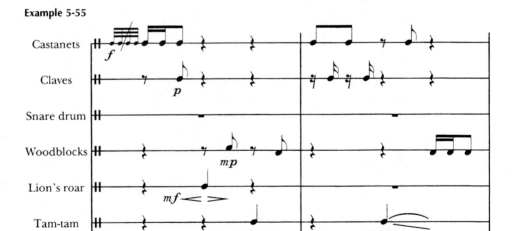

4. The diversity of sounds offers a limitless choice of textures, "chords," and polyphony: Some instruments project forward whereas others provide a background—there could be a constant interplay between instruments that gives the effect of projecting and retreating.
5. Individual "notes" can be fabricated out of combinations of instruments that play at the same time but have different decay times. For example, a short note played simultaneously by a bongo, a snare drum, a temple block, and a tambourine would combine the hollowness of the bongo with the sharp, high-pitched attacks of the snare

drum and the temple block. These initial sounds would quickly give way to the brief jingle of the tambourine.

IMPORTANT POINTS TO REMEMBER

1. The size, shape, and material of a vibrating body, where it is struck, and the size and material of the striking surface all have critical consequences for the pitch, timbre, articulation, and resonance of an instrument. These are also influenced by the force of the stroke.

2. The choice of sticks or mallets can generally be left to the player unless a special effect is sought. The usual specification is "hard," "medium," or "soft." In any case, it is good to mark percussion parts in such as way that the *character* of the passage is clear.

3. Notation should take into account the resonance of an instrument.

4. Beware of ambiguity in designating instruments. For example, "cymbals" could mean crash or suspended cymbal; "bells" could be taken to mean glockenspiel, chimes, or some other kind of bells. Do not confuse the tam-tam with the gong. With instruments that come in tunable sets, such as the bongos, indicate the desired pitch region ("high," "medium," or "low"), even if only one instrument is called for.

5. Keep in mind the mechanics of sticking, especially the problems of cross-sticking, multisticking, and movement between black and white keys.

6. Give players time to change instruments or sticks, change tuning, or make special preparations (for example, for the water gong or a forceful stroke on the tam-tam).

7. For elaborate percussion writing, provide a diagram of the setup, and assign parts to players in an efficient manner.

EXCERPTS FOR LISTENING AND STUDY

Timpani

Berlioz, *Symphonie fantastique*, mvt. 4, mvt. 5
Shostakovitch, Symphony No. 1, mvt. 4 (no. 35)
Prokofiev, *Peter and the Wolf* (nos. 40 and 41)
Egk, *Moira*

Percussion

Saint-Saëns, *Carnival of the Animals* (m. 12—xylophone); *Danse macabre* (five after A— xylophone)
Rimsky-Korsakov, *Scheherazade*, mvt. 3
Hindemith, *Symphonic Metamorphosis*, mvt. 1(B), mvt. 5 (m. 2)
Shostakovich, Symphony No. 15
Copland, *Appalachian Spring*; Symphony No. 3, mvt. 2, mvt. 4
Shankar, Concerto for Sitar
Varèse, *Ionisation*; *Hyperprism*
Messiaen, *Chronochromie*
Nono, *Intolleranza*

Carter, Double Concerto
Stockhausen, *Gruppen*
Tower, *Silver Ladders* (marimba in m. 433)

Drum set

Harbison, *Remembering Gatsby*

CHAPTER 6

The Harp and Keyboard Instruments

The harp, the celesta, and the piano are grouped together mainly because they are so often treated by composers in much the same way—their parts often look much alike, and the roles they play are also very similar. To a great extent, they can be related to the percussion, since the pattern of their sound is basically the same: It begins with a fairly sharp attack and then drops off to a slow decay, over which the performer has no control other than to damp it. In other words, like percussion, they do not sustain. It is not surprising then, to find that they are often used as if they were pitched percussion instruments.

The three instruments are ordinarily placed just below the percussion in the score, but there are many exceptions: Stravinsky in *Agon*, Elliott Carter in his Concerto for Orchestra, and Joan Tower in *Silver Ladders* all put the harp and the piano *above* the percussion. The order in which the instruments appear also varies, but it is often harp–celesta–piano. Some composers place the mallet instruments immediately above or below them, keeping pitched instruments together. When the organ is used, it is generally at the bottom of the group. (Mahler and Stravinsky have also put the mandolin among them!)

THE HARP

The modern orchestral harp dates from 1820, when Sébastien Érard developed the double-action mechanism that is still in use. Earlier harps either could not play in all the keys or, when they could, were too cumbersome to be practical.

Construction

The harp is like an upright piano—it has a vertically oriented frame across which strings are stretched, and a sounding board that amplifies the sound of the strings.

Ed Brown Studio

HARP

The length of a string is the principal determinant of its pitch. There are forty-seven strings, arranged in diatonic order (C, D, E, and so on) from the lowest, which are the farthest from the player, to the highest, which are the closest to the player. The player rests the instrument on the right shoulder, which allows the left hand to reach all the strings, playing on the left side; the right hand can reach down to about *G* on the right side. The range is shown in Example 6-1.

The strings are made of nylon or gut. The C's are red, and the F's are black or purple. Each string is tuned at the top of the frame by means of a tuning key

Example 6-1   Range of the harp

(which looks like a skate key). At the base of the front end of the frame are seven pedals, which are used to alter the pitches of the strings during performance. Each pedal operates a set of metal discs that either impinges on or releases all the strings of the same letter name, thereby changing their tuning simultaneously: For example, a movement of the E pedal changes *all* the strings sounding E-natural to E-sharp or to E-flat.

The pedals are positioned in one of three notches, as shown in Example 6-2. This allows the strings to be tuned to either the natural, the sharp, or the flat version of its letter name. To illustrate, if the pedal for the E string were in position 1, the string would not be affected by the discs, and the tuning would be E-flat. If the pedal were moved to position 2, the vibrating portion of the strings would be shortened by one of the discs, and the pitch would be a half step higher—E-natural. At position 3, the pedal would cause the second disc to shorten the effective string length further, raising the pitch to E-sharp. On most older harps, the pedals do not operate on the lowest strings, DD and CC, or on the highest string, G. Some newer instruments extend the pedal to the DD. The strings that are *not* affected by the pedal can be tuned before, but not during, a piece to flat, natural, or sharp.

Example 6-2

Pedal Settings

There are seven pedals—three on the left side for the left foot, and four on the right side for the right foot. Their arrangement, from left to right, is D, C, B on the left and E, F, G, and A on the right. Occasionally, the left foot can be used to move the E or F pedal, or the right foot the B pedal, but these crossovers are uncomfortable for the player.

Example 6-3 gives the pitch classes available to each string. This shows the basic pitch resources of the instrument. From it we learn which notes each string can play and which can be played on two different strings. (Double sharps and

Example 6-3

double flats are not used in harp parts.) Note, for example, that *the notes Dᵇ, Gᵇ, and Aᵇ can be produced in only one way, whereas all other notes can be produced in two ways.* (For example, D♯ can be played on the D string or as E♭ on the E string, but Dᵇ can be played only on the D string.) This information is vital in determining pedal settings, as you will see.

Possibilities for Playing Chords

Since there are seven strings per octave, only seven notes are available at one time in that octave, and no chord can exceed that number of *different* pitch classes in any octave. Let us suppose that a C major triad is to be played. All the possibilities for doing so are shown in Example 6-4. *The notes in a harp part should always reflect how the pedals are set;* thus, for 6-4a, the C, E, and G strings are played with the pedals set in the natural position for each of those strings; for b, the B string is set in the sharp position and the C string is not played; and so forth for c and d. For g, both the C and the B strings are played, sounding in unison; and so forth for h and i. Of course, these notes could be doubled in other octaves if desired, because the strings in those octaves would automatically be set in the same way.

Example 6-4

The limitations on the content of chords are as follows.

1. There may be no more than seven pitch classes.
2. No chord may contain any of the following groups of notes at the same time, no matter how these pitch classes are spelled.
   a. Gᵇ, G♯, and Aᵇ
   b. Dᵇ, D♯, Eᵇ, and Fᵇ
   c. F♯, Gᵇ, G♯, and Aᵇ
   d. Aᵇ, B♭, Bᵇ, and Cᵇ

   That is, no chord may contain all the notes in a *or* all the notes in b, and so on.

The reason for the limitations in 2 should be apparent from Example 6-3: The three notes Gᵇ, G♯, and Aᵇ, for example, are obtainable only on a total of *two* strings; thus, the four-note groups involving those notes are obtainable only on three strings.

Glissandos

A glissando is made on the harp as it is on the piano—by drawing one or more fingers or some object across the strings in a horizontal direction. Ordinarily, no string is skipped (a gliss could be interrupted and resumed beyond where it had ended), and since glissandos normally (but not necessarily) extend at least two octaves, it is clear that the setting of *all* the pedals is involved. To know which notes may be played in a glissando, then, is, in effect, to know what the limitations of seven-note chords are.

1. There may be from four to seven pitch classes (*different* notes)—no more, no less.
2. No glissando may contain any of the groups given in 2a–d above.

The four-note chords that can be glissed are the familiar seventh chords. A glissando of one of them is actually a fast *arpeggio* of the chord. All the diminished seventh chords are available, but only a limited selection of the other chord types can be played. (Keep in mind the difference between glissandos and *chords* that are played by plucking individual strings—many more chords are possible in the latter fashion.)

The possibilities for glissandos with five, six, and seven pitch classes are too numerous to list. All the traditional major and minor scales are available. The octatonic scales are possible only if one note is omitted (any one), but both of the whole-tone scales are possible.

Notation of Chords and Glissandos

The convention used to be that when a chord had no marking, such as in Example 6-5b, it was played with a slight upward arpeggiation, and that if it were desired *not* to be arpeggiated, brackets were needed to show that, as in 6-5a. For a slower, fuller arpeggiation, a wavy line would be used, as in 6-5c. Today, most harpists would play b unarpeggiated, making a unnecessary.

Example 6-5

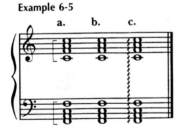

There have been several ways of indicating glissando, including these:

1. Writing out every note, as in Example 7-38.
2. Writing the notes in the first octave, then running a diagonal line to the last note (as in Example 6-6a).
3. Indicating the pedal setting either at this point or before and showing only the first and last notes, as in Example 6-6b. (The duration of glisses for *any* instrument should be clearly indicated. Various methods have been used for this, but there should be no problem if the format of Example 6-6b is used, as long as the first note signifies the full time value of the gliss.)

Example 6-6

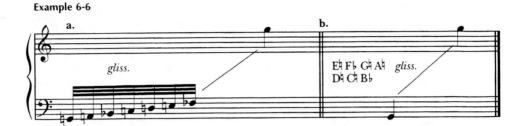

Notation of Pedal Settings

Pedal settings need to be indicated by someone. If the composer does not do it, the player must. Some players prefer to do it in their own way, regardless of how or whether it is marked. Even so, it is well for the composer to do it, since the process forces a thinking-through of the mechanics of pedal settings and changes that can help to avoid unmanageable parts to begin with.

The two most-used systems are the letter notation shown in Examples 6-6b and 6-7a, and the diagrammatic one exemplified in Example 6-7b. The letter notation in a shows each pitch class in the order in which the pedals are located. The diagrammatic representation in b does the same without naming the pitch classes: The first vertical line represents the D pedal, the next the C pedal, and so on. The position of the vertical lines on the horizontal line indicates where the pedal is in the notches: Above the line is the flat setting, on the line the natural setting, and below the line the sharp setting (compare with Example 6-2).

Example 6-7a   **Example 6-7b**

D♮ C♮ B♭ / E♮ F♭ G♮ A♮

A complete initial setting of the harp should appear at the beginning of the piece. After that, only the changes need be indicated (as with a timpani part), and this can be done with letter names, as will be shown. From the standpoint of pedaling, the most comfortable parts have few changes, and there is at least a second between successive changes. Pedal changes are also easier if they are made on, rather than between, beats. Two pedals may be changed at the same time *if they are not on the same side of the harp*, but it may be possible to move two adjacent pedals on one side with one foot, provided they move from the same position to the same new position (for example, both pedals move from flat to natural).

To keep track of the current pedal setting, a chart such as the one in Example 6-8 can be helpful. This chart shows the pedal setting for the excerpt in Example 6-9 and two pedal changes. (The composer did not mark either the setting or the changes.) The numbers indicate the measures in which the setting either begins or changes.

Example 6-8

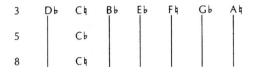

3	Db	C♮	Bb	Eb	F♮	Gb	A♮
5		Cb					
8		C♮					

Example 6-9　Franck, Symphony in D Minor, mvt. 2, mm. 3–8

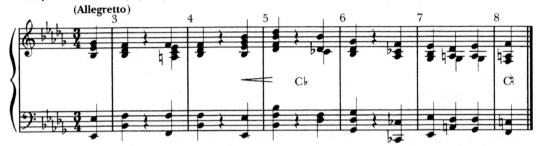

The pedal change from C to Cb is shown in the music between the staves and in the chart as having occurred in m. 5. The complete setting after the change is then readable for future reference. It can be seen that all the notes that are needed can be played with these settings. Note that the second beat of m. 7, spelled Gb–A♮–Db, is really a Gb minor triad. If it were spelled more conventionally, with Bbb instead of A♮ (as it *is* in the cellos and the basses), this would imply the B string, which of course cannot be set to this note. By the same token, the natural sign is needed for *c* in m. 8 to make clear that a pedal change is needed.

Example 6-11a shows the continuation of the passage, and Example 6-10 shows the chart for it. Notice that the harpist always has at least a beat to make pedal changes—still, the changes are quite rapid in m. 15.[1] The pedal changes to

Example 6–10

8	Db	C♮	Bb	Eb	F♮	Gb	A♮
							Ab
9							A♮
10							Ab
11							A♮
13					Fb		
14							Ab
					F♮		
15				E♮			
							A♮
				Eb			

[1]They are all on the right side, which is a great deal of work for the right foot by itself. In this case, the *left* foot is likely to be used for the E pedal.

Example 6-11 Franck, Symphony in D Minor, mvt. 2, mm. 9–16

F♭ and A♭ could have been made at the same time just before the downbeat of m. 14 (as shown below the staff) *if* those pedals were not on the same side of the harp. The same is true of F♮ and E♮ just before beat three of m. 14 and of A♮ and E♭ just before the third beat of m. 15.

In this passage, the harpist might be tempted to consider other spellings of some of the notes, which would mean other configurations of the pedals; for example, he or she might use E♮ instead of F♭. To do so for the downbeat of m. 14 would require quick changes for the following E♭ and F♭ in the soprano, but if it were done only *after* the eighth-note E♭, as in Example 6-11b, the number of pedal changes would be *no fewer* than those in 6-11a. However, to change the tuning of E♭ to E♮ so soon after the note is played could damp that note somewhat.

Quality and Resonance

The attack, quality, and resonance of the registers, from low to high, can be crudely approximated by the sounds "plong," "plung," "plunk," and "plink." Inglefield and Niell give the decay times for representative tones that are played *ff* and allowed to decay to *pp*; these are shown in Example 6-12.[2] As normally played, by

[2]Ruth K. Inglefield and Lou Anne Niell, *Writing for the Pedal Harp* (Berkeley and Los Angeles: University of California Press, 1985), p. 7.

Example 6-12   Decay times for sample tones

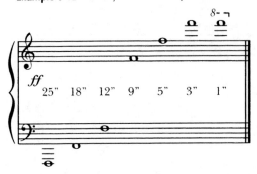

plucking with the flesh of the fingertips, the strings yield a gentle but definite attack. The resonance of the strings from about g^1 downward is an important factor in many harp passages, since the luminous overlapping of tones gives an otherwordly, detached character that has so often been associated with heaven, the heavens, magic, or the sound of water. It is no wonder that the instrument was used so much in opera before it was accepted into the concert orchestra.

Chords, glisses, and arpeggios are glowingly warm. Low notes can approximate low drum sounds or bass pizzicatos, and high notes have a short-lived glitter.

The tuning of a string can slightly influence its resonance—the flat tuning is the most resonant and the sharp tuning the least; for example, a passage written in C-sharp major would be more resonant if played enharmonically in D-flat.

The sound in general is very akin to string pizzicato (the harp often doubles pizzicatos, as it does in the passages in Examples 6-9 and 6-11a) and also to the piano, for reasons that clearly relate to their common features of construction. The orchestrator should remember not only the pronounced resonance of the instrument (and the great variation of that resonance through the range) but also *the essential weakness of the instrument.* In compensation for the latter, Rimsky-Korsakov generally marked the harp louder than he did the other instruments (in *Scheherazade*). As early as Berlioz (*Symphony fantastique*), composers have used two or more harps—Wagner used six in *Das Rheingold*. This also avoids all the problems of producing desired pitches, since a second or a third instrument can play what the first cannot, and increases the strength of the sound.

Another way to increase power is to double notes enharmonically—for example, to play both $f\sharp$ and $g\flat$, rather than just one of these. This is very commonly done for single notes, as well as in chords. (Remember that D♮, G♮, and A♮ cannot be doubled.)

Ongoing harp passages tend to have at least a moderate amount of activity, for the quick drop-off of intensity after the attack does not allow the type of sustained melodic line of which the strings and the winds are capable. Arpeggiations and other constantly moving figurations are common. Slurs are generally meaningless, unless phrasing is to be indicated.

Technique

1. Chords should not have more than four notes in each hand. They may extend as wide as a tenth. Any large intervals within them should be at the top of a chord in either hand (see the third beats of mm. 5, 7, and 8 in Example 6-9).

2. A string should not be played repeatedly at a fast rate, because it will not respond well (especially the lower strings). Thus, the figures in Example 6-13a and c would be more successful if written as in 6-13b and d, respectively, which do not require fast repetitions of the same string.

Example 6-13

3. It is good to allow the two hands to alternate on repetitive or fast-moving figures, thereby avoiding strain. Trills and tremolos should be notated this way (with right-hand notes on the upper staff, left-hand notes on the lower, or as in Example 6-13d). Soft tremolos, giving a rustling effect, are often marked "bisbigliando" ("whispering"), implying that the notes are to be played in random order.

4. Harmonics can be played by touching the string lightly with part of the hand while plucking with the finger or the thumb. The left hand can play up to three harmonics at once if they do not span more than a sixth. The usual harmonics are written with normal noteheads and a small circle above or below. They should be written *an octave lower than they sound.* See Example 6-14a.

Example 6-14

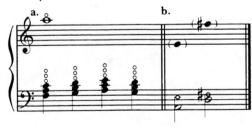

Other harmonics, possible on lower strings, are shown in Example 6-14b. These are notated like artificial harmonics in bowed strings (review the discussion of Example 2-24).

Harmonics are less effective in the highest and lowest octaves.

5. As with certain percussion, the composer should be careful in notating durations. Example 6-12 is a good guide for this (keeping in mind that it is based on notes played *ff*). If there is any possibility of misinterpretation, notes that are intended to last exactly as long as they are written should be marked as in Example 6-15a or 6-15b. Notes intended to ring beyond this should be marked as the upper three notes are in 6-15c ("l.v." stands for either the French "laissez vibrer" or the English "let vibrate"). The damping symbol can be used as it is here to show that some of the notes are to ring and others are not.

Example 6-15

An indication that a series of notes should be damped only enough to prevent overlap is shown in 6-15d, and a more staccato damping is shown in 6-15e.

6. Plucking near the frame produces a nasal sound resembling a ponticello or the guitar. The usual indication is "près de la table" or "table."

7. Glissandos can be executed in either hand (keeping in mind the ranges of the hands) or in both, either in parallel or in contrary motion (Example 6-16a–6-16c). In a, the right hand continues the gliss begun in the left hand—this is stronger than requiring either hand to do the entire sweep. It is possible to gliss with more than one note, as in Example 6-16d. (This notation, incidentally, does not indicate how far the gliss is to go, leaving it up to the player.)

Glisses can reverse direction, as in 6-16e. Typical two-handed overlapping loops can be indicated as in 6-16f.

Example 6-16

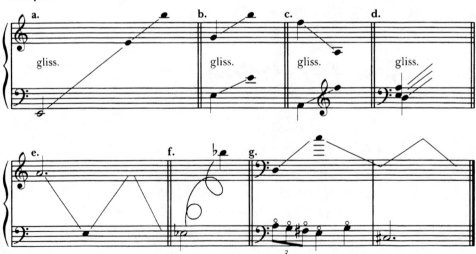

Finally, a melody can be played in one hand while the other accompanies it with glisses (6-16g).

8. The strings can be plucked with the fingernail (use the pictogram for this given in Example 5-3), which gives an even more nasal sound than "table." A plectrum will give a similar effect. The strings also may be struck or rubbed with other objects (Bartók, Concerto for Orchestra, first movement, m. 438), as long as those objects are not injurious to the strings.

9. There are many effects that can be obtained beyond those already mentioned. Most are especially appropriate to chamber music. Here are a few.

   a. The pedal slide (Example 6-17). There is no pitch gliss—simply a change of pitch without a new attack. A modest pitch gliss can be gotten by turning the tuning key after a string has been plucked.

Example 6-17

E♮ – E♭

   b. The pedal trill (Example 6-18).

Example 6-18

C♮–C♯

   c. Striking the soundboard with the fingers or the hand.[3]

The Use of the Harp

The harp is often used to reinforce other instruments, as in Examples 7-38, 7-40, 7-49, and 7-52. In Examples 7-51 and 7-52, glissandos typically contribute an undulant wash of sound that overlays the more defined pitch activity in other instruments. At other times, the harp provides accompaniments, as in Example 6-11 (in this case, to the English horn) or adds ornamental figures to melodic lines in other instruments. Composers like Schoenberg and Webern, however, treat the instrument more independently—more like other pitched instruments. Occasionally, it is called upon to play alone in a virtuoso manner, as in Tchaikovsky's "Waltz of the Flowers" or Rimsky-Korsakov's *Capriccio espagnole*.[4]

---

[3]Many other effects are given by Lucille Lawrence and Carlos Salzedo in *Method for the Harp* (New York: G. Schirmer and Sons, n.d.). Some appear in Chapter 11 of this book.

[4]The cadenza in the *Capriccio* has been made fuller and more idiomatic by Salzedo, whose version is usually the one that is played. A good source that shows idiomatic writing for the harp is *The ABC's of Harp Playing*, by Lucille Lawrence (New York: G. Schirmer and Sons, n.d.), which has a section of piano excerpts that are revised to be played on the harp.

THE CELESTA

The celesta is part piano and part glockenspiel. It looks like a small piano and is played like one. It has a keyboard whose keys activate hammers, but those hammers strike a set of steel bars, as in the glockenspiel, rather than strings, as in the piano. Unlike the glockenspiel's, the celesta's bars are reinforced by wooden resonators. This has the effect of softening the tone and of inhibiting some of the resonance. The celesta has much of the quality of the glockenspiel, with less brightness and resonance.

There is a damper pedal that allows the bars to ring freely when it is depressed. With the pedal off, damping is not complete, owing to the vibration of the resonators; thus, it is not possible to achieve the effect of staccato on the instrument—there are only two degrees of resonance: moderately long and moderately short!

Ed Brown Studio

CELESTA AND TOY PIANO
Celesta
Toy Piano

The usual range is shown in Example 6-19. The upper notes are usually described as silvery, and the low notes have a marimbalike glow with a resonance similar to that of the harp in the same register.

Example 6-19   Range of the celesta

The dynamic range of the instrument is not large, making dramatic use of louds and softs ineffective.

The function of the celesta is similar to that of the harp. In Example 7-51 (where it sounds at pitch), its figurations combine with the keyed glockenspiel (*jeu de timbres*) to add a sparkling glitter to the sweep of the harp glissandos and the thirty-second-note figurations.

The most famous use of the celesta is in one of its first appearances in history—Tchaikovsky's "Dance of the Sugarplum Fairy," which also exploits the tinkling upper register, giving a magical character to the persona of the dancer. If the glockenspiel were used instead, much of the refinement and delicacy of the sound would be lost, and the four-part harmony might cause an unpleasant jangling.

THE PIANO

The piano hardly needs an introduction. There are two types—the upright and the grand, but only the grand will be discussed here. The range is given in the white notes of Example 6-20. The black note indicates the lower extension of the Bösendorfer piano.

Example 6-20   Range of the piano

Construction

The grand piano comes in lengths ranging from a little over 5 feet to 9 feet (the concert grand). When the lid is raised, one can see a metal frame that looks something like a harp, across which are stretched strings of graduated length. The lowest few strings are single; up to about f^1, they are double (that is, in pairs tuned in unison), and above that, they are triple. (In the following discussion, "string" will imply pairs and triples as appropriate.) Below the frame is a soundboard.

The keys act on the hammers by catapulting them toward the strings. When the hammer is at rest, a damper is in contact with the string, and when the key is depressed, the damper is held away from the string as long as the key is held down. After striking the string, the hammer returns to its ready position to allow a quick repetition.

On most American grands, there are three pedals easily accessible to the feet. The pedal farthest to the right is the *damper pedal*, the indication for which is "Ped." As long as it is depressed, the dampers are disengaged from *all* the strings. The indication to release the pedal is _____⌐ or "Ped. up." Half-pedaling somewhat reduces the resonance.

The middle pedal is the *sostenuto pedal*, whose indication is "sost." This releases the dampers only from the notes played just before the pedal is depressed, allowing them to ring; notes played afterward (while the pedal is still depressed) will be damped as if no pedal were down. (Some European pianos do not have this pedal.) The release of the sostenuto pedal can be indicated by _____⌐ or "sost. up."

The pedal on the extreme left is the *soft pedal*, indicated by "una corda." It moves the keyboard sidewise, causing the hammers to strike the strings with a different part of their area, resulting in a more muted tone. When this pedal is no longer to be used, "tre corde" can be indicated.

Quality

The percussion of the hammer produces a fairly abrupt attack, after which the tone decays slowly. (The "woo—ip!" of a piano tone played backward on tape is good evidence that the tone has this shape.) Articulation depends on the timing between the release of one note and the attack of the next—an infinite range of "legatos" and "staccatos" is possible. But for the piano to approximate the legato of a wind or a stringed instrument, the notes should move no slower than about two to a beat at moderate tempo. Thus, like the harp, the piano needs a certain amount of activity, unless the effect is to be fragmentary or percussive.

The lowest tones are sonorous and percussive, having prominent overtones. As one ascends through the keyboard, pitch becomes clearer and resonance decreases. The highest notes are like those of the harp, but much more penetrating, potentially. "Cascading water" effects are well known from rippling high-register passages in Chopin and Liszt.

Many colors can be produced with chords in various spacings: They can be murky or noisy if the notes are closely spaced and low, or bell-like if the notes are spread out and relatively high.

The dynamic range is much greater than that of the harp or the celesta.

Technique

The availability of ten fingers and two hands affords lightning speed, almost instant access of any note in the great range, and powerful massing of notes. Chords should be restricted to the width of an octave in each hand, but since it is possible to play adjacent white or adjacent black keys with the thumb, it is safe to write a ninth if the thumb plays double notes—for example, the notes c^1 and d^1 in Example 6-21. Large intervals within wide-spanned chords should be placed as they are in this example—between the highest notes in the left hand and between the lowest notes in the right hand. This is because the thumb and the second finger can be spread farther than the fourth and fifth fingers can.

Example 6-21

Fast-moving and wide-ranging passages are possible with alternation of the hands, as in Example 6-22a and 6-22b. Fast repeated notes are best accomplished with fingers from alternate hands, making a xylophonelike roll a possibility (Example 6-22c), although, if necessary, fairly fast repetitions are possible in one hand with alternating fingers.

Example 6-22

Glisses over either the white or the black keys can be made by one hand, or by the two hands moving in parallel or contrary motion (see Example 7-60).

The hand, the fist, or the forearm can be used for clusters of notes, as shown in Example 6-23. If only white or only black notes are wanted, this should be indicated separately.

Harmonics can be produced by silently depressing the keys of one or more notes in the harmonic series of a lower note, then playing the lower note sharply and briefly (see Example 6-24). The harmonics will resonate softly—so softly that they may not be heard in a large room, and certainly not if other sound is present.

Example 6-23

Example 6-24

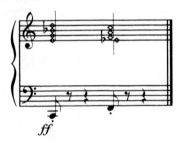

The Use of the Piano

The piano was very rarely used as a member of the orchestra in the nineteenth century, but in recent decades it has become almost commonplace in orchestral scores. Like the harp, it is used both to reinforce or accompany other instruments and as a soloist (Stravinsky's *Petroushka*; Shostakovich's First Symphony, last movement). The percussive low register is used very effectively in the first movement of Shostakovich's Fifth Symphony and in Copland's *Appalachian Spring*. In Example 7-60, the piano is used to reinforce the glisses of the violins. Some works, like Stravinsky's *Symphony of Psalms*, use more than one piano.

The Toy Piano

The toy piano can be a surprisingly effective instrument. The cheaper versions may have only the eight notes of the completed C major scale, whereas others may range from f to f^3 chromatically. The hammers strike metal rods, and the loose action contributes a background clatter to the slightly tinny and wobbly sound of the rods. There are no dampers. The instrument has been used in Crumb's *Ancient Voices of Children* and in Stokes's *Captions*.

THE ORGAN

It is natural that the organ should be used to supplement the orchestra in works written to be performed in church, as it was regularly in the eighteenth century. In that period, it played the *continuo* part, which consisted of the bass line and improvised upper parts that doubled voices or filled in harmonies. In the nineteenth century, a few operas used the organ for an occasional church scene. As Romanticism developed into its late stages, there were frequent allusions to religion in abstract orchestral music. At the same time, the orchestra expanded to accommodate the demand for a grander type of expression. Thus the organ, like the chorus, was occasionally called on as a final element of power and majesty. In the twentieth century, it continues to appear in a few scores.

Naturally, the advisability of including an organ in an orchestral score depends on the availability of an organ in the performing space. Some concert halls have organs and others do not. In the latter case, an electronic instrument may be used, but it will yield only an approximation of the intended sound.

Construction

The organist has available a number of keyboards—often three. Those played by the hands are called *manuals*, and the single keyboard played by the feet is called the *pedal*. The *written* ranges of the manuals and pedal are given in Example 6-25. (Some organs, especially those in Europe, may go only to g^3 in the manuals.)

Example 6-25   Range of the organ

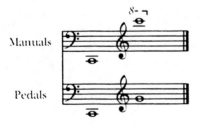

Mechanical action, controlled electrically, causes air to be forced into pipes of various sizes and structures. The pipes that are activated are grouped in *ranks*, or sets of one kind of pipe covering the pitch range of the keyboards. Ranks are grouped into *divisions* of the organ, and each division is played by a given keyboard. *Stops*, manipulated by the hands, are used to select ranks or groups of

Example 6-26

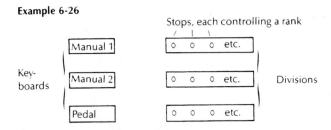

ranks. Example 6-26 gives a schematic diagram of the relation between keyboards, stops, ranks, and divisions.

Although the manuals resemble the piano keyboard, some stops change the pitch from that of the piano. The more usual of these are

16-foot: an octave lower
32-foot: two octaves lower
4-foot: an octave higher
2 ⅔-foot: an octave and a perfect fifth higher
2-foot: two octaves higher
1 ⅗-foot: two octaves and a major third higher

The 8-foot stop gives the normal pitch level. Combinations of these pitch-level stops allow a number of octave doublings to be played while fingering a single line on a keyboard. These stops extend the written range given in Example 6-25 by two octaves below if the 32-foot stop is available, by one octave below if only the 16-foot is available, by one octave above if only the 4-foot is available, and by two octaves above if the 2-foot is available.

Quality

There are two general types of pipe—the *flue* and the *reed*. A flue pipe is like a flute in that air is forced against an edge to initiate vibration. A reed pipe has a freestanding, single metal reed that acts somewhat like a clarinet reed. There are many variations of these types, some with names of orchestral instruments, whom they may resemble only slightly in sound. These ranks vary not only in timbre but also in attack characteristics.

Partly because organs vary widely in the stops that are available, registration (the choice of stops used in a given piece) is usually not indicated in orchestral scores. For example, in his Eighth Symphony, Mahler specifies only "volles Werk" ("all stops"), "halbes Werk" ("half of the stops"), and, at no. 178, "neues Register nehmen" ("change registration"). It is most important to indicate the dynamics desired, as well as the type of expression (for example, "dolce" or "pesante"). Beyond that, it would be well to consult an organist if specific registrations are desired.

Technique

The player can play on up to three keyboards at once, if the pedal is one of them. It is possible to play on two manuals at the same time. Keyboards can be linked by *couplers*, which enable the player to use stops from more than one division while playing on just one of the keyboards. One or two seconds should be allowed to change coupling.

The constant flow of air does not allow the player to vary loudness by pressing a key with more or less pressure, as on the piano: Loudness can be controlled only by (1) the number and type of stops employed; (2) a division, such as the *swell* or the *positive*, whose pipes may be relatively exposed (for louder playing) or relatively enclosed (for softer playing) by shutters; and (3) the use of the *crescendo pedal*, which gradually adds stops up to the maximum or reduces their number. The player can control the crescendo pedal by depressing or releasing it at a desired speed.

The difference between the piano tone and that of the organ is to a great extent a matter of attack and decay. The piano tone has a noticeable attack and a slow decay, whereas the organ tone has *no* decay until the moment of release, and its attack may be less noticeable as a result. Articulation is controlled almost entirely by the length of time a key is held down; thus, legato can be achieved only by effective timing of the release of one note and the depressing of the next—no overlapping of decays is possible, as on the piano, the celesta, or mallet instruments. It is very difficult to produce legato when moving from one chord to the next in one hand. On tracker-action organs (most organs in the United States are of this type), some small differences in attack can be produced by the speed with which the key is depressed: A fast, sharp attack can cause a "chiff" sound that is added to the beginning of a note. A slow depression of the key yields a soft beginning.

The Use of the Organ

The organ blends well with most orchestral instruments, particularly the winds— so well that it may not be recognized if it is playing at soft or medium-loud dynamic levels with the orchestra. Despite the great variety of the timbres it offers, the mechanical nature of the organ's tone production may make it sound relatively bland next to the sounds of orchestral instruments, which have much more control over attack, loudness, and release, and its timbres may not differ enough to offer alternatives to them; thus, the role of the organ is usually to strengthen the orchestra by doubling sound masses, to accompany, or to play solo passages.

The instrument's expression ranges from the powerful to the subtle—staccato chords can have great impact, for example—but its most characteristic feature is a tireless, unchanging sustaining of tone: Pedal tones and sustained chords are very common, especially at beginnings and endings of movements. In some compositions, like Mahler's Second Symphony and Elgar's *"Enigma" Variations*, the organ is brought in only at the end, to emphasize the climax of the work.

Normally, an organ part is written on three staves, the upper two for manual keyboard notes and the lowest for the pedal.

The Harmonium

The harmonium is a small organ with reed pipes. The player can control wind pressure directly by pumping on pedals or indirectly by moving levers with the knees. There are various sizes. The typical range is F^1–f^3. The instrument appears in scores in the early 1900s, but its use has declined until more recently—it is not very available at present. Mahler used both the harmonium and the organ in the last section of his Eighth Symphony.

THE HARPSICHORD

The harpsichord was the secular counterpart of the organ in the eighteenth-century orchestra, playing the continuo part from the bass line. In orchestral scores, the word *organ* or *harpsichord* normally did not appear, because it was taken for granted that the keyboard player would play from the part marked "bass" ("basso"). Often, it was the conductor who played the continuo part. As orchestras became larger and musical style shifted from dependence on a relatively continuous bass line, the practice of playing a continuo part was largely abandoned by 1800.

At the same time, the increasing popularity of the new pianos was forcing the harpsichord into obsolescence. It was not until about the 1930s, under the general influence of Neoclassicism (see the section on this style in Chapter 7) and renewed interest in eighteenth-century music, that such instruments as the harpsichord were again taken seriously. Performers learned to play them, old instruments were reconditioned, and modern versions were made.

Construction

Like the piano, the harpsichord has strings and a key mechanism to make them sound. Unlike the piano, it may have two keyboards and the strings are plucked—when a key is depressed, a jack rises from below the string and a quill attached to the jack plucks the string as it passes by. When the key is released, a damper inhibits vibrations of the string (as on the piano). There are sets of strings that are an octave higher or an octave lower than normal and other sets that have a special timbre and articulation. These can be activated by pedals with the feet or by knobs with the hand.

Example 6-27   Range of the harpsichord

Ranges vary, but the written range given in Example 6-27 is commonly found.

Quality and Technique

As with the organ, the player cannot control loudness from note to note; changes in dynamics can come only from changes of texture—mostly by adding or subtracting doublings through coupling—or by changes in the speed of the notes (faster notes give more attacks per unit of time). As on the organ, a second or two should be allowed for changes in coupling.

The plucking action of the quill makes the timbre somewhat like that of guitars played with picks, but with more resonance (in fact, continuo parts in the early Baroque period sometimes were played by lutes or guitars). The quality is relatively bright, but the sound level is generally quite low. The attack is immediate and the decay rather quick, giving an articulate, clean response—short chords and fast notes can be quite brilliant but also rather noisy. Some instruments have stops that make the sound thinner or more damped, such as harp or lute stops.

The Use of the Harpsichord

The relative weakness of the instrument creates problems of balance in the orchestra, which can be alleviated by amplification, but this alters the quality of the sound. It is most likely to appear in small ensembles, where it can be more of a soloist, since it does not blend readily with orchestral instruments. On the other hand, it offers a contrast of timbre, and its clear articulation is useful for polyphonic textures.

EXCERPTS FOR STUDY AND LISTENING

Harp

Berlioz, *Symphonie fantastique*, mvt. 2; *Harold in Italy*
Franck, Symphony in D Minor, mvt. 2
Tchaikovsky, *Nutcracker*, "Waltz of the Flowers"
Rimsky-Korsakov, *Capriccio espagnole*, mvt. 4
Debussy, *Prelude to The Afternoon of a Faun*
Stravinsky, *Petroushka*

Celesta

Tchaikovsky, *Nutcracker*, "Dance of the Sugarplum Fairy"
Mahler, *Das Lied von der Erde* (four after no. 61)
Stravinsky, *Petroushka* (no. 15)
Prokofiev, *Scythian Suite*, mvt. 3 (m. 7); *Lieutenant Kije*, mvt. 2 (no. 17)
Shostakovich, Symphony No. 5, mvt. 1, (last four measures)
Bartók, *Music for Strings, Percussion and Celesta*
Webern, Six Pieces for Orchestra, mvt. 1, mvt. 6

Piano

Saint-Saëns, *Carnival of the Animals*
Stravinsky, *Petroushka*; *Symphony of Psalms*; Symphony in Three Movements
Shostakovich, Symphony No. 1, mvt. 2 (no. 3, two before no. 18); Symphony No. 5, mvt. 1
    (no. 17)
Piston, *The Incredible Flutist*, Minuet
Copland, *Appalachian Spring*

Organ

Berlioz, *Lelio*
Saint-Saëns, Symphony No. 3
Strauss, *Also sprach Zarathustra*
Mahler, Symphonies No. 2 and 8
Elgar, *"Enigma" Variations* (optional)
Respighi, *Pines of Rome; Fountains of Rome*
Varèse, *Ecuatorial*
Creston, Symphony No. 6

Harmonium

Mahler, Symphony No. 8
Berio, *Passagio*
Penderecki, *De Natura Sonoris* Nos. 1 and 2

Harpsichord

De Falla, *El Retablo de Maese Pedro*
Stravinsky, *The Rake's Progress*
Carter, Double Concerto for harpsichord and piano
Foss, *Baroque Variations*
Ligeti, *Apparitions*

CHAPTER 7

Historical Survey of Scoring Techniques

Although many books and articles have been written about the harmony and form of orchestral music, there has been little systematic study of its orchestration over the course of history.[1] Since many of the basic practices of handling instruments today can be found throughout the history of orchestral music, it is important for us to look at these techniques, not only to learn what they are, but also to see how they *are part of the context in which they appear.* Just as theories of harmony can save time in constructing new works, so can theories of orchestration—but no theory is useful out of context.

Instruments of today are built and played differently than they were in the past. Orchestras are generally larger and have a greater variety of instruments. Conducting, rehearsing, and performing techniques have changed, and so have the places in which orchestras play. We must take these changes into account and try to find general principles that apply to modern situations and suggest new ones.

Instrumentation

In the Renaissance, instrumental music was closely identified with dance and vocal music: Many instrumental works were arrangements of madrigals, chansons, and so on. It was mainly for large stage and religious works that orchestras were required, and there was apparently no standard group of instruments that was regularly employed.[2] The introduction of the true opera about 1600 aided in such standardization. At that time, the bowed string instruments consisted of the new

---

[1]See the works by Carse and Read in the Bibliography, as well as "Orchestra" and "Orchestration" in *The New Grove Dictionary*.

[2]The lack of full orchestral scores from this time is an obstacle to our knowledge. One of the first orchestral scores was the *Ballet Comique de la Royne* in Paris, 1582.

violin family intermingled with the older, fretted viols (the bass viol has retained its shape and name to this day but has lost its frets; its name, too, is giving way to other forms, such as "contrabass," "double bass," and "string bass"). The wood-winds consisted of early forms of the flute, the oboe, and the bassoon. These were incapable of playing a full chromatic scale and were best suited to playing in certain keys, especially D major. The oboe seems to have been more technically developed than the flute at this time, which may explain the relative absence of the latter in earlier eighteenth-century works.

Brass instruments included earlier forms of the trumpet, the horn, and the trombone. Although the trombone was close to its modern form, the trumpet and the horn had no valves and thus were "natural"—they could produce only the tones of the overtone series appropriate to their tube lengths. Although other tones could be produced by hand-stopping techniques, they were of inferior quality and uncertain pitch, and composers generally avoided them when possible.

The orchestra in the seventeenth century seems to have been mainly a body of strings supported by a keyboard instrument, along with plucked stringed instruments and/or bassoons that played the basso continuo. Other wind instruments were occasionally added for descriptive purposes or because they were associated with specific imagery. Timpani were also used in a limited manner. Side-by-side with the earlier forms of modern instruments were several older instruments that gradually became obsolete. In addition, there were various sizes and types of oboes, trumpets, and other instruments that fell by the wayside. More modern versions of the violin family, the flute, the oboe, the clarinet, and the horn were developed toward the end of the seventeenth century.

As in much of the eighteenth century, brass and percussion players were likely to be drawn from military bands, although there was also a rich tradition of ensemble and solo music for brass instruments.

Historians usually place the beginnings of the orchestra as we know it somewhere in the seventeenth century. Early in the eighteenth century, orchestral concerts began to have an existence independent of operas or other stage productions. The symphony as a form gradually became distinct from the opera overture and the orchestral suites and concertos from which it evolved.

BACH AND HANDEL

Johann Sebastian Bach. The orchestra in Bach's four orchestral suites consisted of 2 oboes, 1 or 2 bassoons, strings, 3 trumpets, and timpani. The last two of these appear in only two of the works. The *continuo*, a keyboard instrument not usually specified in the score (but usually a harpsichord), played the bass line with the left hand and improvised accompanying figures or harmony notes in the right hand. This orchestra is similar to the one usually used in the Haydn and Mozart symphonies, and its treatment is also similar, in spite of the basic differences between the Baroque and Classical styles.

Texture.   Voice lines in Baroque music tend to move continuously in a more or less steady rhythm. The strings normally play each voice in tuttis (a *tutti* is a section in which all instruments play). The voice parts are normally assigned in score order—the highest to the first violins, the next highest to the seconds, and so forth. In tuttis, the oboes are likely to double the violins (and violas, if there are three oboes) and the bassoons usually double the bass line. When there are two oboes, the viola is left undoubled, which reflects the Baroque emphasis on the two highest parts and the bass.

At times, the doubling takes the form of *shadowing*. This is the sustaining of some of the more important notes, as shown in mm. 5–10 of Example 7-1, where the oboe shadows the upper notes of the second violins. The last five measures of Example 7-2 exhibit a combination of shadowing and *simplifying*, where the trumpet plays some of, but not all, the first violin notes. Simplification makes the wind parts less tiring and lightens or clarifies the line. In some cases, it allows a brass instrument to avoid notes that are not in its overtone series.

Example 7-1   Handel, Opus 3, No. 2, mvt. 1, mm. 33–44

Example 7-1 *(continued)*

Example 7-2 Bach, Orchestral Suite No. 4, Gavotte, mm. 26–33

Winds and Timpani. At times, a group of solo winds offers relief from the constant tuttis. It is mostly in these passages that the winds are independent of the strings. The trumpets are more likely than the oboes to be independent, although they play less often and are more restricted in pitch choice. The timpani, tuned always to the tonic and the dominant below it, play only when the winds are playing and usually match the rhythm of the winds or the bass.

In Example 7-3, the timpani are written in C major, as was customary, which means, in this case, that they must be tuned a major second higher than written to sound in D. Notice that the rhythms and pitches of the part approximate those of the bass line (Continuo). In the fourth measure, this results in some momentary dissonance when the bass line moves to a C♯ against the timpani's D (sounding). This is hardly noticed for two reasons: The dissonance is very short-lived and unaccented, and the timbre of the timpani is so different from that of the other instruments that it sometimes has the effect of a nonpitched instrument.

Example 7-3   Bach, Orchestral Suite No. 4, mvt. 1

Example 7-3   *(continued)*

In works other than his suites, Bach used a variety of wind instruments, including the flute and the horns. Flutes and oboes both double the violins in tuttis. Bassoons ordinarily play together on the bass line, as in the suites. Occasionally, trumpets take part in the doubling of the violins—usually at the beginning or ending of a passage, and very often in a simplified version.

George Frideric Handel.   In his concerti grossi, Handel used two oboes with strings, both to double the violins and as soloists. None of his Opus 3 concertos, however, used trumpets, and bassoon parts are not always indicated in modern editions (which is to say that they *may* have played along on the bass part). At times, the oboes fill in the string texture by playing a part that lies between the first and second violin parts—this is a more modern technique. Occasionally, an oboe might switch its doubling from one violin part to another, as in the sixth measure of Example 7-4. Handel's oboes sometimes shadow the violins, as do Bach's. In the works of both composers, the more homophonic movements—the dances, in particular—tend to treat the orchestra in a block fashion in the main section, the winds literally doubling the strings, whereas, in contrasting sections, such as Trios, the orchestra is treated in smaller units—for example, the strings or

Example 7-4   Handel, Opus 3, No. 5, mvt. 2, mm. 9–15

the winds playing alone. This practice was carried forward directly into the dance movements of Haydn and Mozart.

HAYDN AND MOZART

Instrumentation.   The symphony grew in the context of increasing numbers of public concerts and the demand for larger forces. There were great disparities in size from place to place: Some court orchestras would be considered chamber orchestras today, whereas those in large cities sometimes approached the size of a modern orchestra. The number of instruments grew in the later symphonies of Franz Joseph Haydn and Wolfgang Amadeus Mozart, and the texture became correspondingly fuller. At the same time, the winds and the percussion (the latter consisting usually only of the timpani) were treated more independently. The practice of using a keyboard instrument to play from the bass line and fill in upper notes was gradually given up toward the end of the century.

Texture.   In the period generally referred to as eighteenth-century Classicism, the continuous voice lines of the Baroque period were both incorporated into and alternated with a more homophonic texture. Most of the activity now took place in the highest voice, which had a greater variety of rhythms, and the regular eighth notes that were formerly part of the rhythm of the melody lines were transformed into repeated notes in the lower voices. Movements or passages began to appear in which these subdivisions were not heard at all. This created a thicker, more sustained texture that is typical of the nineteenth century.

Winds and Timpani.   During this period, two horns were added to the basic Baroque orchestra. As before, brass instruments changed from one overtone series to another by inserting crooks of various sizes into the instrument (one at a time).

Only certain crooks were used, which limited these instruments to a few keys, mostly C and D major. Horns were less limited than trumpets because they more readily played high overtones, making more notes available, and hand-stopping provided other notes. Timpani were still tuned mostly to the dominant and tonic notes for the duration of a piece. At first, flutes were used only occasionally, then later more often, when the clarinets also made a tentative appearance. The opera, being a less abstract medium, employed a wider variety of instruments than the symphony did.

As in the Baroque, wind instruments were used in pairs much more often than singly. The upper woodwinds were generally kept above the strings, doubling them an octave higher or playing a "filler" part (one that fills in the space between the soprano and the bass) an octave higher. This practice continued well into the nineteenth century and beyond.

Many of Haydn's symphonies changed instrumentation from movement to movement, as was done also in Baroque pieces. The strings almost always predominated in the slow movements, and the violins (but not the lower strings) were muted. In the third movements—the Menuettos—the main section was usually scored like a Baroque tutti, the winds doubling the strings as far as possible, and the Trios furnished contrast with a reduction of forces and separation of families (that is, the families did not double one another but played different things)—the winds might be omitted or, on the contrary, *featured* either as a group or with soloists. Cello parts began to be somewhat distinct from the contrabass part, whereas previously the parts for those instruments had always been identical. Occasionally, solo string players were called for, but only violins or cellos. The viola part was rarely of interest in itself except in contrapuntal passages.

Highlighting. A more modern combining of instrumental voices can sometimes be found. In Example 7-5, the oboes play only certain notes of the violins,

Example 7-5   Haydn, Symphony No. 44, mvt. 4, mm. 142–147

with the purpose of emphasizing them by reinforcement. This will be called high-lighting. It is one of the most common devices in the history of orchestral music.

Linking.   Example 7-6 is even more unusual for its time. It breaks a continuous melody into fragments that are taken by different instruments or groups of instruments. In m. 45, the clarinet and the bassoon join the E-flats of the violins and continue the melody while the strings drop out. The joining, or "linking," allows the melodic line to be smooth, in spite of the changes in instruments: If the violins had ended on their previous E-naturals, there could be a gap between the E-naturals and the E-Flats, since the violinists would tend to phrase their line, thinking of the E-natural as its end. In m. 46, the linking is not as smooth as the line returns to the violins—the strings do not enter on the woodwinds' last note; this is appropriate, since the B-flats in the winds are the end of a figure, whereas the next B-flats in the violins begin the next subdivision of the melody.

Example 7-6   Mozart, Symphony No. 40, mvt. 1, mm. 44–55

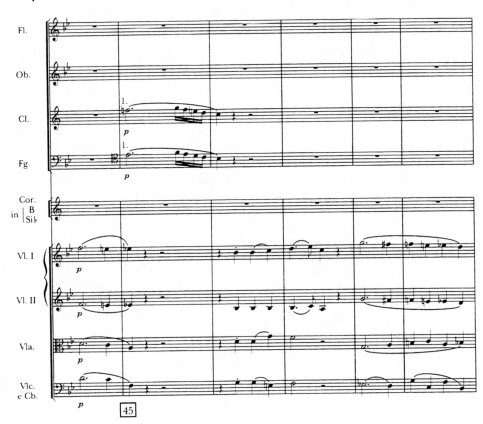

Example 7-6 (continued)

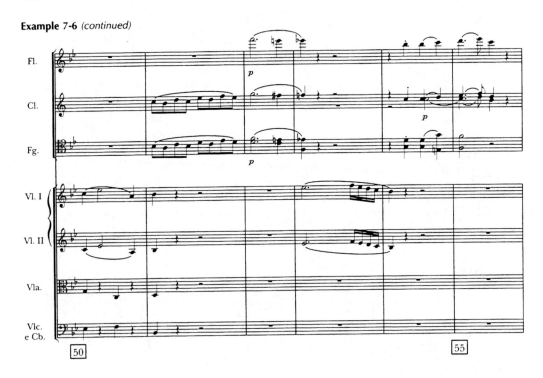

In m. 51, there is another overlap when the wind line begins on the same note with which the violins end. *Overlaps are more successful on the beat than off, and on strong, rather than weak, beats.* The device of continuing a melody in other instruments occurs quite often in later music. When it occurs between like instruments, it may be hardly noticeable, but between unlike instruments, as here, it can cause an abrupt change of color in the course of the line.

Octave Doubling.   In the later symphonies of Mozart and Haydn, the practice of octave doubling within families became more common, and we see this not only between the cellos and the basses, but also between the violins and the violas, two clarinets, or two oboes. A further thickening of the texture comes with tripling of the woodwinds in thirds, as we see in Example 7-7. This became a favorite device of Beethoven, Brahms, and others. When the violins are in octaves, the violas are often divided into alto and tenor notes (the cellos remaining, as usual, on the bass line) to maintain the usual four voices in the family. See Example 7-8. The violas may supply not only harmonic fillers but also, as here, rhythmic subdivisions.

Example 7-7   Haydn, Symphony No. 94, mvt. 1

Example 7-8 Mozart, Symphony No. 40, mvt. 1

Intensification.   Another modern touch is found in Example 7-9, where each appearance of the main theme is scored with more instruments than before, giving the effect of intensification. This technique is to be found almost everywhere in later music. It avoids static restatements and engenders a feeling of growth or greater excitement over the course of a section of music or even a whole movement.

Instrumental Effects.   Here and there we find unusual instrumental devices that became common in the twentieth century. In Symphony No. 97, Haydn asked the strings to play sul ponticello. In Symphony No. 102, he muted both the trumpets and the timpani.

SUMMARY OF BACH, HANDEL, HAYDN, AND MOZART

1. The basic orchestra consists of 2 oboes, 2 bassoons, 2 horns, and strings (sometimes 1 or 2 flutes, clarinets, trumpets, and/or timpani).
2. The strings usually carry all the important voices, and their lines are usually doubled, shadowed, or simplified by the other instruments.
3. Toward the end of the eighteenth century, the nonstrings increase in number and become more independent. The texture becomes thicker with filler parts, more octave doublings, and octave triplings.
4. Early examples of highlighting, linking, and intensified repetition or recurrence appear.

Example 7-9   Haydn, Symphony No. 94, mvt. 4

Example 7-9 *(continued)*

THE EARLY-TO-MIDDLE NINETEENTH CENTURY

Instrumentation.   During this period—roughly 1800 to 1870—the orchestra increased dramatically in size, adding new instruments and new versions of older ones. The woodwind section occasionally included the piccolo, the English horn, the bass clarinet, or the contrabassoon. The new brass included trombones (previously not used in the symphony), the cornet (mostly in France), and, in later years, the tuba.

For some time, the use of the newer instruments varied considerably from country to country: The cornet and the harp were used more in France than elsewhere, and the same was true of the tuba in Germany. Some instruments were made differently in various countries: The English and the Italians used a three-stringed contrabass for much of the century, while elsewhere the four-stringed version was replacing the three- and five-stringed basses. Bassoons made in France differed from those made in Germany. To this day, such disparity exists, and some wind instruments are even made differently within the *same* country.

New Developments.   Perhaps the most important development of all was the invention of devices to make it easier for wind instruments to play all pitches within their range. By the middle of the century, the complete chromatic scale was possible for all of them. New keys were added to woodwind instruments, along with new mechanisms to operate them. Valves were introduced in brass instruments, making seven tube lengths easily accessible. The harp, too, became fully chromatic with its new pedal system. These new developments were accepted only gradually, but their advent is clearly reflected in a new reliance on these instruments for important melodic parts.

The development in percussion was slow at first. The instruments formerly associated with Turkish music—the triangle, the cymbals, and the bass drum (still used for that in Beethoven's *The Ruins of Athens*)—were now used for their own sake. The timpani were tuned to tones other than just tonic and dominant, and the tuning could be changed from movement to movement (after Beethoven) or even within movements. Berlioz called for three timpanists in his *Symphonie fantastique* (1830) and for sixteen in his Requiem.

Texture.   In the first half of the nineteenth century, there was a change from Classical to Romantic texture. The rhythmic impulse was generally softened (except in stylized pieces such as marches and dances) in favor of a more lyrical character, and all voices became more melodic. Accompaniments now tended to have legato weaving figures rather than staccato repeated notes, and in general, the effect was thicker, darker, and more sustained than before.

A study of some of the principal composers of this period shows that many techniques of scoring found in today's scores were already present in their works. As the wind families expanded in number, they were more often treated as units in themselves, and their members were also more freely combined with other families. The interaction between families and the choices of instruments for thematic lines became important factors in the delineation of form.

BEETHOVEN

Doubling.   In his first symphonies, Ludwig van Beethoven took up the fuller texture of Haydn's last works, doubling both the strings and the woodwinds separately, and expanding at times to four octaves. Doubling in contrapuntal passages could be inconsistent, with some lines doubled at the unison and others at the octave. In more homophonic textures, the soprano line might be the only one doubled.

Instrumentation.   The basic orchestra now consisted of 2 flutes, 2 oboes, 2 clarinets, 2 bassoons, 2–4 horns, 2 trumpets, occasionally 2 or 3 trombones, timpani, and strings: Each of the melodic families could provide a complete texture. Before the valves were adopted, the brass were the least likely to do so.

In Example 7-10, the violins play the thematic line in octaves, supported below by an accompaniment of repeated notes in the eighteenth-century manner. The strings are harmonically complete in themselves. The melody is imitated by the flute, the clarinet, and the bassoon in two octaves, supported by the other woodwinds, the brass, and the strings. The woodwinds, too, are complete except for the note G, which is supplied by the second horn. In mm. 2 and 3, the winds,

Example 7-10   Beethoven, Symphony No. 1, mvt. 1, mm. 33–35

Example 7-11 Beethoven, Symphony No. 1, mvt. 1, mm. 39–43

like the strings, are split between the functions of melody and accompaniment while the strings are relegated to accompaniment only. A few measures later, the woodwinds, doubled over three octaves, join the strings for three notes, highlighting the thematic figure A–C♯–D (see Example 7-11).

Spacing. In tutti passages, the strings have to be spread out to cover the full pitch range because there are only five sections of them, whereas the more numerous individual woodwinds are concentrated more in upper octaves and are more closely spaced. Example 7-12 gives a brief illustration of this. (In later years, with more string players, divisi was often employed to give a fullness comparable to that of the woodwinds.)

Example 7-12 Beethoven, *Leonore* Overture No. 3, mm. 57–64

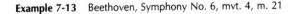

The overall spacing in Beethoven's tuttis can be characterized generally as close in the upper and middle registers and open in the bass, as illustrated in Example 7-13. The spacing is close from *f* upward and in open octaves below. In this example, note the consistency with which many like instruments are doubled in octaves—the two flutes, the clarinets, the horns, and the two halves of the first violins.

Example 7-13 Beethoven, Symphony No. 6, mvt. 4, m. 21

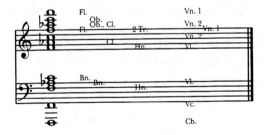

In his disposition of wind instruments in a chord, Beethoven used all the possibilities for arranging pairs of like instruments in four parts:

1. *Juxtaposition.* For example:
    Flute
    Flute
    Oboe
    Oboe
2. *Overlapping.* For example:
    Flute
    Flute/Oboe
    Oboe
3. *Interlocking.* For example:
    Flute
    Oboe
    Flute
    Oboe
4. *Enclosure.* For example:
    Flute
    Oboe
    Oboe
    Flute

In wind instruments, where timbre differences are at times quite noticeable, the choice of arrangement can affect how well the group blends. In order of blending potential, these can be ranked from the most to the least blending as follows: (1) interlocking, (2) enclosure, (3) overlapping, and (4) juxtaposition. Interlocking mixes, and therefore blends, the two types of sound by placing unlike instruments next to each other. Enclosure mixes unlike instruments on the outside (top and bottom) but not on the inside. Overlapping and juxtaposition emphasize differences in timbre by placing *like* instruments close to each other—overlapping softens the contrast by doubling unlike instruments (in some cases, it might create a better blend than enclosure).

Beethoven very often placed the woodwinds in score order—that is, with the flute on the highest note, the oboe, which is next in the score, on the next highest note, and so forth. Any departure from this is known as inversion.

Use of Clarinets, Bassoons, and Horns.   As did countless composers after him, Beethoven often used the clarinets, the bassoons, or the horns—all good blending instruments—to fill in the string texture, or to double inner parts, usually the violas. He often added a pair of these instruments to the strings in the later part of a phrase, usually horns in octaves (see Example 7-14). This device became a cliché, particularly in Italian opera arias. It could be said to create a subtle increase of warmth as the climax of the phrase is reached. It is also used for *instrumental transition,* a bridge between instrumental groups. In this passage, the horns, as wind instruments, "reintroduce" the clarinet and the bassoon when they are inserted almost unnoticeably into the string texture in preparation for a more prominent role for the winds.

Example 7-14 Beethoven, Symphony No. 2, mvt. 2, mm. 82–87

Example 7-15 Beethoven, Symphony No. 1, mvt. 4, mm. 258–266

Reintroducing an Instrument. Related to this is the omitting of a wind instrument in a tutti passage so that when it comes back in, it will have the effect of a relatively fresh sound. Example 7-15 shows such a passage: The oboes are not included in the first five measures of *ff* that are shown, and when they reenter at m. 6 with a new idea, that idea attracts attention partly because it has a fresh color.

Orchestral Crescendo. Along with the technique of intensification, Beethoven often employed "orchestral crescendo"—the adding of instruments *during* a passage. In Example 7-16, the notated crescendo is greatly enhanced by the addition of the first flute, the first oboe, the first bassoon, and the violas, then several other instruments, and finally the trombones. The orchestral crescendo was made famous by Rossini, who generally applied it to repetitive passages. It

Example 7-16 Beethoven, Symphony No. 6, mvt. 5, mm. 52–56

became a stock-in-trade for all later composers, even when no crescendo indication was specifically given.

SUMMARY OF BEETHOVEN

Main features are

1. A basic orchestra of two each of flutes, oboes, clarinets, bassoons, horns, trumpets, and timpani
2. Doubling of main lines in up to four octaves in the strings, the woodwinds, or both
3. Complete textures in either the strings, the woodwinds, or both
4. Separate functions for strings and woodwinds
5. Tutti spacing in which the bass register is open and the upper registers are close
6. Woodwinds arranged generally in score order (juxtaposition), but also (when in four parts) in either interlocking, overlapping, or enclosure
7. The manipulation of instrumental entrances or omissions to add warmth, reserve a color for a new idea, provide a transition from one family to another, or give the effect of crescendo

WEBER AND MENDELSSOHN

Although Carl Maria von Weber and Felix Mendelssohn were more than twenty years apart, their styles have much in common. Using the basic orchestra of Beethoven, they introduced a greater variety of color and a more flexible interaction between families.

Spacing. The brass now often represented the full complement of the harmony—alone or in tuttis—and occupied most of the middle of the texture, with strings and woodwinds distributed over the upper and lower portions. Example 7-17 shows the brass playing every note of the chord from c to c^2. The woodwinds are not represented in the area of $d-e^1$, nor are the strings in $d-c^1$. The woodwinds are interlocked, as are the upper strings (which are playing tremolo for maximum strength). The brass can be considered in two groups, both of which are harmonically complete and close to numerically balanced (an equal number of instruments per note): the horns, in close position, and the trumpets/trombones in open position. That the horns are complete, as are the other brass as a whole, avoids the problem of overstressing certain harmony tones, since the horns match each other, more or less, in power and quality, whereas the trumpets and the trombones are more similar to each other than to the horns in the same respects. This is a typical treatment of the brass in tuttis, particularly in nineteenth-century German scores. Weber and Mendelssohn began to approximate the numerical balances that became the norm in the twentieth century. In Example 7-18, most of the tones are played by two wind instruments or two string sections, providing a rough equality of strength.

Example 7-17 Weber, Overture to *Der Freischütz*, m. 279

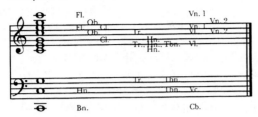

Example 7-18 Mendelssohn, Symphony No. 3, mvt. 1, m. 213

Use of Families.   In an apparent quest for new colors, the composers now used new combinations of instruments by more freely mixing families and used inversions within or between families. Both are shown in Example 7-19, along with some subtle instrumental voice leading. The clarinets are mixed with the strings, taking an inner voice: Composers now were beginning to exploit the use of the low register of the clarinet for its blending character as well as its special color.

Example 7-19 Weber, Overture to *Oberon*, mm. 16–21

Inversion is used in two ways. (1) Within the strings, the cellos are placed above the violas, an arrangement favored by later composers. The first cellos, playing the main voice line in mm. 16–18, are in their strongest register. The violas, paralleling them just below, are relatively dark, as they descend to their lower strings—the blend is not as "good" as if the instruments were not inverted. Apparently, Weber was more interested in the richness provided by the cellos for the melodic line than in the best blend with the lower voices. (2) The clarinets, which are treble or alto instruments, are placed below both the violas and the cellos.

Instrumental Voice Leading.   A final point of interest in this passage is the instrumental voice leading. In contrast with pure voice leading, which is associated with choral music and wherein each voice moves characteristically by small intervals and remains in its own "territory," instrumental voices can move into and out of each other's pitch areas, providing subtle changes of color while giving the *effect* of pure voice leading. In the first two measures of the example, the instrumental voice leading is pure—the first cellos act as sopranos, the violas as altos, the clarinets as tenors, and the second cellos as basses until the third measure, when the upper strings cross over the clarinets, causing the latter momentarily to become the soprano on their half-note c^1 (sounding a). This a is immediately joined by the second violins as they enter, and the viola and the cello assume the function of inner voices. Following this, the entrance of the first violins makes it sound as if the soprano line has moved from the a of the clarinets and the second violins back to the d^1 from which the line descended on the second beat of the measure in the cellos. When the first violins rise to e^1, and so on, the clarinets take over the d^1 (sounding) they had just left, making the soprano note d into an alto note as the violins leave it. On the following fourth beat, the second violins and the violas repeat what the first violins and the clarinets had played previously—they join on d^1, replacing the clarinets, and the violas proceed upward (inverting over the second violins). This play of colors takes place through the mechanism of doubling a note in a line with a new color, then continuing the line with the new color alone. It is a form of the linking technique shown in Example 7-6, applied to various lines within a texture.

Reorchestration.   We have seen techniques that match orchestration changes with changes in form—intensified repetitions and orchestral crescendos. Another one is *reorchestration.* This is the rescoring of a recurring idea in various ways to avoid monotony. It is illustrated in Mendelssohn's *Hebrides* Overture by the melody

Example 7-20 Mendelssohn, *Hebrides* Overture

shown in Example 7-20. This melody appears several times, always accompanied by sustained tones:

	m. 1		m. 3
Melody:	Violas/Cellos/Bassoon		Violas
Accompaniment:	Violins		Violins/Clarinets

	m. 5	m. 9	m. 11
Melody:	Violas/Cellos	Violins	Violins
Accompaniment:	Violins/Clarinets/Oboes	Horns	Horns/Trumpets

	m. 13 (melody altered)		m. 17
Melody:	Violin 1		Violin 2
Accompaniment:	Horns/Flute		Oboe/Horns

Notice that in each case, the melody is played by one or more string sections, and that after m. 2, the accompaniment notes are always (at least partly) played by winds; yet, no two settings are the same. Other examples of reorchestration occur in this overture, especially in the development section (mm. 96–123).[3]

Repeated Notes in the Oboe. At m. 553 in Example 7-21 (see page 204), all the woodwinds but the oboes are asked to play rather fast repeated triplets (the tempo is about dotted quarter note = 150). The same is true of a similar, more extended passage at the beginning of the movement. These are two of many examples where composers are careful not to overburden the oboist's tongue. The overture to Rossini's *La Scala di seta* has a fast staccato passage for the oboe, but it has been played with interpolated slurs, which relieve the tongue. There are times when the oboe is given fast repeated notes, but the success of such passages probably depends on the player.

SUMMARY OF WEBER AND MENDELSSOHN

Main features are

1. A typical tutti texture with the brass completely representing the harmony and with the strings and woodwinds in the outer registers
2. Tutti doubling that sometimes approaches numerical equality—an equal number of wind instruments or string sections on each note
3. A more deliberate mixing of families—e.g., the clarinet playing as an inner voice among the strings
4. Reorchestration of an idea that is heard several times to keep the sound fresh
5. The exclusion of oboes from wind ensembles executing fast repeated notes

---

[3]An example of a whole theme that is repeated several times, each time with different orchestration, can be found in the third movement of Rimsky-Korsakov's *Scheherazade*, mm. 70–126. This is discussed in Chapter 8.

Example 7-21   Mendelssohn, Symphony No. 4, mvt. 1, mm. 548–563

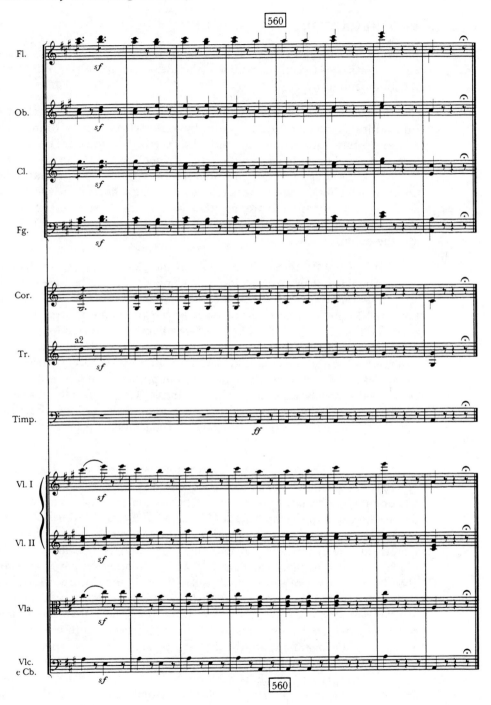

BRAHMS, TCHAIKOVSKY, AND WAGNER

Johannes Brahms, Piotr Ilyich Tchaikovsky, and Richard Wagner represent a variety of approaches to composition and the use of the orchestra in the latter half of the nineteenth century.

Instrumentation. Around the middle of the century, the valved brass became widely accepted (although never by conservatives such as Brahms). The tuba and the contrabassoon were occasionally called upon to strengthen or color the bass, and the English horn and the bass clarinet were added to the midrange and baritone areas. Wagner required whole sets of new brass instruments, creating, in effect, subfamilies of tubas and trumpets. The harp became a symphonic, as well as an operatic, instrument: Wagner used as many as six at a time. New percussion instruments, such as the xylophone, and keyboard instruments, such as the celesta and the piano, appear in scores.

The Use of Families. There was an increased emphasis on lyricism and a fluid stretching-out of form: Melodies became longer and had greater range. The score took on an increased heaviness that followed two lines of development, as Carse tells us in *The History of Orchestration:* the Germanic approach, which was to reinforce lines by mixed doubling between families, and reinforcement of a line by doubling *within* a family and separation of functions by family color. The second method was followed in non-German countries—especially Italy, France, and Russia—that favored opera (in which it is important to differentiate melody and accompaniment) over purely orchestral music. Carse considered the Germanic approach to be relatively colorless and tiresome in its lack of diversity, and the non-Germanic, particularly in the case of Tchaikovsky, to be relatively clear and brilliant.

Spacing. The tutti texture, even at lower dynamic levels, was often very full. Whereas the spacing in earlier composers tended to be close in the treble register and open in the bass, now it was often open at the extremes and close in the middle, as illustrated in Example 7-22. (The middle of this chord is not entirely close, since there is a gap between c^1 and a^1, but in the same chord at the end of the movement, the gap is filled in by string pizzicato.) Notice the consistency with which like instruments are arranged in sixths: trumpets, upper trombones, flutes, oboes, both sections of violins, and violas. (The clarinets' third can be considered an inverted sixth.) As in earlier music, the brass is concentrated in the middle, with the woodwinds and strings spread (the strings more than the woodwinds) to cover the extremes. The brass is harmonically complete, both in the horns, which are in close arrangement, and in the "sharp" brass—the trumpets and the trombones—which are in open position.

In Example 7-23, Brahms achieves a marvelous sequence of harmonic and orchestral color through changes of instrumental types and spacing: There is an alternation of almost pure wind and string groups. In m. 227, the instruments are

Example 7-22 Brahms, Symphony No. 3, mvt. 1, end

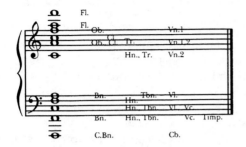

Example 7-23 Brahms, Symphony No. 4, mvt. 1, mm. 227–230

for the most part either interlocked or enclosed, producing a rich blend. A soft effect results from the placing of each instrument in a middle register, where it is neither weak nor especially brilliant.

There are other interesting features: The bassoons are below the horns, as they usually are when those instruments are closely associated. There is close to the same number of instruments playing each note. In mm. 228 and 230, the strings achieve a special resonance through double stops in interlocking large intervals. (This is the usual way in which double-stopping or divisi is arranged between and within sections.) Resonance is further enhanced by the open C and G strings of the violas and the cellos in the last measure. The spacing in the outer measures is typical of the open–close–open practice. The violas are inverted over the violins in m. 228, providing some contrast with the accompanying strings, and the imitating figure in m. 229 carries forward the solo string tone in the cellos. In this measure, the "softer" instruments of the woodwinds and brass are combined in midregister, and the horns are typically complete and in close position.

Groups of Like Instruments.   Wagner often used ensembles of like instruments. Like many composers after him, he seemed to subdivide both the woodwinds and the brass into two groups—a "sharper" one and a "softer" one. The double reeds constitute the sharp group of the woodwinds, and the trumpets and the trombones are the comparable members of the brass. Any brass instrument, when muted or stopped, takes on the quality of a sharp instrument. (The corollary of "sharpness" in the strings is playing sul ponticello.)

Wagner's *Tristan und Isolde* features a long English horn solo at the beginning of the first scene of the third act. The choice of that instrument is by this time especially meaningful because it has been associated with the "Love Potion" motive that begins the opera and is heard many times in the course of it. The motive begins in the cellos, linking with the English horn (see Example 7-24), which takes over their $d\sharp^1$. The first oboe continues the motive in another voice. Since the high cellos tend to sound somewhat nasal, the linking from their $d\sharp^1$ in m. 2 to the nasal English horn is a transfer of somewhat like colors. The wind group in mm. 2 and 3 is entirely double reed, except for the clarinets, whose function is merely to highlight the lowest two notes and then to drop out. The second oboe highlights the soprano entrance of the first oboe. (This changing of color during a line is typical of Wagner and, after him, Mahler, Schoenberg, and others. In conjunction with changes of harmony, it affords almost unnoticeable shadings of musical, and perhaps psychological, meanings.)

Sharp and Soft Instruments.   Later in the Introduction, small string and woodwind ensembles alternate playing a figure, as shown in Example 7-25 at no. 3.

Example 7-24   Wagner, *Tristan und Isolde,* Prelude

Example 7-25   Wagner, *Tristan und Isolde*, Prelude, mm. 33–42

Example 7-25 (continued)

Here the violas, interlocked with the cellos, take the soprano line. They are echoed by the oboe, which is accompanied by the English horn and two (softer) clarinets. This is one of countless examples of composers associating a double-reed instrument with the violas, especially when the latter are relatively high and more nasal. (A famous example is the melody beginning at m. 183 in the overture to Tchaikovsky's *Romeo and Juliet*, given to the English horn and the violas in unison.) Composers seem to consider the viola a relatively sharp instrument.

Shared Lines.   Example 7-26 shows Wagner linking the softer tubas in m. 3 with the sharper trombones and double reeds. This emphasizes the despair of Wotan, who sings, "Götternot!" ("Grief of the Gods!") at this point.

Example 7-26   Wagner, *Die Walküre*, act 2, scene 2, mm. 36–37
(strings and voice omitted)

Wagner and others also used linking extensively to divide continuously moving fast passages. In these passages, like instruments share lines that would be fatiguing or unnecessarily difficult if each player had to play all the notes. Example 7-27 shows a fast descending arpeggio and a rising scale line that is divided between first violins and violas, then between the second violins and the firsts, who in turn link their $f\sharp^2$ with the violas. The interaction gives the effect of one section playing continuously.

Example 7-27   Wagner, *Die Walküre*, act 3, scene 1, m. 103

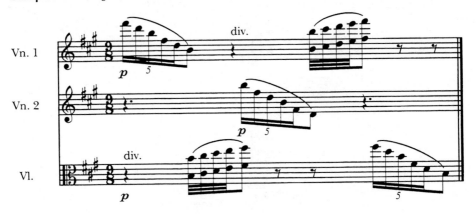

Although the dividing of the line makes the passage easier for individual players, it also creates a performance problem: Individual figures such as these are likely to have some accentuation, and the endings, particularly those that do not end on a beat, are likely to be tapered off; therefore, the result overall may not be as smooth as it would be with all players playing every note.

Surreptitious Entrances.   Brahms often changed color by sneaking an instrument in while others are playing, then dropping the "old" instruments out. See Example 7-28. The clarinet, which is eminently capable of a soft entrance, joins the oboes on their eb^2. This provides both the sustaining feature that is often added near the ends of phrases (as in Example 7-14) and a preparation for the clarinet's emergence. When the oboe descends into the pitch area of the accompanying strings to end on a lower E-flat, the clarinet appears to continue the melody in a higher octave. Notice also how the violins shadow the oboe's bb^1, c^2, and so on, which also helps the oboe to retreat into the accompaniment.

Combined articulation is another group effect. At m. 98 of the last movement of Brahms's Second Symphony, the strings and the woodwinds play in unison but with different articulations: The woodwinds and the contrabasses have slurred four-note groups while the violins, the violas, and the cellos play each note three

Example 7-28   Brahms, Symphony No. 1, mvt. 2, mm 42–45

times in a quasi tremolo. This allows the strings to be stronger (since the bow moves much faster than otherwise) and yields a mixed articulation—a kind of colored, articulated sostenuto.

Cross-voicing is a voice-leading technique in which instruments (usually of the same kind) alternate notes that belong to each other's "line." Normally confined to accompaniments, it is used for the first hearing of the *main theme* at the beginning of the finale of Tchaikovsky's Sixth Symphony (Example 7-29a). Comparing this with Example 7-29b, which is a later version using exactly the same notes, we find that in the first version, the violins cross-voice with each note played—the second violins switch from the soprano $f\sharp^2$ to the alto a^1 while the firsts move from the alto b^1 to the soprano e^2, and so on, and the violas and the cellos similarly cross-voice the tenor and bass lines. It is scarcely perceptible to the ear that the two

Example 7-29   Tchaikovsky, Symphony No. 6, mvt. 4

versions are orchestrated differently, since the strings as a family are so homogeneous in color. Still, it is a dramatic demonstration of the difference between an instrumental and a vocal handling of voice lines. This device is rarely found in the nineteenth century, but it became a favorite of Stravinsky and others later. Like other combining techniques, it gives individual parts a more instrumental character (namely, more activity) than they would have with pure voice leading.

The Use of Families to Clarify Form.   Earlier examples have shown how changes in orchestration are associated with form. The expanded orchestra made it possible for each family (aside from percussion) to carry either a melodic or a harmonic function by itself, offering more possibilities to delineate formal units through the interaction between families. With horizontal expansion—the lengthening of each section of music—it was now expedient to build toward a climax by first alternating families and then combining them for greater strength: At the most intense moments, each instrument plays the line that is in its strongest register, with colors mixed in unison doublings. Separation, then, is used as an effective way to *approach* a climactic moment.

An example of this procedure can be seen in Example 7-30. At m. 128, the first theme is played by the woodwinds in octaves, with one secondary idea in the horns, another in the violins and violas, and a bass line in the lower strings—each family has a separate function (the strings have two), and each is doubled in octaves for strength. As the theme progresses, intensity builds, and at m. 134, literal doubling begins to cross family boundaries—the horns and the woodwinds double inner voices, leaving the melody to the upper woodwinds, while the tuba enters to double the bass line (in the strings). This acts as a transition to the climax at m. 142, where the second theme returns in all the strings except the basses, doubled by flutes and first bassoon, the accompanying harmony and rhythm in horns and the other woodwinds, the lower brass doubling the strings in the bass.

Cross-function—the switching of roles between two instrumental units—is another formal device. The third movement of Brahms's First Symphony begins with the clarinet playing the leading line and the upper strings entering at the end of the first phrase as a highlight of it. When the theme begins again in m. 19, it is the *strings* that play the leading line while the clarinet plays an accompanying figure, and other *woodwinds* enter at the end of the phrase, much as the strings had done previously. Cross-function sometimes is applied to the return of a theme over a longer period of time. It is a special form of reorchestration.

The movement just cited also illustrates the use of an instrument as if it were a theme all by itself, somewhat like the English horn in *Tristan und Isolde.* As we saw, the clarinet plays the first theme, then accompanies the restatement of the theme. After a transition section, the clarinet begins the second theme (at m. 45) and then gives way to the oboe, but reappears in m. 62 to play a fragment of the first theme and then the full return of that theme. The following Trio begins with a dialogue between the woodwinds and the strings, excluding the clarinets. In the next phrase, the clarinets and the horns answer with their own dialogue with the strings. For the rest of the Trio, the clarinets are submerged in a full use of the winds. In the retransition from the Trio to the first theme (mm. 109–114), the clarinets are again omitted. Thus, when the first theme returns with the clarinet, both the theme and its associated color are renewed.

Example 7-30   Tchaikovsky, Symphony No. 5, mvt. 2, mm. 125–142

Example 7-30 *(continued)*

Example 7-30 (continued)

Numerical Balance. In matters of balance, composers now approached twentieth-century practice more closely. Example 7-31 illustrates an apparent attempt to keep the upper and lower octaves close to equal with respect to the numbers and strengths of the instruments. As the line goes up or down, instruments move into or out of strong registers, and small adjustments are made in the number playing each octave: On the downbeat of m. 5 the composer does not bring the first bassoon up to c^2 with the first and third horns, presumably because that note would be too weak or difficult. As the line descends, the trombones and then the tuba are added for greater power, and the instruments that are already playing adjust the balance by moving to the upper octave. *The modern equation for balance between the horns and the other brass at* forte *level is: Two horns equal one of the others;* therefore, 3 horns = 1 trombone + 1 horn, and the bassoons balance each other. Notice that *the distributing of the bassoons over the two octaves avoids the problem of calculating the power of the bassoons against that of the brass,* since each type of instrument is balanced against instruments of the same kind. Second, the blend is better if there is one bassoon in each octave than it would be if only bassoons were in one octave and only brass in the other. On the second note of m. 6, the principle is again applied—two trombones are added, one to each octave, maintaining the equality of numbers. On the next eighth note, the fourth horn joins the upper octave just before the tuba enters, partly to offset that new addition and partly to avoid going into the weaker low register of the horn. On the final three notes of the measure, the opposition of forces is 1 bassoon against 1 bassoon, 4 horns against 2 trombones, and 1 trombone against the tuba.

Tchaikovsky's contemporary, Rimsky-Korsakov, estimated that two woodwind instruments roughly equal one brass instrument. Using the equation that at *forte* level, 1 trumpet, 1 trombone, or 1 tuba equals 2 horns or 2 bassoons (this last is quite a rough estimate), we find that for the passage, the tonal weights in "trumpet units" in the two octaves are

$$f^1:1.5 \quad c^2:1 \quad ab^1:1.5 \quad \ldots \quad eb^1:2 \quad \ldots \quad c^1:3 \quad bb:3.5 \quad ab:3.5$$
$$f:1.5 \quad c^1:2 \quad ab:1.5 \quad \ldots \quad eb:2 \quad \ldots \quad c:3 \quad Bb:2.5 \quad Ab:3.5$$

Example 7-31   Tchaikovsky, Symphony No. 4, mvt. 1, mm. 5–6

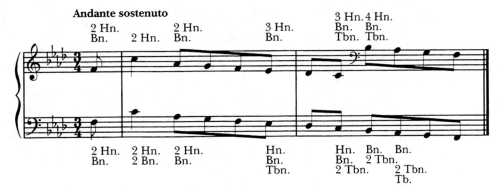

Andante sostenuto

The Use of Percussion.   The percussion now had a more varied role than before. Added to the traditional devices of rhythmic delineation and accentuation was the modern device of *pitch-level matching.* This device follows the "rule" that lower-sounding nonpitched instruments play with lower pitches (in pitched instruments) and higher-sounding nonpitched instruments play with higher pitches. Example 7-32 provides a clear example: The cymbals ("P." for "Piatti") match the partly syncopated rhythm of the relatively high line of the flutes, oboes, clarinets, horns, trumpet, and first trombone, while the bass drum ("Gr.C."—"Gran Cassa") reinforces the rhythm of the bass line.

Another practice is to match lower percussion with accented beats and higher percussion with unaccented ones, or offbeats, as is also the case in Example 7-32. Of course, composers did not treat nonpitched percussion only in those ways. They might simply have these instruments keep time by playing on every beat. The triangle is often used in this way.

Instrumental Colors.   Composers were becoming increasingly more sensitive to sonic characteristics of instruments. Brahms, for example, liked to exploit the lowest open strings of the string section for their ringing sound, as in Examples 7-23 and 7-33. In m. 5 of Example 7-33, the cello's open C string is used for an expressive change of harmony. (See also mm. 49, 230, and 256 in the first movement, m. 114 in the second movement, and mm. 113 and 128 in the last movement.)

The ringing of the open E string of the violin is emphasized in the last movement by *bariolage,* the playing of the same note on two strings alternately (Example 7-34). This ringing is matched by the first trumpet, which sustains the same pitch. Notice also the cross-voicing between the violin sections. (A very similar matching of the violin's E string with trumpets was used by Shostakovich in his First Symphony.) The Russian composers of this time loved the sound of the open strings, often incorporating them into double- and multiple stoppings.

SUMMARY OF BRAHMS, TCHAIKOVSKY, AND WAGNER

1. Tutti spacings are close in the middle and open in the extremes.
2. In tuttis, four horns tend to be harmonically complete in close position, whereas the sharp brass are also complete but in open position.
3. Family groups are employed in various ways, principally in alternation for color contrast or to prepare a climax by separating family functions first, then uniting them in literal doublings for greater strength at climaxes.
4. Sharp instruments of the woodwinds are often associated with sharp brass, muted brass, or violas. Soft wind instruments are often associated with each other in contrast to sharp ensembles.
5. Linking can be used to change color in a line when unlike instruments are involved or, when like instruments are involved, to divide a line that would be more fatiguing or difficult if undivided.
6. Cross-voicing is occasionally found, allowing instrumental voices more activity than they would have with pure voice leading, and to create variety.

Example 7-32 Tchaikovsky, Overture to *Romeo and Juliet*, mm. 342–344

Example 7-33   Brahms, Symphony No. 4, mvt. 1, mm. 1–6

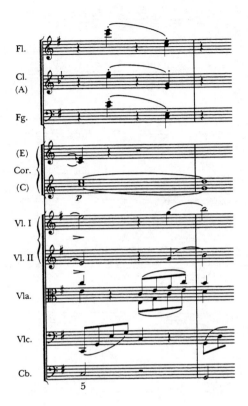

Example 7-34   Brahms, Symphony No. 4, mvt. 4, mm. 69–71

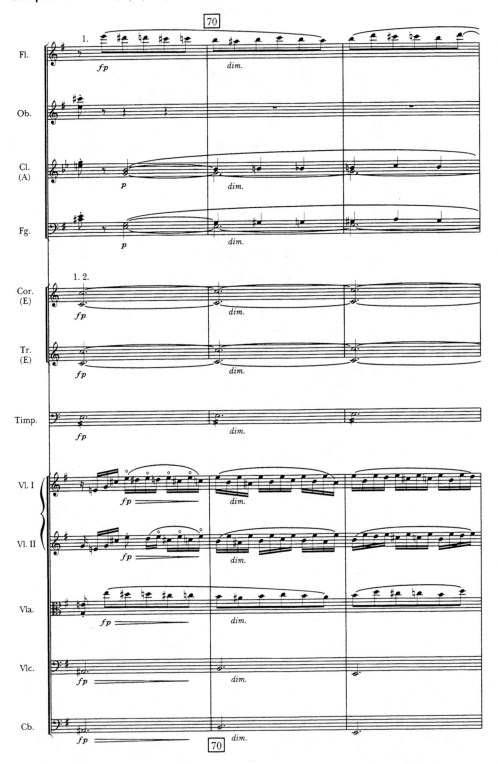

RIMSKY-KORSAKOV, STRAUSS AND MAHLER

Nicolai Rimsky-Korsakov, Richard Strauss, and Gustav Mahler wrote their best-known works from about 1885 to 1915. Rimsky-Korsakov and Tchaikovsky are rather similar in style, whereas Strauss and Mahler are closer to Wagner. It follows, from what was said earlier, that the Russian composers liked *melodies to be clearly differentiated from accompaniments,* and the Germans tended to make the entire orchestral fabric out of melodic lines, *sometimes obscuring the relationship between melody and accompaniment.*

Instrumentation. The woodwind section grew in Mahler's works to 4 flutes, 3 or 4 oboes (with possibly 2 English horns), up to 5 clarinets (plus possibly piccolo and bass clarinets), and up to 4 bassoons (plus contrabassoon). The brass expanded to as many as 8 horns, 6 trumpets, 3 or 4 trombones, and tuba. Occasionally added to the usual instruments were the organ, the mandolin, the guitar, or voices. The wind machine, sleigh bells, switches, and cowbells were occasionally added to the percussion. At times, the operatic device of offstage instruments (used as early as Beethoven's *Fidelio*) was employed. Perhaps because of Wagner's example, greater demands were made on orchestral players' endurance, virtuoso playing, and ability to produce unusual effects. In all these composers, the activity level of all instruments is much greater than before.

Spacing. Rimsky-Korsakov's tutti chords tend to be very full, with no gaps between about *e* and *e³*. The chord shown in Example 7-35 consists only of the notes F-sharp and B, showing great consistency in the choice of instruments wherever there is a perfect fifth—all the fifths are played by like instruments: 2 oboes, 2 trumpets, 2 bassoons, 4 horns, 2 trombones, viola divisi, and celli divisi.

Example 7-35 Rimsky-Korsakov, *Scheherazade,* mvt. 2, end

The tutti chords of Mahler, on the other hand, often have gaps, partly because his texture is so linear that the gaps are needed to give instruments room to move into them melodically. Example 7-36 has gaps below both D-flats, which are strongly doubled. These D-flats move melodically downward into the gaps. The heavily scored *bb* is also part of a line—this line moves into the gap above it.

Notice that the oboes, the clarinets, and the trombones are all in close position. This disposition of like instruments, a relatively modern one, is even more evident in Example 7-37, where each of the wind instruments except the trombone–tuba group is placed in a close-spaced grouping. The violins and the violas also form such a group. Notice that the upper winds—flutes, oboes, clarinets, and trumpets—are all in high registers, as are the upper strings. Strauss's tutti chords tend to be very full, but otherwise are like those of Mahler's.

Example 7-36   Mahler, Symphony No. 1, mvt. 4, five before no. 4

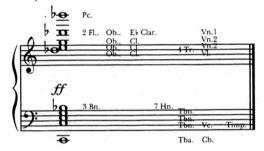

Example 7-37   Mahler, Symphony No. 2, mvt. 3, nine after no. 50

The Swirl.   A relatively new effect is the combining of instruments in a single "swirl"—a confusion of rapidly moving groups of notes, creating something of a blur more than a clearly defined line. Example 7-38 shows a mild example. The simple scale lines in the flute and the clarinet are combined with a glissando in the harp. The harp moves from just below the clarinet's first note to the high point of the flute's line (exclusive of the following f^3) and back, crossing both of the woodwind players' scales with its glissando (really an *arpeggio* of the harmony), moving about twice as fast. Swirls become very important later as composers realize the possibilities provided by group effects. (More elaborate swirls will be seen in later examples.)

Example 7-38   Rimsky-Korsakov, *Scheherazade*, mvt. 3, m. 161

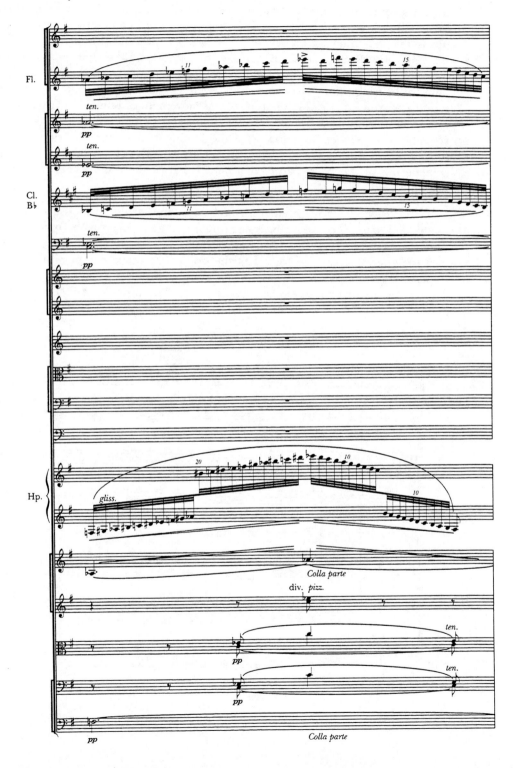

Matching. As the orchestra expanded and doubling became a more routine procedure, composers began to match some characteristic in one instrument by doubling it with a similar characteristic in another instrument. A typical example is the matching of pizzicato in the strings with staccato in the winds. In Example 7-39, Rimsky-Korsakov matches two piccolos, violin harmonics, and the triangle, all of which have in common not only high pitches but also a somewhat penetrating ring. The harp lends itself well to matching. Individual notes can sound like string pizzicatos (see the second movement of Franck's Symphony in D Minor, illustrated in Chapter 6). Its resonant and percussive low strings can also resemble low percussion sounds (see the ending of Mahler's Fourth Symphony, second movement, where low harp octaves are combined with the tam-tam). The shimmering of the harp's arpeggios match that of the quiet string tremolos in Example 7-40.

Consistency. With greater resources to draw from, composers showed a tendency toward a certain consistency in the content of instrumental combinations. In Example 7-41, the two-measure figure of mm. 70 and 71 is repeated an octave higher, keeping the format of the original accompaniment, which consists of pizzicatos, and the melody, carried by a trio of woodwinds composed of two of the same *soft* instruments on the upper notes. The notes in the corresponding

Example 7-39   Rimsky-Korsakov, *Scheherazade*, mvt. 2, mm. 175–184

Example 7-40 Rimsky-Korsakov, *Scheherazade*, mvt. 2, mm. 416–420

Example 7-41 Rimsky-Korsakov, *Scheherazade,* mvt. 1, mm. 70–75

instrumental parts are in the same register, respectively: The cello notes move from the highest to a middle string, as do those of the viola, and the clarinets move from mid- to upper register, as do the flutes.

Detailed Specifications. Composers now more frequently specified certain details about the orchestra or how it was to play. Strauss indicated the number of players he wanted in each string section for his *Don Quixote:* 16 first and 16 second violins, 12 violas, 10 celli, and 8 basses. That is not much different from the numbers called for by Berlioz, Wagner, and later composers, and it corresponds well with the size of many professional orchestras of today. One reason for designating precise numbers of sections might have been a concern for balances.

Another kind of specification is seen in Example 7-42—different dynamic levels for different instruments. There is a texture of three independent lines at no. 5—one in the violins, another in the flute and the solo violin, and a third in the clarinet and the trombone. The two violin sections are pitted against pairs of

Example 7-42 Strauss, *Don Quixote*

Example 7-42   *(continued)*

instruments, but the violins are marked *p* and the pairs are marked *mf.* The flute and the solo violin (which, is muted, probably for color) have the double advantage of carrying the highest-sounding line and of playing in their strongest registers. The trombone is one of the most powerful of instruments, but its volume (not its cutting power) is reduced by the mute. Thus, the balance seems about even, partly because the dynamics are adjusted to compensate for these various factors.

Also note in this example the consistency of color within the pairs, which consist of members of different families; the cello solo's final a^1 linking to the flute and the solo violin; and the interaction of the trombone and the clarinet—at first the clarinet highlights the trombone; then the trombone, after dropping out, highlights the onbeat notes of the clarinet. The passage as a whole is characterized by clarity and fine coloring.

Mahler's texture is also very linear. In loud passages, the orchestra is divided into large subdivisions, mostly along family lines, as in Example 7-43. Sometimes, melodic lines interfere with each other, or merge, as in the upper two lines of this example, but generally they are clearly separated by pitch, as the lowest line is from the others.

Example 7-43   Mahler, Symphony No. 1, mvt. 1, no. 30

3 Fl., Ob., 2 Cl., Eb Cl.

Ob., Cl.

Vn. 1

Vn. 2, Vls., Hns.

2 Bn., Vc.

C. Bn., Cb.

Mahler's scores show an almost constant exploring of orchestral resources. We encounter not only the traditional markings but also many new ones that describe some unusual way of playing. Although very large orchestras are required for his symphonies, his textures are often *relatively* thin, like that of Example 7-43, composed for roughly equal lines of counterpoint, and clearly differentiated by pitch level and color. Some of the new effects are

1. The use of glissandos in both wind and string instruments: In m. 42 of the last movement of the Fourth Symphony, the English horn, the bassoon, two horns, and cellos all are asked to slide from $c\sharp^1$ to *a*. (Obviously, only the cellos can produce the complete gliss, and the winds approximate it, creating a kind of swirl.)

2. Instructing the strings to "remove mutes gradually" during a passage—that is, in staggered fashion, so that the sound changes gradually from muted to open (Symphony No. 2, first movement, no. 23).

3. Scordatura violin. In the second movement of the Fourth Symphony, the violin soloist is to tune the instrument a major second higher than normal, to make it sound like a folk fiddle. The part is written as if the instrument were "in D"—that is, a major second lower than it is intended to sound.

4. The use of a switch, struck "on the wood" of the bass drum (in the third movement of the Second Symphony).

5. The combination of muting and open sound in both brass and strings (Symphony No. 2, first movement, eight after no. 5, and second movement, nine before no. 14).

6. Variable dynamics—several different dynamic levels all at once (see Example 7-44). This is rather common in Mahler, although not in a unison passage such as this. His desire was evidently a mixture of colors and strengths, aimed at a special quality.

Example 7-44 Mahler, Symphony No. 2, mvt. 4, two before no. 21

2 Fl. (*ff*), 2 Ob. (*ff*), 2 Cl. (*p*), 2 Bn. (***ppp***)

7. "Schalltrichter auf" ("bells up"), not only for brass but also for oboes and clarinets, for a more penetrating sound (Fourth Symphony, first movement, m. 268).

8. Beginning a tremolo in the middle of sustained tone (Symphony No. 1, first movement, six after no. 23).

9. "Snap pizz.," causing the strings to rattle against the fingerboard (Symphony No. 7, third movement, three after no. 161).

10. Much coloring of lines by highlighting, shifting of color, and instruments dropping in and out. Example 7-45 is an illustration of all of these. Notice that the dynamic level of the muted violins is *pp*, in contrast to the *f* in the flutes.

Example 7-45 Mahler, Symphony No. 4, mvt. 4, mm. 4–8

SUMMARY OF RIMSKY-KORSAKOV, STRAUSS, AND MAHLER

Main features are

1. Very full tutti chords, usually with groups of closely spaced like instruments
2. Swirls
3. Matching of like sounds and effects by unlike instruments
4. Consistency of scoring in like passages
5. Unusual uses of instruments, such as glissando, scordatura, and snap pizzicato
6. Mixture of open and muted sounds
7. Variable dynamics
8. Coloring of lines

DEBUSSY, RAVEL, AND EARLY STRAVINSKY

Style. Claude Debussy and Maurice Ravel were the most famous of the French Impressionists, writing their best-known works between 1890 and 1925. Their style was highly influential over such diverse composers as Stravinsky, Berg, and Bartók, until about 1917. Impressionism emphasized color and "mood"; clarity of outline or shape was often avoided in favor of subtly moving lines and masses of sound. Impressionistic melodies are often accompanied by other melodies, rather than by the same melodies in imitation, as in traditional counterpoint. They tend to have a static quality that comes with frequent repetitions, and may end before having been fully developed.

The sense of melodic incompleteness is emphasized by an orchestral texture that folds one line into another and brings several components into one, using the techniques of highlighting, linking, and divided lines. The static quality brings color to the fore, since repetitions require changes of color. The basic movement tends to be slow, with energy going into surface activity, like waves and splashes over a general, riverlike flow.

Spacing. Tutti chords are not common in Debussy and Ravel; more often, the winds encompass the full range of the harmony while the strings play in octaves. The chords may have gaps in the area of the upper bass staff. All three composers follow the previous composers in placing like instruments together in close spacing in such chords and leaving most of the treble staff to the brass. In general, the treatment of spacing and register—at *all* times—is one of the most important of the modern features of this group of composers. In contrast to earlier music, which relied on relatively continuous melodic lines and accompaniments that stayed more or less in the same registers and in a relatively consistent four-voiced spacing (with doublings), the music of the Impressionists and the early works of Igor Stravinsky actively explored the possibilities of using spacing and register changes as an important element in formal structure. Typically, a "pitch band," or pitch area, is emphasized, usually with close spacing. This is aided by the narrow range of some of the melodies.

Pitch Bands. Debussy's "Fêtes," as shown in Example 7-46, begins with a high pitch band followed by a low one. These are alternated until the texture expands, increasing the intensity to its fullest extent. The middle of the movement contracts the texture to three closely spaced trumpets, and expansion begins again. Example 7-47 shows abrupt shifts of register and timbre, coinciding with changes in motivic material and tempo. After the opening chord, there are three narrow bands in high, low, and medium registers. The tutti that follows expands the texture by incorporating the previously used bands and adding a higher one in the closely spaced flutes.

The favorite pitch bands seem to be high (roughly, on the treble staff and above) and low (roughly, on the bass staff and below) ones. High bands are favored by Stravinsky: Most of *Petroushka* emphasizes that area, giving the ballet a very bright, toylike sound that seems to evoke the world of the puppet stage (the main characters are puppets). Example 7-48 shows the beginning of the ballet.

Accompaniments typically are made up of quasi-melodic, ostinatolike patterns that either move stepwise or arpeggiate, often covering more than an octave in their movements. These accompaniments are static as a whole but have individually active parts. In Example 7-49, the accompaniment of undulating sixteenth notes is restricted to a band of Bb to bb^1.

Other Features. Melodies are often reharmonized and reorchestrated when they reappear. At times, voice leading emphasizes parallel motion, which encourages the use of blocks of like instruments. New types of harmonies—sometimes lush and full, with chords of many notes, and at other times more starkly bare, with modal or dissonant qualities—are set with appropriately lush or stark sonorities.

In Impressionism, orchestration became a more essential ingredient than it ever had been before. Most of the techniques were not new, but what had formerly been incidental now became standard, and the unusual became basic.

Example 7-49 illustrates several things. First is the special color created for the melody beginning at no. 4, which is carried by the oboe, doubled below by the harp, the solo cello, and the bass pizzicatos. This line, therefore, not only exists on several octave levels but also blends a variety of timbres and articulations. The other instruments contribute to the line by elaborating it with arpeggios to other chord tones. Some elements move faster than others, thickening the rhythmic density of the fabric. When the oboe and the cello arrive at their dotted half note, this note is quietly highlighted by the first violins in the two octaves above, acting as "enhanced overtones." At this point, the bassoon enters with a countermelody that is somewhat obscured by or merged with the ongoing strings, since it plays not only some of the same notes but also some of the same rhythms as they do.

Combining. In Example 7-49, we see several components collaborating to project a single line whose color is not pure, but very mixed, and whose outline is equally unclear, since it is elaborated by decoration. The harmonic element is formed by a homogeneous blend of strings and harp.

Example 7-46   Debussy, "Fêtes"

Example 7-46 *(continued)*

Example 7-47 Stravinsky, *The Rite of Spring,* no. 56

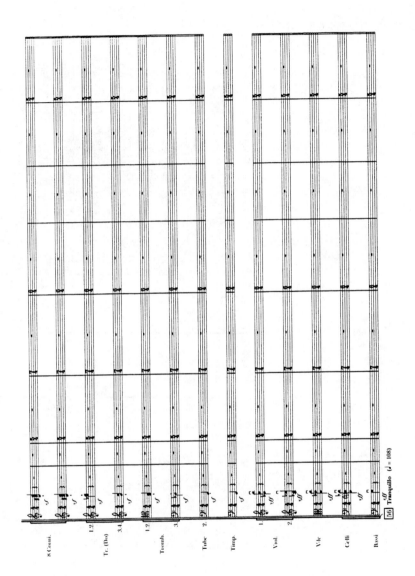

Example 7-47 *(continued)*

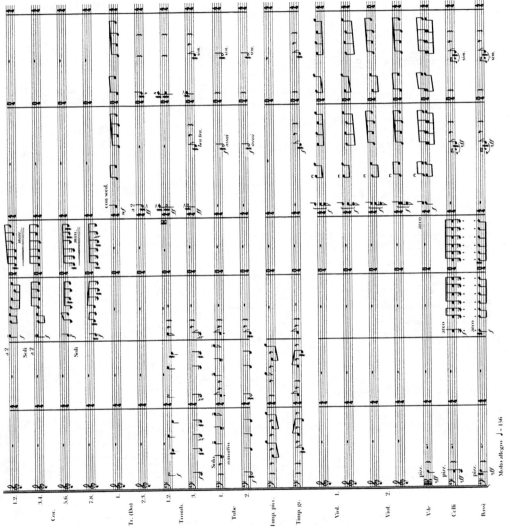

Molto allegro ♩ = 156

Example 7-48 Stravinsky, *Petroushka*

Example 7-49 Debussy, *La Mer*, mvt. 1, two before no. 4

Example 7-49   *(continued)*

Example 7-50 shows another example of many components contributing to what is essentially one line. The sustaining parts are again in a homogeneous group, this time the double reeds. The A-natural in that block is elaborated by a

Example 7-50 Debussy, *La Mer*, mvt. 1, three after no. 10

Example 7-51 Ravel, *Daphnis et Chloé*, one before no. 168

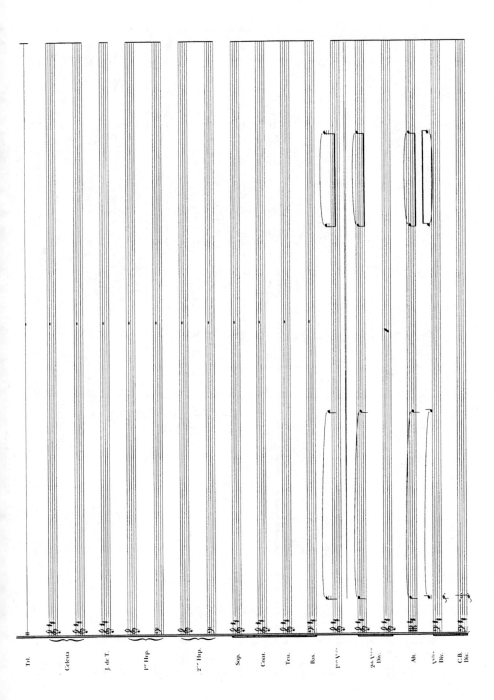

Example 7-51   (continued)

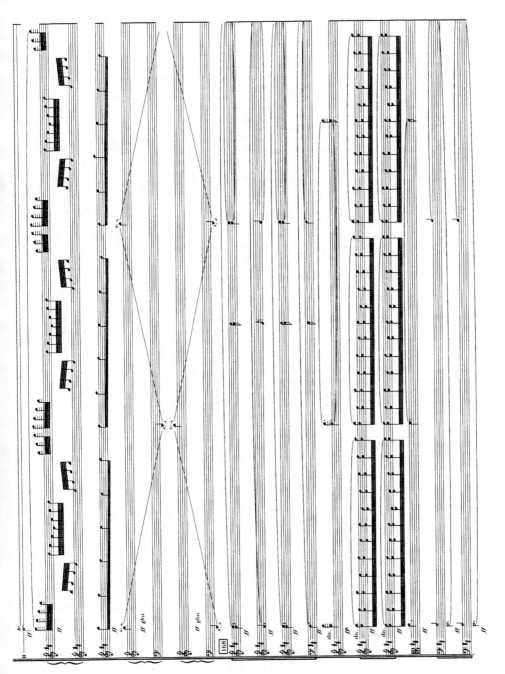

Example 7-52 Ravel, *Daphnis et Chloé,* one before no. 221

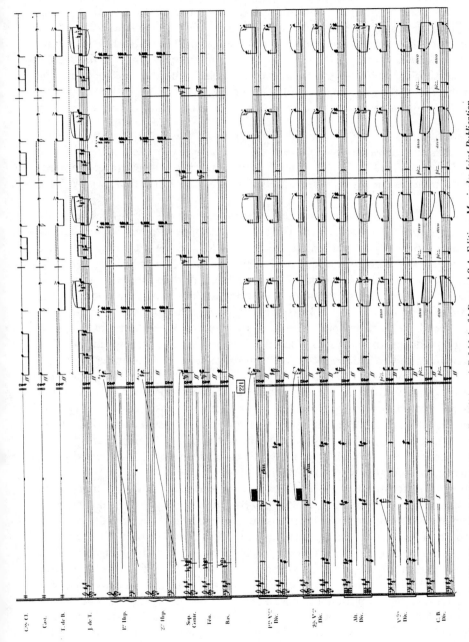

counterfigure that alternates between the flutes/clarinets and the second violins/violas (each of which is in itself homogeneous). The alternation of the wood-wind–string figure just mentioned is bridged by a scale in the first violins and the cellos that takes over the g^1 of the clarinets and moves to the a^2 of the second violins. The dividing of this figure allows the quick crescendos to be played with greater strength, since they are isolated, enhancing the effect of these "splashes" of sound. The accented notes of the double reeds are rhythmically highlighted by the second violins, the violas, the double basses, and the cymbal, while the low horn and the scale in the first violins become part of their crescendo. The basses punctuate the end of the horn note, and the cymbal matches the high point of the scale line.

New Effects.   Both Debussy (in "Sirènes") and Ravel (in *Daphnis et Chloé*) used wordless choruses as part of the texture. These are treated somewhat like another wind section—in blocks, legato, and sustaining. Other novel elements of scoring include the use of instruments such as the oboe d'amore and the saxophone.

The Impressionists made much use of muting, tremolo, harmonics, and glissando, both in the strings and in the winds. Various types of pizzicato and bowing devices are also common, including sul ponticello and jeté. Combined effects include large-scale swirls for background shimmer, as in Example 7-51, and for a dramatic rise in pitch, as in Example 7-52. In the first of these, a four-part circular arpeggiation in the upper strings and woodwinds is blurred by different arpeggiations in the celesta and the glockenspiel, the three arpeggiations all moving at different speeds. The entire pitch range of the texture is blanketed by contrary-motion glissandos in the harps (the settings for the harps are not given, but they surely are intended to produce the same notes as those in the other arpeggiations). The main melodic line (violin 1, and so on) and the countermelody (chorus) are enveloped in the faster-moving but hazy background. Finally, the rolls in the timpani, the cymbal, and the triangle cast a rumbling, misty cloud over all else.

In the second example, the swirl is composed of a sixteenth-note line in octaves in the upper woodwinds, slower arpeggios in the middle strings, long glisses in other strings, and all-embracing glisses in the harps. To add activity, the string arpeggios and glisses are played with bowed tremolo.

Stravinsky used similar devices in his earlier works. He was particularly fond of combining effects. Examples 7-53 and 7-54 show how systematically he used cross-voicing. Example 7-55 is a condensation of the tones that result from the interchange of lines in the string parts for the first five notes at no. 7 in Example 7-54. These are doubled in the winds, which are not cross-voiced. Giving each wind instrument a value of 1.0 and each string subdivision a 0.3 (since the string sections are divided into thirds), it can be seen that, by and large, a numerical balance is preserved between the parts and from note to note. Notice also that there is cross-articulation, the winds slurring while the strings detach. This is of advantage to both families, because continuous staccato playing would be more difficult for the winds than for the strings, whereas the unequalized articulation of the winds

Example 7-53   Stravinsky, *Firebird* Suite, mvt. 1, mm. 7–8

would be less effective for the strings than for the winds (see Chapter 2, under "Equalization").

Stravinsky created unusual sounds in many ways. One of them, undoubtedly suggested to him by the works of Rimsky-Korsakov, was writing for instruments in extreme registers. A famous example is the beginning of *The Rite of Spring*, which places the solo bassoon in the extreme upper register of e^1–d^2. See Example 7-56.

Example 7-54   Stravinsky, *Firebird* Suite, mvt. 2

Example 7-55 Stravinsky, *Firebird* Suite, mvt. 2, no. 7

Composite:

F#3	1.3	F3	1.3	E3	1.3	C3	1.3	B2	1.6
D3	1.3	C#2	1.3	C3	1.3	A#2	0.3	A2	1.3
Bb2	1.6	A2	1.6	A#2	0.3	G#2	2.6	G2	1.6
F#2	0.3	F2	0.3	G#2	1.3	F#2	0.3	F2	1.3
D2	1.6	D#2	1.3	F#2	0.3	E2	2.6	D#2	1.6
Bb1	1.3	C#2	0.3	E2	1.3	D2	0.3	C#2	1.3
F#1	2.3	B1	1.3	D2	0.3	C2	1.3		
		G1	1.3	C2	1.3				
				G#1	1.3				

It is soon joined below by other instruments that normally play *above* the bassoon—the clarinet and the English horn—thus emphasizing the unusual color of the bassoon by inversion. This opening number of the ballet is notable for its richness of color and detail, achieved with an expanded woodwind section that is accompanied only by a light string fabric and a few notes in the brass.

At a time when percussion was becoming more important, Stravinsky popularized the percussive use of the *strings* by featuring successions of short, sharp notes, often played at the frog in multiple stops. The dry and brittle quality that this produced separated him clearly from the Impressionists and was highly influential on later styles. It constituted a clear break with the Romantic liking for sustained sound and encouraged a new concept that required an expanded use of percussion instruments. (As an example, the final movement of his *Rite of Spring* uses percussion in 147 of the 276 measures.) Wind instruments, too, were often treated percussively.

Example 7-56 Stravinsky, *The Rite of Spring*, beginning

Example 7-56   *(continued)*

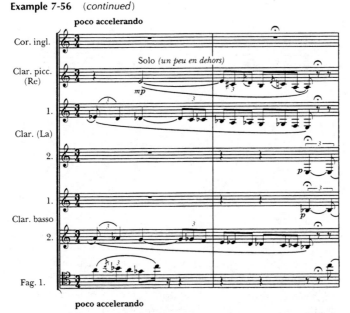

SUMMARY OF DEBUSSY, RAVEL, AND EARLY STRAVINSKY

Main features are

1. Combinations of various components in a single line or figure (see item 4)
2. Mixed doublings (that is, of unlike instruments)
3. Large-scale swirls
4. Highlighting, linking, and divided lines
5. Frequent use of muting, harmonics, tremolo, sul ponticello, glissando, pizzicato, and other techniques
6. Systematic cross-voicing

BARTÓK, SCHOENBERG, AND WEBERN

Style.   The expressionistic composers Béla Bartók, Arnold Schoenberg, and Anton Webern were among the leaders in the revolutionary changes that took place about 1910–1930. All of them emphasized the linear aspects of texture, Schoenberg and Webern following the Strauss–Mahler pattern. Those elements of the texture that were not linear tended to be rhythmically static (as, for example, ostinatos) or momentarily sustaining. The Expressionists, like the Impressionists, sought new types of sound quality for their new harmonic, tonal, and melodic patterns, but with a very different character, for, whereas the Impressionists cultivated very delicate, subtle, or exotic sounds, the Expressionists sought sounds that were strident, strange, and even terrifying. Both styles therefore emphasized new combinations of instruments and new ways of making them sound.

Texture.   The texture emphasized independent, ongoing lines, in contrast with the Impressionists' combined lines, hazy backgrounds, and secondary lines. All but Webern (in his later works) liked transparent textures with octave doubling of important lines. They also liked to set melodic lines in blocks of like instruments (for example, the trombones and the tuba in Example 7-60). Bartók's spacings can be either narrow or widespread. He used the contrast between the two as a means of setting off formal units.

Webern's textures are very spare, filling the pitch space with single lines that move mostly in leaps and almost constantly shift from one instrument to another, in different registers. When he writes chords, they tend to be compact and scored for like instruments.

Aside from Webern and occasional passages, the textures of these composers is more like that of the music *before* Impressionism than Impressionism itself. (Alban Berg, who is usually associated with Schoenberg and Webern, often used Impressionistic devices, such as a stream of parallel chords.)

Instrumental Color.   Schoenberg broke new ground in his Five Pieces for Orchestra (1909). The movement called "Farben" ("Colors") for the most part consists of chords played by groups of instruments linking to each other. The result is a kaleidoscope of color changes with very limited pitch movement. In his 1949 revision of the work for smaller orchestra (the original called for quadruple woodwinds, and so on), the first ten measures alternate the two combinations of instruments shown in Example 7-57. Except for the bassoon in the first combination, the groups represent an alternation of soft and sharp instruments. The English horn seems to sound an octave higher than the flute, whose note it takes over—undoubtedly because overtones are more prominent in sharp instruments, and the contrast with the relatively low flute is particularly striking.

Later, more mixed combinations are used, such as bassoon with clarinet, violins, muted trombone, and muted horn; and violin with English horn, muted trombone, and bass clarinet. The composer specified that the conductor should

Example 7-57   Schoenberg, "Farben"

not attempt to achieve an even balance among the instruments, but should let stronger instruments come out naturally. (This built-in variable dynamics, reminiscent of Mahler, is an important feature in some later composers.) At the end of the first section of "Farben," three solo basses and four solo cellos, playing high (up to *ab*) on the C string, add an unusual sound. The heterogeneous combinations given above are very usual in both chordal and polyphonic settings. Great contrast between linear elements is common; for example, at measure 250 of Schoenberg's Variations for Orchestra, the elements are (1) two low flutes, flutter-tonguing, (2) two bassoons and two solo basses, and (3) a solo violin, highlighted by the celesta.

Combined Phrasing.   Related to combined articulation, this is the combining of several instruments on a line, each phrasing the line differently. In his arrangement of Bach's "Schmücke Dich, o liebe Seele," Schoenberg combines different phrasings and different articulations (see Example 7-58). There is also a shift of texture when the piccolo drops out and a shift of color when the second flute is added to the English horn and the clarinet.

Fragmented Linking.   Webern's arrangement of Bach's Ricercare from *The Musical Offering* emphasizes heterogeneity and contrasts of color. (See Example 7-59.) The melodic lines are divided into one- or two-note groups given to different instruments without overlapping tones. This has the effect of breaking up the melodic line in such a way that certain intervals or intervallic patterns are brought out and new phrasings emerge, as with cross-phrasing.

Example 7-58   Schoenberg, "Schmücke Dich," mm. 9–10

Example 7-59   Webern, Ricercare from Bach's *Musical Offering*

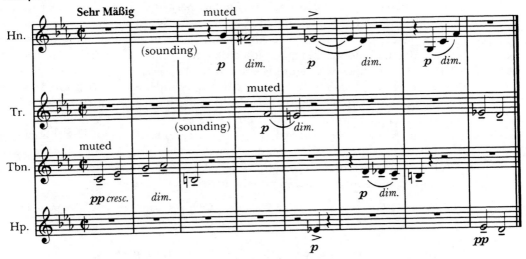

Webern's mature works are notable in their brevity and smallness of scale. His Symphonie, for example, is scored for one clarinet, one bass clarinet, two horns, harp, and strings (without bass). If grace notes are not counted, no more than three notes are ever slurred. The texture is consistently thin: Except for some spots in the second movement, rarely is more than one note attacked at the same time, and there are no unison- or octave-doubled lines. There are also no combining devices such as linking, cross-voicing, and highlighting. The apparent purpose of this scoring technique is to provide a clarity that emphasizes the progression of pitches (this work is strictly twelve-tone); the diversity of color creates shapes that bring out certain aspects of the pitch organization. For example, at the beginning a double canon is presented as follows:

CANON 1

Notes (of the row):	1–4	5–8	9–12[4]
Leader:	Hn.2	Cl.	Vc.
Follower:	Hn.1	B.Cl.	Vl.

CANON 2

Notes:	1	2–4	5	6–8	9–12
Leader:	Hp.	Vc.	Vn.2	Hp.	Hn.2
Follower:	Hp.	Vl.	Vn.1	Hp.	Hn.1

[4]Theorists in more recent years number the notes in tone rows from 0 to 11. Here they are numbered in the older fashion: 1–12.

Comparing the instrumental sequence of the leader with that of the follower in the two canons, we see that like instruments play like portions of the row; for example, in Canon 1, Hn.2 is imitated by Hn.1, the Cl. by the B.Cl., and so on.

Bartók, applying impressionistic techniques to make pitch outline obscure, employed combinations and swirls to color general pitch movement. In Example 7-60, the trombones/tuba figure is colored by the lower strings, which articulate the second note. A counterpointing swirl in the upper strings is colored by the piano gliss and by flutter-tonguing and trills in the woodwinds, then by swirls. The roll in the timpani provides another obscuring element.

At m. 63 of the first movement of his Concerto for Orchestra, Bartók built a very methodical orchestral crescendo. (See Example 7-61.) With each reiteration of a five-note figure over thirteen measures, he added an instrument or moved it an octave up or down to make a gradual increase in intensity.

m. 63:	The ostinato, played by lower strings, is partly doubled by bassoons in octaves.
m. 65:	One clarinet is added to each bassoon.
m. 66:	The first bassoon is dropped to the lower, stronger, octave while the first oboe takes its place.
m. 68:	The second oboe is added to the upper octave.
m. 70:	The first flute is added to the upper octave.
m. 71:	The second flute is added to the upper octave.
m. 72:	The first flute moves an octave higher.
m. 73:	The second flute, the first oboe, and the first clarinet join the first flute on the highest octave.
m. 74:	The first flute is raised an octave higher.
m. 75:	The second flute joins the first.

This is a good example of how carefully and consistently composers in the twentieth century tend to calculate effects when working with large numbers of instruments that are freed from many of the technical limitations of the past.

Many other interesting examples can be cited from these composers, but for the most part they would fall into one of the types listed in the summary.

SUMMARY OF BARTÓK, SCHOENBERG, AND WEBERN

Main features are

1. Emphasis on the linear, employing contrasting elements to set off each line, sometimes with unequal balance
2. Unusual combinations of instruments
3. Cross-phrasings
4. Isolation of figures in a line by change of color (from one instrument to another)

Example 7-60 Bartók, *The Miraculous Mandarin*, no. 34

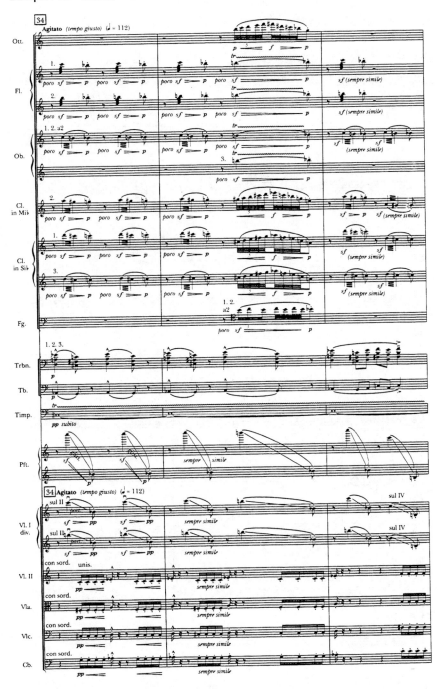

Example 7-61   Bartók, Concerto for Orchestra

NEOCLASSICISM AND NEOROMANTICISM

Style. A large number of Europeans and Americans working from about 1930 to 1950 fall into the categories of Neoclassicism and Neoromanticism. Representative composers are Stravinsky, Milhaud, Hindemith, Copland, Shostakovich, and Britten. Their music grafted new features onto older ones and drew heavily on the eighteenth century (Neoclassicism) and the nineteenth century (Neoromanticism). The mood-pictures of Impressionism and the psychodramas of Expressionism gave way to a generally light character and a more clearly defined sense of form in the Neoclassicists, whereas the Neoromantics returned to the lyrical, sustained character of the nineteenth century.

The orchestral fabric continued to stress the linear, but there was also a definite return to melody and accompaniment. Unusual combinations of instruments or treatments of them were not as important as the clarification of form through *changes* of instrumentation. Family separation was popular, often in blocks of like instruments (for example, a brass group). The Russian composers used much percussion, and in many cases, sections of music were set off by a change from one kind of percussion instrument to another. The piano, the harp, and the celesta were now more common. Their function was usually to support main lines by doublings, highlighting, and accompaniments. The melodic percussion, such as the xylophone, tended to double melodies, sometimes in a simplified form, with only the main tones. Nonpitched instruments occasionally matched the rhythm of melodies—for example, the snare drum playing sixteenth notes along with the violins.

Balances tended to be numerically calculated, although at times only the highest voice may be doubled. In a departure from the time-honored octave doubling of cellos and basses, the basses were frequently divided in octaves, freeing the cellos to play another line or to double the *upper* strings. The cello–bass doubling, however, was more usual.

Subtle part-writing effects were common, such as cross-voicing, which was sometimes employed among a large number of instruments. Related to this is "cross-doubling," a device favored by Stravinsky and Copland and illustrated in Example 7-62. The soprano line is played by the flutes, doubled by the first violins until the third measure, where the violins drop out; the doubling shifts momentarily to the horn, whose line moves to the flutes' eb^1. As the flutes continue, the violas merge with them on f^1 in the next measure, after which the violins and then the horn resume their doubling. (Instruments not affected are not shown.)

This period of music favored sectionalized form, and the nineteenth-century method of using families to set off sections was very much in evidence. Solo lines were usually accompanied by backgrounds consisting of a different timbre. A favorite device was to begin a section with strings alone and then to introduce a solo wind instrument against it.

Example 7-62 Copland, Symphony No. 3, mvt. 1, seven after no. 41

SUMMARY OF NEOCLASSICISM AND NEOROMANTICISM

Main features are

1. Blocks of like instruments
2. Basses divided in octaves
3. Sections set off by changes in the use of percussion and by changes of instrumentation in general
4. The use of the melodic percussion, the piano, the celesta, and the harp to highlight, simplify, or double other instruments
5. The matching of the rhythms of other instruments by nonpitched percussion
6. Numerically equal balance
7. Some cross-doubling

SCORING TECHNIQUES SINCE 1950

Style. The period since 1950 encompasses a wide range of individual styles, only a few of which will be touched upon here. The influence of Webern sparked a continued exploration of twelve-tone techniques. The concern for precisely chosen successions of pitches favored fragmentation of the orchestra into individual lines, many of which were themselves fragmentary. These lines now were used against each other in great profusion and density, such that fast-moving notes often merge into swirl-like figures and are integrated with nonpitched percussion in such a way that lines can sound partly pitched and partly nonpitched (for example, in Edgar Varèse's music before 1950 and Elliott Carter's since). The traditional melody/background and line-against-line polyphony is often abandoned. Pitches may be combined in tight clusters or dense tone masses and not restricted to the usual tuning, which sometimes gives a noiselike, nonpitched effect (for example, the music of Krzysztof Penderecki and Iannis Xenakis). Instruments are sometimes juxtaposed in such apparent "confusion" that the unarticulated, fluid character of some electronic music is approached (for example, in the music of Henri Pousseur and György Ligeti). Some composers call for improvisatory passages; others write in such a way that certain passages *sound* improvisatory.

More recent years, however, have brought back some of the older textures and styles along with many of the newer effects. The new and the old may alternate in a single piece.

Representative composers are Stravinsky (in his later works), Pierre Boulez, Karlheinz Stockhausen, Luigi Berio, Carter, Xenakis, Penderecki, John Adams, Joan Tower, and David Del Tredici. The later works of Varèse, mostly written before 1950, can be included.

Only a sampling of new scoring devices can be given here. Although it would seem that orchestration practices might have changed as radically as some of the practices of using pitch and rhythm, it is surprising how many of the now-traditional devices are still used. It is notable, for example, that orchestral families continue to be separated by function. Even in very dense textures, strings tend to play as a group, as do the woodwinds, the brass, and the percussion. This is perhaps largely because certain characteristics of the instruments are emphasized (for example, tremolo in the strings), and when a group effect is desired, which is often, it works well to keep it in the family. Xenakis and Ligeti go further by dividing string sections down to individual players and giving each one the same kind of effect, such as tremolo, pizzicato, or glissando. This may be followed, for example, by a block of brass playing flutter-tongue, or glissando, and so on. Amorphous effects are achieved by multi–part writing in all families, including percussion, with overlapping and crossing lines. A mass of pitches then emerges, rather than a clear line (see Example 7-63).

In Varèse's scores, percussion is used about as much as any of the other families, and he tended to use the other families as if they were percussion: Their melodic movement is relatively static, and they play in blocks of tones so arranged spatially that they produce a rather metallic, almost pitchless quality. In addition, frequent use of extreme registers and dynamics elicits timbres that are nontraditional.

Most of what is new in orchestrational practice in this period comes under three categories: unusual instruments, unusual use of instruments, and new types of notation associated with these.

Most of the unusual instruments are percussion. These either are drawn from folk instruments in various cultures (David Amram) or are sound media that were not originally designed for musical purposes (for example, wine glasses or brake drums). Occasionally, a composer invents an instrument.

Example 7-63 Ligeti, *Melodien*

Many works feature large percussion sections, calling for several players. Nonpitched instruments may be arranged in "pitch" order—that is, from highest to lowest (for example, Stockhausen in *Gruppen* and Carter in his Double Concerto for Harpsichord and Piano)—these instruments being designated by numbers, rather than by name, for quick identification by players and score readers.

Instruments normally associated with popular music or band music, such as the drum set or saxophones, occasionally appear in orchestral scores. Toy instruments (with precedents in Leopold Mozart's *Toy* Symphony and Tchaikovsky's *Nutcracker*) are also encountered. Electronic sounds, played either live on synthesizers or on tape, add a new dimension. Until recently, it seemed to be difficult to integrate them successfully with orchestral instruments, because the sound sources were basically so different. Like the organ, electronic sound has a certain mechanical "flatness" or regularity that is foreign to acoustic instruments, which are so variable and more intimately controlled by the performer. With the recently developed technique of manipulating acoustically generated sound, this may change, since this technique allows close matching with orchestral instruments. Another problem has been and may continue to be that the orchestra is such a rich source of sound possibilities in itself that more variety is not needed. At present, electronics are more likely to be used in chamber music or by themselves.

Perhaps most important is the way instruments, both new and old, are treated individually. Some scores, especially those written in the 1960s, require more nontraditional uses than traditional ones. Directions such as "con sordino," "snap pizzicato," "glissando," and "white tone," and many unique instructions, can occur in quick succession. Composers may use a set of notational symbols that are explained at the beginning of the score or in footnotes. A sample: "Break a bottle in a bag" (Lukas Foss, *Baroque Variations*), "Flick snare drum with a nail" (Egardo Simone, *Entrada*), "Rattle a comb in the bell" (Eric Stokes, *Captions*), "Take mute out slowly" (Stockhausen, *Gruppen*), and (for strings) "Left hand finger not all the way down" (Ligeti, *Atmospheres*).

Another feature of recent scores is unusual seating of the orchestra. Frank Zappa's *Dupree's Paradise*, for example, calls for percussion groups on the right and left side of the stage and winds placed in a half-circle around a few stringed instruments, and the conductor at the center. Other works divide the orchestra into smaller orchestras. Offstage placements, although not new, are more common than before.

SUMMARY OF SCORING TECHNIQUES SINCE 1950

Main features are

1. Lines produced by tone masses (generally in blocks of like instruments) or combining effects of interacting individual swirls
2. Mixing of nonpitched and pitched sounds, where the former are part of the line, rather than background
3. Noiselike or electronic effects achieved by spacings, extreme dynamics and registers, lack of rhythmic definition, and nontraditional tunings
4. Nontraditional seating and offstage placement of instruments

This chapter has outlined a history of scoring practices from about 1700 to the present. Most of the features discussed have proven themselves effective enough to have been retained, in some form, so that, as a whole, they form a catalog of models for today's and tomorrow's practitioner. A full understanding of them, however, can come only with extensive listening to and studying of the examples in the context of the whole pieces from which they are drawn.

CHAPTER **8**

Guidelines for Scoring

In music, we are always trying to reconcile the aesthetic with the practical side of an issue. An orchestrator attempts to develop techniques, just as a performer develops coordination—this is the practical side of orchestration—but *the way in which the techniques are used* is the *art*, or the aesthetic side, which will ultimately determine how successful his or her music is. As with other compositional elements, such as harmony and form, the composer looks for models from successful works so that he or she does not always have to invent techniques from scratch; in fact, it is almost impossible *not* to be influenced by what one has heard and liked. If the techniques of previous composers can be listed in some rational way, much time and effort can be saved. That is what has been done in this chapter. But the creative side of the orchestrator's mind should decide *how* to use those techniques, and even when to invent *new* ones, for the best results come when the creator is the master of the tools, and not the reverse. Then the aesthetic side and the practical side work together as one!

BALANCE

Problems with balance can take up a significant portion of an orchestral rehearsal. Typically, the conductor tells certain players to play softer so that others may be heard. If the problem persists, the number of players who are too loud might be reduced, or the number who are not heard well enough might be increased. Although it is possible that the players are at fault in not playing the proper dynamics, it is also possible that the *orchestrator* is at fault for improperly balancing the components of the texture. Such defects might have been avoided if one or more of the following factors had been taken into account.

Factors That Influence Balance

A. *Numbers.* How many wind instruments or string sections are playing each note? All other things being equal, equal numbers of one or the other or both per note tend to produce an even balance.

B. *Family representation.* Generally, individual brass and percussion instruments are stronger than string sections, and string sections are stronger than individual wood-wind instruments. Within the brass, the horns are weaker than the other brass at *forte* levels and above. If a texture contains instruments of different families and the scorer desires an even balance, it is safest to mix the doubling in such a way that each family is balanced *in itself* and there is a consistent mixture on each note. To take a specific case, suppose we want to use a flute, a clarinet, a bassoon, a horn, and a trumpet in a five-part texture, with each voice equally heard. All the instruments are in their middle registers and marked *mf.* Here are two very different arrangements:

1. Flute

   Trumpet

   Clarinet

   Horn

   Bassoon

2. Flute/Trumpet

   Clarinet/Trumpet

   Bassoon/Horn

   Bassoon/Horn

Arrangement 1 is in danger of being out of balance because some instruments are woodwinds, others brass. Arrangement 2 is more likely to be evenly balanced because there is one of each family of each note. The *color* and overall strengths of the two will differ—arrangement 1 will be more "colorful," owing to the contrasts within it, whereas arrangement 2 will be stronger, owing to the greater number of instruments overall.

C. *Register.* See Chapters 2, 3, and 4.

D. *Playing requirements*

1. Strings tend to be stronger when playing chords, tremolo, sul ponticello (which is more penetrating, not heavier), or with bow strokes of short duration. They tend to be weaker when muted and when playing sul tasto, col legno, or with bow strokes of long duration. (Seeking new sonorities, Mahler, Schoenberg, Webern, and others combined strength and weakness factors when they muted the strings and marked them *fortissimo* or "sul ponticello.")

2. Woodwinds tend to be stronger when playing flutter-tongue. They tend to be weaker when muted. (Muting is rare. See Chapter 3, under "Muting.")

3. The brass tend to be stronger when marked "cuivré" or "bells in the air," or when playing flutter-tongue. Muting for them is like sul ponticello for the strings—the sound becomes rather penetrating with higher dynamic levels or accents. The brass tend to be weaker when stopped, muted (at low dynamic levels), or playing into the stand.

4. Percussion instruments have more weight when notes are rolled than when they are allowed to decay naturally. The use of small, hard sticks or beaters will produce a more penetrating sound than will the use of softer sticks.

E. *The relationship of the parts to each other.* All other factors being equal, the following will be true:

1. The top line will be most easily heard.

2. The bass voice will be next most easily heard.

3. Inner voices will be least easily heard.

F. *Spacing.* The farther a line is away from adjacent voices, the more likely it is to be heard.

G. *Activity.* Lines will be more hearable if
    1. They move faster than others.
    2. They move in a different direction from others.
    3. They are generally more diverse than others, especially in rhythm and contour.
    4. Their articulation is different from that of the others.
H. *The dynamic markings of the individual parts.*

As an illustration of how these factors work, let us examine Example 8-1.

Example 8-1

Spacing. Example 8-1 shows four different arrangements of the same four voices, each favoring a different voice or voices because of the way it is spaced. In Example 8-1a, the distances between the voices are about equal, at least at first, which eliminates the factor of spacing; thus, the outer voices should be the easiest to hear (see E in the foregoing list). Example 8-1b adds to the strength of the soprano by moving that voice farther from the adjacent alto than the other voices are from each other. Example 8-1c brings out the inner voices by putting them farther apart than in the other arrangements. Example 8-1d strengthens the bass by moving it farther from the tenor than before.

Activity. The excerpt is rather polyphonic, owing to the fair amount of diversity between parts: No two have the same rhythm. The bass and the tenor are the most different. The tenor is the fastest-moving and the bass is the slowest, and these voices move in opposite directions. The tenor, furthermore, moves in contrary motion to all the other parts. The soprano and the alto are most alike—their contours are similar and they have about the same number of notes. Thus, on the basis of activity and diversity, the tenor and the bass should be more easily heard than the other voices.

Instrumental Assignments.   Let us assign instruments to the parts in Example 8-1a as follows:

Soprano: Violin 1
Alto: Clarinet 1
Tenor: Trombone
Bass: Timpani

This rather unusual combination is chosen strictly for purposes of discussion!

The violin 1 line has the advantage of being the highest, and, as part of the string section, the violins are somewhat stronger than the woodwind instrument just below it. Its bowing style—short strokes—favors it also, but it is in its middle register, which is not a strong one.

The clarinet has several disadvantages: It plays an inner line; that line is close to the surrounding ones; the instrument is a representative of the weakest family; and its notes are in the throat register, which is the weakest.

The trombone is placed on an inner voice, but it is a member of one of the strongest families, and it is in a strong register.

The timpani are also members of a strong family. They are further strengthened by being on the lowest part, and their notes are strong ones—well within the ranges of the usual drums.

Example 8-2 shows four-part texture that is taken from a composition. It is also somewhat polyphonic. The lines are not very rhythmically diverse until m. 17, where the soprano departs from quarter-note motion (although still implying it in the dotted eighth notes on the beat), and the first bassoon momentarily lingers on a half note. Overall, the four voices have somewhat varied contours. The tenor is the least adventuresome, whereas the others have occasional leaps. Contrary motion is found most notably between the bass and the tenor and between the bass and the soprano. There are subtle changes of spacing that tend to bring out different voices at different times; for example, the distance between the inner voices suddenly increases on the second beat of m. 17, which momentarily calls attention to the alto, especially since the soprano and the tenor slow down at that point. Similarly, the space between the lowest voices spreads on the fourth beat, emphasizing contrary motion. At the end of the excerpt, the lower three voices return to the compactness of the beginning, momentarily obscuring their individuality.

Because all the instruments are woodwinds, one would expect a generally even balance. The soprano is carried by the clarinet, mostly in its bright clarion register. It is thus favored by register and position in the texture. The articulation of its line is slightly different from that of the other instruments, which also sets it

Example 8-2 Bizet, *L'Arlésienne* Suite (Allegro deciso), No. 1, mvt. 1, A

off a bit. The alto is the only one that is doubled. The flute is in its weak low register, and the English horn is in its relatively weak middle to upper register. The strength of numbers therefore compensates for the weakness of the registers and the inner voice.

The tenor and the bass, played by bassoons, fairly well balance each other—the second bassoon descends to a little stronger Ab, but generally they are both in an upper, fairly thin register that will not be obtrusive.

It is unusual for such a passage to have a variety of dynamics at the same time. The clarinet and the flute might have been marked louder than the others because the English horn and the bassoons are double reeds. Perhaps it was to enhance the clarinet as a leading line and to support the weak register of the flute. The passage cited in Example 8-2 is unusual, then, in that the dynamic levels of the instruments are not all the same and the numerical distribution is not even.

As was pointed out in Chapter 7, composers seem to adjust balances much more often by numbers than by dynamics, preferring to give each instrument the same dynamic indication and to equalize the numbers for even balance or to use more instruments on lines or notes that they wish to bring out. Good reasons for this can be offered: The ear is less sensitive to differences in loudness than to differences in pitch, and an individual tends to adjust his or her dynamic level to that of other players and may not be aware that other players have different dynamic indications.

Example 8-3a presents a curious, but instructive, phenomenon of balance that is influenced by register. Even though the piccolo remains above the flute, the second flute note, d^2, predominates so much that its first overtone, d^3, seems to be played by the piccolo, as if the piccolo part were written as in Example 8-3b. Not only is the flute's d^2 a distinctly bright tone, but also, against it, the piccolo descends to a written $f\sharp^2$, which is a weaker note for that instrument, and this narrows the distance between the instruments, increasing the chance that their lines will be confused.

Example 8-3   Rodrigo, *Fantasia para un gentilhombre*, mvt. 1, m. 23

Octave Doubling.   Octave doubling of a line obviously makes it stronger—about as strong as unison doubling. The two types of doubling, however, differ in other respects: If, for example, a flute were to double the clarinet an octave higher in Example 8-2, there would be three changes in the character of the soprano line: an increased brightness, owing to the register in which the flute would be playing; an increased strength; and an increased *fullness*, or volume. Alternatively, if the flute were to double the clarinet at the unison, there would probably be little change in the brightness of the line, although it would have a different color; and although there would also be an increase in strength, there would probably be a smaller increase in fullness or volume.

Obviously, the more the parts that are doubled in octaves, the greater the sense of fullness the passage as a whole will have. One does have to take care, however, that unintended crossing of parts does not result. If, for example, the tenor part in Example 8-2 were doubled an octave lower, the first four notes of the tenor line would then lie *below* the bass line (as well as above it), changing the harmonic structure. The bass line would also have to be doubled an octave lower to prevent that. With so many octave doublings, the orchestrator should consider whether the revised spacing is a desirable one—notes that are closely spaced below about *c* can have a thick, dark, and unclear effect. If *every* part were doubled at the octave, the texture could become very dense (review the typical spacings shown in Chapter 7).

Keep in mind that the factors just listed are independent of each other and that one factor can either add to or offset the effect of another.

Balance in Homophonic Textures

In textures where inner voices are not intended to be stronger than outer ones, it is customary to allow either outer voice, or both outer voices, to be stronger than the inner ones; therefore, *in such textures the soprano, the bass, or both can be doubled at the unison or at the octave, and the inner voices should balance each other, but not be stronger than either outer voice.*

Errors in Balance

Before leaving the subject of balance, let us look at two cases in which famous composers apparently made some miscalculations. Example 8-4 shows a passage containing two chords—I and V^6_5 in D-flat major. The first chord is nearly balanced numerically, with two or three instruments on each note. The upper two notes are well balanced in that each has both a relatively strong horn and a relatively weak clarinet. The second chord increases the texture from three to four notes, and two horns move from the inner note, f^1, to double the bassoons. This results in an audible weakening of the inner parts, now played only by one clarinet each, against two and four instruments on the outer voices, respectively. When the passage reappears at m. 267, the balance is more satisfactory. The first chord is again almost evenly balanced numerically, and on the second chord, two horns take one of the inner voices—eb^1, the seventh of the chord—leaving one clarinet on the fifth of the chord, c^1. This imbalance is in accord with the relative importance composers often gave to the members of seventh chords, the fifth often being omitted.

Example 8-4   Beethoven, *Egmont* Overture, mm. 259-261, 267–269

Beethoven was very probably aware of the problem in m. 261. Since he was using horns in F and E-flat, to get a gb^1 (the seventh of the chord) on either one of them, he would have to ask for a note that was not in the overtone series. That note would have been not only of poor quality but also weaker. He might also have wanted the f^1's to be prominent, as a reference to the unison F that begins the work. A modern composer might have put one horn on each note and interlocked the clarinets with the bassoons.

A second example is found in a work that is otherwise cited as a remarkable piece of orchestration: Debussy's *Prelude to The Afternoon of a Faun*. See Example 8-5. In m. 45, there are two melodic lines—one in the highest staff and the other in the second staff. In the following measure, those lines converge on a sustained D-flat while the clarinets and the English horn play a new line, marked "trés en dehors" ("bring out strongly"). Although this new line is played by three wind instruments, note these considerations:

1. They are woodwinds (the weakest family).
2. They are not in strong registers.
3. They begin on a note that is played by other instruments and move to other notes that are also being played by other instruments (f^1, g^1, f^2, db^2, db^1)—in other words, only four of their nine notes are not already heard at the same time.
4. They are surrounded by horns and other instruments in close proximity.

Example 8-5 Debussy, *Prelude to The Afternoon of a Faun*, mm. 45–46

Thus, it is not surprising that conductors usually ask all but the "très en dehors" players to play much softer than their indicated *forte*. This is a good illustration of the need for a prominent inner voice to have "breathing space" (see again item E3 under "Factors That Influence Balance").

BLENDING

In this discussion, "blending" refers to how much two or more instruments sound like one; that is, if two instruments blend well, it is relatively difficult to tell them apart.

Factors That Enhance Blending

1. The instruments are in the same family, and especially in the same *subgroup* (e.g., double reeds).
2. The instruments play adjacent voices in the texture.
3. The instruments play parts that are similar or are treated similarly, especially in articulation.
4. The instruments are evenly balanced.
5. The interval between the instruments is relatively consonant.
6. The timbre of an instrument is not such that it attracts attention away from another instrument.

Factor 1 was mentioned several times in Chapter 7. Factor 2 also figures in that chapter in connection with the terms *juxtaposition, overlapping, interlocking,* and *enclosure* (see p. 197).

Blending is so closely associated with balance that it is sometimes difficult to separate the two. In factor 6, however, the distinction between the two is clear. If a blending instrument plays with a less-blending instrument, the dominant timbre will be that of the latter; this form of blending is different from the kind that results from factors 1, 3, and 5, which involve *sameness* of sound.

Returning to Example 8-2, we see a division of the texture into double reeds and non–double reeds, producing a two-color composite in juxtaposition. If the passage were scored like this:

Oboe
Clarinet
Clarinet
Bassoon

the inner voices would blend, but there would be less *overall* blend. The maximum blend, of course, would be a quartet of clarinets or horns, for example.

Factor 5 may need a little explanation: Consonant intervals generally differ from more dissonant ones in that the vibrations of the two notes are more in agreement with each other. For example, in the unison, the vibrations are exactly the same. In the octave, vibrations coincide on every two cycles, and in the perfect fifth every six cycles. With decreasing consonance, there is less correspondence, and the effect is one of decreasing smoothness, or blend, and increasing roughness. Many other variables are involved, such as timbre, intensity, and intonation, so the factor of consonance is no more precise than any of the others, but there does seem to be some influence. We saw several examples in Chapter 7 in which like instruments are deliberately written in octaves, the result being a satisfying blend. In Example 7-13, for example, the flutes, the clarinets, and the violins are each in octaves. As another case, we often find two bassoons at the bottom of a texture in a consonant interval, as in Examples 7-17, 7-22, and 7-23. Sustained octaves in like instruments seem to be as common in scores as spices are in prepared foods!

In Example 8-2, there are few dissonant intervals. The most prominent of them is probably the seventh, $bb–ab^1$, on beat two of m. 17. This interval, in addition to those already mentioned, could help to separate the instruments playing the inner voices.

In Example 8-6, there is a delicate interplay of balance and blend: Four muted horns are marked *piano,* and two bassoons and the bass clarinet are marked *pianissimo.* All are in registers that produce a dark quality, and each is a blending instrument. The mutes take away some of the soft and blending character of the horns but also reduce their power, and this might be why they are marked at a higher level. The bass clarinet is at first obscured by a bassoon and then enclosed *between* the bassoons; in both chords, however, it is part of a dissonance that could help to bring it out somewhat. In the second chord, blending is enhanced by the octaves formed between the two horns and between the two bassoons. The numerical imbalance of the first chord is "corrected" in the second chord.

Even consonant intervals can produce a rough effect if the notes are close and lie well above the treble staff or anywhere below the bass staff. This is especially true if they are also intense. Dissonances are decidedly more strident or indistinct under those conditions. In the case of two notes that are high and close, if the texture is very spare, the interaction between the notes can produce *difference tones* that could be dissonant with lower tones. Example 8-7 shows such a hypo-

Example 8-6 Copland, Symphony No. 3, mvt 1, m. 4

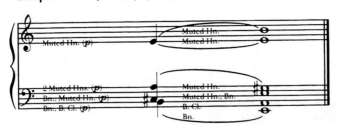

Example 8-7

thetical case: The notes f^3 and d^3, as they are normally tuned, could produce the difference tone bb. If a $b\natural$ were sounding, there could be a clash between the two.

FUNCTIONS

A good first step in composing for orchestra is to write out the music in short form on two or three staves, just as it sounds, so that, if desired, it could be played by one or two pianists. Any music to be transcribed could also be written in that form, if it isn't already. The next step is to decide how the texture can be broken down into *functions. This is possibly the most important step in the whole process of orchestration.*

The usual functions are

1. Melodic line
2. Harmony
3. Accompaniment
4. Highlighting

A texture may contain more than one of these, or some may be absent. Functions may overlap: An accompaniment might have enough interest to make it a secondary melody, or, conversely, a leading melody might sound as if it could be an accompaniment. "Harmony" involves isolated notes that are not an important part of some line or accompanying figure but that add to the harmonic fabric.

Functional Analysis. Example 8-8a is a short score of an excerpt from a symphony. (Here we have reversed the process, making a reduction to show how the excerpt might have looked before it was scored. This, incidentally, is an excellent way to study how a piece is orchestrated.) Example 8-8b shows one way to separate the excerpt into functions—lines 1–5. Line 2 has the most melodic interest, and all the other functions are clearly accompaniment. Lines 3 and 4 form a pair, as do lines 1 and 5. Example 8-8c is another way of breaking down the texture. Here, three of the functions are melodic—lines 1, 2, and 5. Lines 1 and 5 are partners that seem to imitate one another, and 2 merges with 1. (Alternatively, 2 could be considered an accompaniment.) The remaining functions—lines 3 and 4—can again be grouped together as accompaniment. This is clearly a more satisfactory version, because melodic activity is much more clearly defined.

Instrumental Assignments. A look at the actual score (Example 8-8d) reveals that version c is used as follows:

Line 1: Clarinet
Line 5: First bassoon
Line 2: Violins, alternating
Lines 3 and 4: Flutes, oboes, second bassoon, horns, and lower strings

Because Schumann put notes in the accompaniment that are the same as, or very close to, melody notes, there tends to be some confusion between the two functions. The contrast of articulation (legato for the melodies, staccato for the accompaniment) and some contrast of timbres helps to overcome this; yet, that confusion is what makes the version in Example 8-8b also a somewhat reasonable one, and one that some listeners might perceive, if the performance does not prevent it by emphasizing balance and blend differences. (It is possible, though, that the composer *intended* the functions to be ambiguous!)

Example 8-8 Schumann, Symphony No. I, mvt. 3, mm. 17–20

Scoring. Suppose we wish to score the excerpt shown in Example 8-9a. (This is from a piano piece.) A straightforward assigning of functions is shown in 8-9b. Line 1 has the most melodic interest because of its diversity of rhythm and contour. Lines 2 and 3 are also of some melodic interest, but melodic focus is somewhat diluted by changes from single notes to two- or three-note "harmonies." These lines are set off, however, by their individual consistency of rhythm, and 3 is further distinguished by its consistency of phrasing and melodic patterns. The "extra notes" suggest that the lines can be subdivided.

Examples 8-9c and 8-9d show ways in which this can be done. Those tones that seem to make the clearest melodic line—the highest notes, in this case—are chosen for lines 2a and 3a, and the remaining tones are assigned to harmonic functions in lines 2b and 3b, although they still retain some melodic character. If the highest notes were *not* chosen, it is possible that, because they *are* the highest, they might interfere with lower notes that might otherwise be chosen. Yet other factors, such as smoothness of voice leading or consistency of some kind, might encourage us to choose lower notes in other cases. Line 3b can further be subdivided as in Example 8-9e.

The final step—the assigning of instruments—involves many considerations, some of which are listed here.

1. How clearly differentiated the functions are. Is one more prominent than all the others, are two equally prominent, or are they all about equal?
2. How well each function as it stands suits the various instruments available to play it. This involves such things as the playing ranges, strengths, characters, and techniques of those instruments.
3. How orchestral the short score will be when instruments are assigned.

These considerations will be part of the discussion that follows. A separate treatment of 3 will be found under "Achieving an Orchestral Sound."

The differentiation of functions for the Brahms excerpt (Example 8-9a) has already been touched on. There seem to be three clear melodic functions (1, 2a, and 3a), a brief divergent line (3b2), and harmony notes (2b and 3b1). Line 1 is the most prominent. Line 3, owing to its activity, is next in interest, followed by lines 2 and 3b2. Since all of these have at least some interest, it seems advisable to score them with a more or less even balance. They are not very distinct from each other in rhythm; therefore, to assign these lines to similar timbres would tend to merge, rather than differentiate, them. If one prefers to emphasize the polyphonic potential of the lines, contrasting timbres would be appropriate. For a more homophonic setting, the entire texture could consist of strings only, or winds only. Otherwise, one or more lines could be given to one family and the rest to one or more different families.

Example 8-9 Brahms, Op. 118, No. 2, mm. 3–4

Harmony Notes.   What should be done with the few harmony notes? One might think that they should be played by some instruments not already in use, just as they stand. However, there could be problems with that solution. First, we want them to blend with the line whose harmony they fill out. Second, and more important, for an instrument to enter for just one or two notes could distract from, rather than support, the melodic lines. For example, the first note in 2b would be attacked as an *entering* note, not as a note slurred from the one before, as is the *g#¹* in 2a that it supports. Conversely, the second note of 2b *ends*, unlike the *a¹* it accompanies.

Made-up Lines.   To avoid the problem of harmony notes that are rendered as isolated notes that just drop into and out of the texture, one can create new lines that weave back and forth between existing lines and harmony notes. In this way, there is no stopping and starting that could interfere with the texture as a whole. Some examples of this are shown in Example 8-10. In this setting, line 1 is given to the clarinet and violin 1; line 3a is given to the first bassoon and the cellos (with some exceptions); and line 2a is given to the second violins. (The relatively short bow strokes in violin 1 help to bring that line out.) The harmony notes of 2b are taken by the violas, which weave a made-up line out of notes in 2a, 2b, and 1. In the fourth measure, rather than continuing to double line 2, they move to double the stressed downbeat of 1 and then leave it. The homogeneity of the strings allows some liberty in creating made-up lines.

The harmony notes of 3b are taken by the second bassoon and divided cellos, similarly weaving back and forth between lines 3a and 3b. To avoid awkward leaps, the first *d* is made a quarter note that moves smoothly to *c#*, in keeping with

Example 8-10   Brahms, Op. 118, No. 2, mm. 3–4

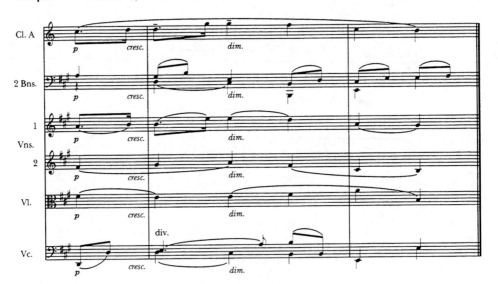

the general quarter-note motion and legato character of the passage, while the leaping eighth notes of 3a are shared by the first bassoon and the upper cellos. To avoid the sound of an entrance on its $g\sharp$, the first bassoon begins on a, doubling the soprano and filling in part of the gap between D and $f\sharp^1$. On the third beat, the cellos, not being able to play the BB, take the two B's above the original BB, filling in the gap between BB and $f\sharp^1$. The lower of these, B, continues the step-wise motion begun with the d. Another harmony note—$c\sharp$—is added in the first bassoon in m. 4 to make a smoother connection and to fill in part of the gap between E and $c\sharp^1$. Note that *all harmony notes are played in timbres that are the same as those playing the lines they support—this helps to clarify their function.*

Embroidery. This setting of the Brahms excerpt could be enriched by devices that *embroider* the functional lines. For example, the simplifying of the bass line by the quarter note $c\sharp^1$ in the second bassoon could be carried further by an instrument playing the line shown in Example 8-11. This could be reinforced by basses playing pizzicato.

Example 8-11

Adding Instruments. Another kind of embroidery is the adding of an instrument to double just part of a line, thereby stressing it, as in Example 8-12. Such an addition should be made with care. If it is not made at a point where a phrase could be subdivided, it might distort the structure of the phrase. The doubling could be at the octave higher, but with the risk that it might be heard as a separate entrance, or that the melodic line would suddenly seem to jump from one octave to another.

Example 8-12

Oboe

mf dim.

In some cases, the composer or arranger might *desire* to break up a melodic line. An extreme example of that was shown in Example 7-59. In the setting of the Brahms piano piece, there are many possibilities—for example: using the oboe as in Example 8-12, but as a replacement of the clarinet and the first violins; giving the original two-note figures in the bass *alternately* to the bassoons and the cellos; and shifting the entire texture abruptly from strings to woodwinds or brass at some dividing point in the phrase.

Highlighting. As we saw in Chapter 7, this technique is often applied with only one or two notes; thus, percussion instruments or percussive effects on other instruments can be effective. Since highlighting tends to accentuate, musical sense dictates that it be applied to points of stress, such as the first beat of m. 4. A note on the triangle or a soft roll on a drum could provide an interesting color. An important consideration is whether the character and pitch level of the highlighting sound enhance, rather than clash with, the character and pitch level of the instruments carrying the texture. Like so many other things, this is a matter of the scorer's taste and intention. A triangle note, of course, is much higher in "pitch" than the a^1 in the soprano. It could add a pleasing sparkle or, on the other hand, an inappropriate clamor, depending on one's viewpoint. A roll on the timpani (on a well-chosen pitch) would impart a completely different character—perhaps an ominous one, perhaps one that is subliminally comforting. A single timpani note is another possibility, if the contrast of its articulation with the rest of the texture is not disturbing. The reader would benefit by trying to imagine other possibilities.

Let us now consider Example 8-13, which shows a treatment of a late Baroque keyboard work. Example 8-13a is the original. One way of assigning functions is shown in 8-13b. Lines 1 and 3 are more or less continuous and distinct enough to qualify as melodic. Line 2 is much more fragmentary and dependent on the others. It is not the usual type of accompaniment *because* it is so fragmentary. To set lines 1 and 3 should not be very difficult, since they are so clearly melodic. One problem with 3 is that the two entrances after a sixteenth rest are difficult to execute at the presto tempo—such entrances are likely to be late and rushed. The same problem is found in line 2, which is very discontinuous—it would be difficult for the player(s) to understand how the part relates to the other instruments.

Other problems with line 3 are the quick leaps in the second measure and the wide range of D to g^1. The cellos, a bassoon, or a bass clarinet could negotiate it without going into a difficult register. A horn or a trombone could play the notes, but they would be very tricky at this tempo. For the horn, the lower notes would not be ideally responsive.

Example 8-13c shows a breakdown that should alleviate some of these problems. Line 1 is the same as before. Line 4, a reworking of old line 3, now has no leaps or sixteenth rest in the second measure (although the sixteenth-note motion after a tied-over sixteenth is about as difficult as a rest). The line is much smoother: Some notes have been interpolated in the bass line, filling out its essential motion from f to e to d. (Whether this is too great a departure from the original is for the scorer to decide.) The notes d^1, $c\#^1$, and f^1 have been taken from old line 3 and given to new line 2, which is now much more melodic than before. New line 3 is a smooth progression that begins comfortably on the beat with a filler a^1 and continues with the "bass line," ending with a filler d^1. The sixteenth rests in old line 2 have been eliminated in new line 2, which moves continuously between old lines 2 and 3, adding a d^1 on beat three of m. 2 that not only resolves the leading-tone $c\#^1$ but also fills a gap.

Whenever made-up lines such as new line 2 are created, there is always the danger that they could be projected more prominently than the more important lines, or equally so, neither of which is desirable. To minimize that danger, they can be assigned to more blending instruments or in some way made weaker than the other lines. In that case, two flutes could play line 1, one clarinet line 2, one clarinet line 3, and two bassoons line 4.

Example 8-13   D. Scarlatti, Sonata for Harpsichord, K. 18, mm. 1–2

The more experienced composer may find it convenient to skip step 1 (writing out the composition in short form), except to be able to play the piece on the piano, and to conceive the composition from the first in a functional breakdown. This encourages an orchestral concept. The functional breakdown, being midway between a short score and the full score, has some of the advantages of both.

FORM

The relationship between orchestration and form, as we normally think of it, is complex. In a deeper sense, orchestration is as much a part of form as the arrangement of pitches and rhythms. Thus, a piano piece and an orchestral transcription of it do not have exactly the same form, although one is very likely to say that they represent "the same music."

Consider the basic elements of form:

1. Identity (anything that can be remembered by being heard more than once)
2. Change
3. Contrast

Identity can be established not only by recurring melodic, harmonic, or tonal patterns, but also by recurrences of instruments, groups of instruments, or miscellaneous orchestral sounds. Clearly, change and contrast are also possible.

It should be evident, then, that the two things—pitch/rhythmic form and orchestrational form—are independent, and they can work with or against each other in innumerable ways. For example: (1) A theme (pitch/rhythmic identity) could recur with the same orchestration or with a different one; (2) a transition section could have changing or static orchestration; (3) two lines might contrast with each other (in speed of movement, contour, and so on), whereas the orchestration of those lines either emphasizes that contrast or does not.

One might expect that the most effective orchestrational form is one that reinforces the pitch/rhythmic one; yet, this is often not the case, as we saw in Chapter 7—a recurring theme or phrase is often more fully orchestrated than the original. However, more is involved than a simple change of texture; it will usually be found that many of the original elements of the orchestration are retained, and the increase of texture is more a matter of adding things than of changing color completely. (See Example 7-7, for instance.) Thus, the reorchestration can be said to preserve much of its own identity while adding an element of *change*.

Another example is the second theme of the third movement of Rimsky-Korsakov's *Scheherazade,* mentioned in Chapter 7. Example 8-14 shows the first measure of this theme in each of its four appearances. In the original (8-14a), the clarinet has the leading line. The accompaniment is composed of string pizzicatos and the snare drum, which combine to approximate the rhythm of the melody. In the second version (8-14b), the leading line is again in the clarinet, now doubled an octave higher by the second flute. The downbeat pizzicatos are now amplified

Example 8-14 Rimsky-Korsakov, *Scheherazade*, mvt. 3

Example 8-14 (*continued*)

by the *upper* strings and some of the woodwinds. The rhythm formerly given to the snare drum is transferred to the first flute, and new percussion instruments help with the downbeat and the later eighth notes (the thirty-second notes in the snare drum's version are mercifully slowed down to triplets for the low flute). The violas' former notes are given to the first violins an octave higher. This version retains the families and some of the instruments previously used, but expands the texture upward and considerably brightens the color by raising many of the notes an octave higher and replacing the relatively low-sounding snare drum with the high-pitched triangle and the tambourine.

The third version (8-14c) continues the expansion and the brightening and adds brass. The clarinet sound is thickened by octave doubling, and the pizzicatos, also thickened by the harp chord, are extended to a rising arpeggio in the rhythm of the accompaniment. The repeated-note part previously played by the low flute is now played by a trumpet, with some similarity in sound. The snare drum returns, with a roll replacing (and intensifying) its earlier thirty-second notes.

The final version (8-14d) is more sustained in character, under the influence of intervening passages. The leading line is still in the clarinet, amplified by a flute and the violins. There are still arpeggiated pizzicatos, as in the previous version, but percussion is absent. The horns and the bassoons, with a softer sound than the trumpet, take over the repeated notes.

We can see, then, that the pitch/rhythmic identity of the theme, which hardly changes, is somewhat stronger than its orchestrational identities, which do change. Certain elements of the latter *are* consistent, though—the placing of the leading line at least partly in the clarinet (always in the same register) and the pizzicatos in the lower strings. The addition of flutes and the piccolo to the leading line is a rather small change of color, as are some other changes—the moving of the repeated notes from snare drum to flute to trumpet to horns/bassoons and the various changes in percussion.

The changes give an archlike form to these recurrences of the theme—a steady expansion, then a slight contraction. But there is also transformation of character at the end, aided by the prominence of the most blending instruments. This treatment of repetition is typical of Rimsky-Korsakov—he sets off the predictability of literally repeated music by changes in orchestration. But it is important to note the continuity from one version to the next. This kind of continuity (retaining one or more elements while others change) is also used to link orchestration of *contrasting* material (see the discussion of transitions in Chapter 7).

The interaction of the two kinds of form is quite different at the beginning of Schoenberg's "Farben" (Example 7-57), where pitch is at times completely unchanging while color changes, and in Webern's Ricercare (Example 7-59), where the notes in a line are assigned to instruments in a manner that not only seems to fragment it into subgroups of a few notes each but also suggests some threads of identity provided by the reentrances of instruments: The first notes in the trombone might be linked to its later ones (especially since both trombone fragments end with *b*) and the same for the trumpet, horn, and harp (whose fragments are sequential). This constant fluctuation of color is typical for Webern. In his composed music, such as the Six Pieces for Orchestra, Op. 6, there are several passages with a comparable rate of change. This could be related to the fast rate of change in his pitch structure.

Chapter 7 illustrates devices such as transitions and orchestral crescendo (or diminuendo) that reinforce or counteract ongoing changes in pitch and rhythm.

The Long-Term Plan.   Over the course of a long piece or a long movement, the choice of colors and textures should be planned carefully, both with respect to the order in which they appear and in their distribution. As with choice of pitches and rhythms, orchestration can become predictable. A striking orchestral effect, for example, can easily lose its power if repeated many times, or even once. It is advisable to find a balance between the usual and the unusual—too many unusual things can verge on chaos or an unpleasant nervousness, and too few of them could result in dullness.

The degree to which the orchestration changes is another consideration. Abrupt changes emphasize breaks in the form; smooth changes, such as transitions, can bridge such sharp breaks.

CONTEXT

One of the unpredictable aspects of scoring is the effect of context on timbre. It is common, for example, to imagine that one hears wind instruments while listening to a string orchestra. In the same way that visual colors can change when accompanied by first one color and then another, instrumental timbres seem to change when the timbres around them change. Confusion of timbers is likely to occur when instruments blend well; otherwise, it is difficult to give guidelines for predicting such things.

Another influence is harmony and tonality. Listeners may attribute "sadness" or "brightness" to an instrument's timbre when the character of the pitch relations around it is sad or bright in effect. A good test of this, for example, is to compare the sound of the strings in the famous Air from Bach's Third Orchestral Suite with the same instruments in Bartók's Music for Strings, Percussion and Celesta (when they are not playing with mutes).

Finally, articulation is a critical influence on timbre. It is well known to music psychologists that recognition of an instrument depends to a great extent on the character of the attack. Tones that are artificially deprived of an attack lose some much of their recognizability. (It is surprising how difficult it is to recognize a piano when a tape of it is played backward—the attack now comes *at the end* of the tone!) Instruments probably sound most recognizable when playing notes of moderate length. Very short notes may cut off enough of the "steady state" sound to alter the timbre considerably.

Careful listening to instruments in various contexts is the best way to become sensitive to this phenomenon.

ACHIEVING AN ORCHESTRAL SOUND

Each idiom has a characteristic sound, whether it be choral, chamber, solo, or orchestral music. Solo music (for a single player with or without accompaniment) tends to be either quiet and intimate on one hand, or very showy and virtuosic on the other. Chamber music has intimacy of a different type—that of equality among partners interacting polyphonically. The orchestra, with its eighty-plus instruments ranging from the heavy and low-pitched to the lightweight, brilliant, and high-pitched, requires a certain gravity or weight for its music to sound natural. Its family and subfamily units also make subdivisions of its mass, as well as joint action of those units, a natural part of the way it is treated.

Judging by the way composers have used the orchestra up to the present, the following are some of the scoring features of idiomatic, successful orchestral writing.

1. A certain variety of color
2. A certain heaviness, power, or solidity of sound
3. A certain fullness of texture, affecting both spacing and pitch range
4. A certain complexity of activity among individual components of the whole
5. Idiomatic use of instruments

If any of these factors fall significantly below that "certain" level (which is difficult to define objectively), the effect, if it persists, may be more suggestive of the chamber orchestra, or even chamber music (which is not *wrong*, but simply *inappropriate*, from a practical standpoint).

It is this consideration that should prompt the scorer to expand the scope of an original, if that original does not already have the variety of color, the solidity of sound, the fullness of texture, or the complexity of activity appropriate to an orchestral composition. If one is transcribing a piano piece, for example, the best result is one that sounds as if it had originally been written for orchestra.

With that in mind, let us look again at some of our examples. Example 8-8d is an orchestral rendering of the "original" in Example 8-8a. Its orchestral features are a variety of color provided by the melodic strands in the clarinet, the violins, and the bassoon and the use of both arco and pizzicato in the strings; a solidity and fullness in the depth of the bass notes in the accompaniment and the full harmonies in the winds on the third beats; and a complexity of activity in the implied counterpoint between the violin sections, the merging of horns' eighth notes with the woodwind chords, and the counterpoint between the clarinet and the bassoon.

Example 8-10 is a close-to-literal rendering of Example 8-9a. It does not have much variety of color, since woodwind and string sounds are almost uniformly mixed. One would expect more variety as the piece progresses. The original already has an orchestral solidity of texture, and the few gaps in it have already been closed up. Either here or later, the texture should be expanded (probably upward more than downward) by octave doublings or added parts and perhaps also, for variety, narrowed or thinned. There is already an appropriate level of activity in the original.

In his orchestral works, Brahms made accompanying parts interesting by giving them more activity than may be perceived, often dividing repetitive figures among like instruments. Examples 7-29 and 7-54 show other examples of such activity, using cross-voicing. If one desired to add to Example 8-10, accompanimental versions of some of the lines might be appropriate, as in Example 8-15. These flute parts, marked discreetly soft and set in a register that is not brilliant, merely weave between the more sustained notes in the second violin and the viola (except for an interpolated e^1). A similar sort of active, but not intrusive, use of the flutes can be found in the second movement of Mendelssohn's Fourth Symphony at m. 11.

Example 8-15 Brahms, Op. 118, No. 2, mm. 3–4

Example 8-13a is a different matter. The original texture is not very orchestral—the lines are fairly spread apart, the texture is quite thin, and the pitch band is rather narrow, ranging mostly from d to f^2. Of course, since this is the beginning of the composition, it could be effective to begin with a literal setting of this texture in the expectation of expanding and thickening it at later times. Example 8-13c already adds a few notes that fill out the harmony and some of the voice lines. Transcriptions of Baroque music such as this often add octaves to the voices, as well as sustaining harmony (usually in the brass in climactic moments). The distinction between lines, so important in this music, is often achieved by contrasts of family. Line 1 might be assigned to flutes and oboes in octaves, and line 4 to cellos and basses, also in octaves. Lines 2 and 3 could be taken by violins and violas. Some slower-moving harmony notes might be added by clarinets and bassoons. This setting is shown in Example 8-16.

As has been mentioned, the fullness of this scoring might be more appropriate for a later part of the piece than for the beginning. The first bass note, to add emphasis, is played pizzicato. In the low register of both instruments, it will have great resonance. The contrast with the following arco notes helps to set it off from the melodic bass line, which really begins with the sixteenth notes, in imitation of the soprano. The choice of woodwinds instead of violins for the soprano was dictated by the difficult leap from a^2 to f^3, which *can* be negotiated by at least moderately accomplished violinists but is risky enough that a few players, even professionals, might not get the f^3 in tune; it is more secure in the flute. In an even heavier setting than this, both flutes and violins would work well.

Example 8-16   D. Scarlatti, Sonata for Harpsichord, K. 18, mm. 1–2

The made-up parts in the inner voices are marked at a lower dynamic level to minimize interference with the original lines. The blending clarinets and bassoons, not in strong registers, enter a beat later than the violins to avoid an undesirable emphasis in the middle of the phrase. As the other parts become more active, the clarinets and the bassoons drop out to avoid interfering with them. The second violins are divided to strengthen the viola line and to provide some continuity, reducing the possibility that the viola entrance will sound like a new idea.

If this passage were to occur near the end of the piece, a heavier setting might be effective. It could mix families for strength rather than separate them for contrast, with all instruments playing in their strongest registers. Here the brass could be called to double inner lines, and possibly add to the active bass (trombone and tuba) if the tempo were somewhat relaxed. Percussion could be discreetly used to give a sustained effect with rolls (especially on the timpani). A more modernistic touch would be a doubling or shadowing of lines on the xylophone or the marimba, or a highlighting of selected notes on the triangle, the glockenspiel, or the celesta.

IDIOMATIC USE OF INSTRUMENTS

A review of Chapters 2–6 would be helpful for a survey of what is idiomatic for the various instruments. It would also be well for you to study exercise books written for the instruments to gain an idea of what kinds of figuration, rhythms, and articulations seem typical. A look at solo literature is also recommended, but it might not be worth asking orchestral players to master a very demanding or intricate passage if the effect could be achieved in another, less demanding way. Occasionally, however, solo passages that are concertolike do appear in orchestral literature, and players enjoy the opportunity to show off. To have a section of strings execute such a passage, however, might be either very effective or disastrous, depending on its complexity and the ability of the players: Even if the passage can be mastered, it may not be worth the rehearsal time needed to coordinate a section of individuals.

Writing idiomatically means writing in such a way that the part "plays well": It is not awkward, and it shows off the best qualities of the instrument without undue effort on the player's part. Ideally, the player should enjoy playing the part. A good scorer usually makes use of a range of sounds and effects. It is generally not a good idea to keep an instrument in one register most of the time, to give it only one or two types of articulation or figuration, to keep it always muted or at one dynamic level, and so on.

Over the years, instruments have taken on stereotyped images, such as "the sweet violins," "the noble horns," and "the comic bassoon." These characterizations can be helpful for the novice, but they tend to limit one's thinking, whereas one should be ever alert for new ways to use instruments. The strings, for example, can sound quite "military," as in the Finale of Beethoven's Ninth Symphony at m. 164, where, at the same time, the brass are lyrical (see Example 8-17); thus, the two families switch their usual roles. The bassoon can play very affectingly, as in the wonderful melody at m. 274 of the second movement of Tchaikovsky's Fourth Symphony, as well as the last five measures of that movement.

The inexperienced scorer might continue the exploration of the "idiomatic" by considering the following various ways an instrument produces sound.

The strings play either downbow or upbow, and each stroke has its own characteristics. There are various bowing styles. Each of the four strings on the instruments has a different sound, and bowing across them can allow arpeggiation of chords, as in Examples 2-5, 2-14c, and 7-41. Double and multiple stops are avail-

Example 8-17 Beethoven, Symphony No. 9, mvt. 4, 164–167

able, as well as the colors of open strings, harmonics, and glissando. Consider also the various placements of the bow on the string, muting, and pizzicatos of various kinds.

The woodwinds breathe and tongue. There are varieties of articulation, including double-tonguing and flutter-tonguing. With proper breath control, notes can be shaped by subtle dynamic and timbre changes. Registers offer a variety of color: Register breaks can even be exploited, as we have seen. Staccatos can be soft and gentle or dry and biting. Fast-moving slurred notes are generally very clean, and upward-moving arpeggios brilliant.

The brass radiate the feeling of power and weight, even in *piano.* Breathing and tonguing like the woodwinds, they are more dependent on the overtone series; thus, arpeggios are very natural figures for them. The impact of tonguing styles can be very pronounced, especially in trumpets and trombones. Muting and stopping can be employed with dramatic effect. The resonance and smoothness of a well-integrated brass ensemble can provide either a marvelous, sustained background or a choralelike entity in itself. In lively passages, hardly anything can be more boisterous than these instruments.

The percussion make up for some overall deficiency in the ability to produce sustained melodies by offering an almost unlimited range of articulations and timbres, along with an unmatched dynamic range. The act of striking an object has an enormous number of variables: how to strike, where to strike, and with what to strike. Drumming figurations can be stunningly virtuosic, shaped into characteristic figures by the interaction of the two hands. Rolls, on more resonant instruments, allow subliminal background effects, matching of sustained notes in other families, or an overwhelming mass of sound. The choice of instruments is very large (even when limited to those that are generally available), and changes from one to another can often be made instantaneously. Resonance can be altered by various means of damping. The mallet instruments are capable of virtuoso passages as well as supportive ones. As a whole, the percussion section can act as a collection of "single tones" contributing to a thicket of ever-changing sounds and effects (for a good example, listen to Elliott Carter's Double Concerto for Piano and Harpsichord).

The harp, the piano, and the celesta are essentially self-sufficient instruments with bell-like percussive qualities, among other things. The piano has the greatest power. Marvelously resonant low notes emanate from both the piano and the harp, especially when written in octaves, and the celesta provides a more delicate, mysterious, and ethereal presence.

Keep in mind that *context* has a powerful influence over the way an instrument sounds—both its timbre and its overall character. One of the joys of discovery is to find that a "sad" instrument can be made to sound "happy," or a "heavy" instrument "light," and so on. Twentieth-century composers, beginning with Ravel and Mahler, have constantly looked for new ways of making instruments sound. The exploration continues unabated with today's composers.

TRANSPOSITION

Whether writing directly for the orchestra or transcribing from another medium, the scorer should consider the pitch level of the orchestral result. Pitch level can affect three things: timbre, range availability, and ease of execution. If the music is in a key, or at least has tonal centers and a scale of some sort, the key or tonal center might have a characteristic sound, owing to the various resonances of instruments. To experience this effect, one should find places in an orchestral work where the same music is heard in different keys and, if possible, scored in similar ways. One such spot is in mm. 557–564 of the first movement of Beethoven's Third Symphony, where a fragment of the main theme is first heard in D-flat major and then in C major. Although there are some differences in the second hearing—the higher dynamic level, the string tremolos, and changes in the high woodwinds—for the most part, the instruments simply play a half step lower than before. The listener will probably hear a different color. Although some of this may be due to the tonal context (the key or chordal relationships), much of it must be acoustic (for example, the open strings of the violas and the cellos) and simply the "C major sound," as opposed to the "D-flat major sound."

Such differences in timbre have been noted at least as early as the Baroque period, when certain keys were very often chosen for specific types of expression or images. C and D major, for example, were commonly associated with power or joy, C minor with turbulence, and F minor with sorrow. Closer to the present, the orchestral works of Debussy, still in "keys," offer good examples of a composer's sensitivity to pitch level. His use of D-flat major at m. 63 of *Prelude to The Afternoon of a Faun* and the first and third movements of *La Mer* shows that he may have considered this key as one of serenity; for more activity, he moved to other keys. The first two movements of his *Nocturnes* reveal a kaleidoscope of key colors, including the D-flat major in "Fêtes" for the quietest spot in that movement. How much brighter is the sound of the instruments when, later, there is a turn to A major! Similarly, the final section of *Daphnis et Chloé* moves from B major through a succession of keys to finish in a brilliant A major. Therefore, the choice of tonal level—the same as the original, or not—can have some bearing on the timbral aspect of the orchestral sound. A "bright" key original might be made "darker" or more subdued by transposition, or vice versa.

The second and third consequences of pitch level are more practical ones: By raising or lowering the pitch level, the scorer can make it possible for some instruments to play notes that otherwise would be out of their range. Finally, some keys are easier to play in than others (for example, see the section on the clarinet in Chapter 3).

PERFORMANCE AND THE PERFORMER

Performance difficulty is not limited to technically challenging passages. There are also many problems associated with ensemble performance that are not self-evident. A few are listed here, along with suggestions for alleviating them.

A. *Ensemble hazards*

1. Overlapping parts. They are more likely to sound smoothly connected if

    a. They have one or more notes in common.

    b. Both the last note in the ending line and the first note in the beginning line are *on* the beat, preferably a downbeat. See Example 8-18.

Example 8-18

2. Doubling of a line by players who are seated at some distance from each other, especially if they are unlike instruments. Examples:

    a. The oboe and solo cello in the second movement of Schumann's Fourth Symphony

    b. A melody played simultaneously by a flute and the glockenspiel

    It may be difficult for the players to see or hear each other, and one could be located much closer to the conductor than the other, which could cause different perceptions of when the beat occurs. Even small differences in distance can be a factor when coordination is critical. Example 8-19a shows such a passage involving two string sections. If rescored as in 8-19b, coordination should be better, since the players playing different parts are sitting closer to each other. An example of such a troublesome passage—very exposed and difficult to get together—is found at m. 135 in the overture to Mozart's *Marriage of Figaro.*

Example 8-19

3. Doubling of exposed, single staccato notes in instruments that have sharp or powerful attacks. A good example is in Copland's Third Symphony, which calls for heavy, isolated notes played both on two timpani (played by one player) and on the bass drum. See Example 8-20. Del Mar remarks that it is difficult for two pianists to strike a chord together.[1] Isolated pizzicatos are difficult to coordinate with staccato notes elsewhere in the orchestra.

Example 8-20   Copland, Symphony No. 3, mvt. 3, three before no. 87

© *Copyright 1947 by Aaron Copland; Copyright Renewed. Reprinted by permission of the Estate of Aaron Copland, Copyright Owner, and Boosey & Hawkes, Inc., Sole Licensees.*

4. Quick entrances after rests or a fast succession of syncopations, as in Examples 8-21 and 8-22, respectively, especially when rhythmic precision is required. Some way of allowing the player to play *on* the beat would be helpful, as line 2 in Example 8-13c does.

---

[1]Norman del Mar, *The Anatomy of an Orchestra* (Berkeley and Los Angeles: University of California Press, 1981), p. 458.

Example 8-21

Example 8-22

    B. *Ensemble intonation problems*

        1. Two instruments playing the same tone at the same time in an exposed position, especially if their timbres or vibratos are different. An example is the offstage horns at no. 29 in Mahler's Second Symphony. Another example is m. 38 of the first movement of Schubert's *Unfinished* Symphony, where two bassoons and two horns are suddenly exposed on a unison d^1. The strength of the horns and the difference in vibratos may contribute to the problem here. In Mahler's Symphony No. 1, third movement, just before no. 13, overtones of the tam-tam and the bass drum clash with the *G*'s of the harp and the timpani. A single player or three players in unison are safer than two; yet, doubling by two players is common.

        2. A pretuned instrument, such as a keyboard instrument (piano, celesta, glockenspiel, and so on) or a harp, playing in close proximity with other instruments playing the same notes, especially in chords. A glaring example is at m. 303 of the first movement of Beethoven's *Emperor* Concerto, where the piano repeats a chord first played by the whole orchestra. See Example 8-23. (Incidentally, this is a good example of the difference between typical orchestral spacing and typical spacing in piano music.) Another is at the end of the second movement of Gershwin's Piano Concerto, where the woodwinds reach a sustained D-flat major triad and the piano enters, moving scalewise up to high A-flats.

Example 8-23   Beethoven, *Emperor* Concerto, mvt. 1, mm. 303–305

C. *Ungrateful parts.* A score that *avoids* the things listed here is more likely to be learned by the orchestra in a shorter time than otherwise (a factor that is vital in professional situations, especially recording sessions); to sound better; and to be more favorably received by the musicians—it may even determine whether or not the piece will be played.

1. Poor manuscript. This is probably the easiest way to alienate an orchestra.

2. Unidiomatic treatment of the instrument or notation. Unusual things should be checked out with a performer to ensure that they will "work."

3. Repetitious or otherwise fatiguing passages (for example, the string parts in the last movement of Schubert's Ninth Symphony, which are infamous).

4. Parts that are unnecessarily difficult either to learn or to play when learned.

5. Parts that allow either very little rest or too much rest.

6. Scores or parts that have many errors or imprecise notation. (A rigorous use of the checklist in Appendix E and double-checking of notes between score and parts should avoid most problems.)

7. Parts that are generally uninteresting. If possible, allow every instrument to play, or at least share, a leading line at some times. Accompaniments should be made interesting. Schubert (at times), Dvořák, and Brahms were good at this. Any part that can be played by a beginner can lose an accomplished player's interest and respect: The professional welcomes a reasonable challenge to his or her ability.

THE USE OF FAMILIES: A SUMMARY

Chapter 7 illustrates many uses of families with respect to function and form. Here we will gather together some main points from that chapter and this one.

Strings

The strings are the most homogeneous group in the orchestra, with the fewest blending and balance problems within it. There is also more uniformity in technique than in other families, with allowances for size and response. The strings provide a warm, rich sonority that is most characteristic in singing passages; such passages typically have many slurs—otherwise, they will not sound idiomatic. In fullness of texture, through multiple divisi, this family is unrivaled. Its range of effects (bowings, pizzicato, harmonics, and so on) is wide. In tuttis, it tends to be spread rather evenly over the entire pitch range.

Woodwinds

The woodwind family is less homogeneous than the brass or the strings. It excels in both lyrical and staccato styles. Its colors can be bright and glowing, without the intimate warmth of the strings, or pungent and whimsical. Differences in technique and register strength should always be kept in mind. However, differences in character offer interesting contrasts within the group. Horns are used so often with woodwinds that they could functionally be considered "in-laws."

In tuttis, woodwinds tend to be concentrated in the extremes of the pitch range, with only the bassoons and the bass clarinet on lower notes.

Brass

The brass are capable of remarkable homogeneity, especially below the *forte* level, but care must be taken to integrate the horns with the more clearly defined timbres of the rest. Except when muted, the brass exude presence and power at almost every dynamic level. Tonal qualities include great brilliance and solid lyricism. Muting and stopping offer more pungent, pointed textures that blend well with double reeds, the violas, and the ponticello sound of the strings. In tuttis, the group usually ranges in pitch from about C to f^2.

Percussion

Here is by far the most heterogeneity of every kind—range, attack, decay, timbre, power, and character. The least characteristic type of articulation is legato, and the most characteristic is staccato, but there is a multitude of possibilities between those extremes. It is more difficult to blend this family with the others than to blend the others with each other. Pitch area is a vital consideration when this is to be attempted, as is the articulation style of the nonpercussion instruments that are playing. Great virtuosity can be displayed by many of the instruments—mostly the mallets (excluding the glockenspiel, for practical purposes) and the drums (especially the snare drum, and least of all the bass).

Percussion is capable of carrying leading parts, but since it is so different from the other families, it tends to be used more for accompaniments and highlighting. Subliminal additions to the texture can be extremely effective.

The Harp, the Piano, and the Celesta

These instruments are the most self-sufficient. The harp and the piano have extensive ranges, and the piano has the most power of projection. All have a distinctive color. The virtuosity of the piano is well known, but it is rarely exploited in the orchestra.

Typically, these instruments are treated much like mallet instruments—to double leading lines, to highlight, and to provide accompaniments. Occasionally, they are given solo parts.

THE ORCHESTRA AS ACCOMPANIST

The orchestra is typically used to accompany instrumental color (for example, in concertos or single pieces), vocal solos (arias and the like), and ensembles (instrumental, choral, or operatic). Space does not permit a thorough examination of this role, but a few general principles should suffice for most purposes.

1. Balance considerations are the most important. Scrupulous attention to strength, spacing, and pitch factors is mandatory. A study of concertos reveals that no matter which instrument is being accompanied, the following are true:

    a. Important lines in the solo are generally placed either well above the pitch level of the orchestra, below that pitch level, or in a large gap, with no instruments playing in the same pitch area. Piano solo parts sometimes have the right hand playing above the orchestra at the same time the left hand plays below it.

    b. When accompanying an instrumental solo, the orchestra is often reduced in size. Wind instruments—especially woodwinds and horns—may be reduced to single players, and the heavier instruments may not be used at all. The strength and carrying power of the soloist is an obvious factor. All woodwinds benefit from a chamber-orchestra scale of accompaniment, which is not a bad idea for any but the most powerful of solo instruments. Although the contrabass may seem like a powerful instrument, it is surprisingly weak as a soloist, especially in the singing, upper register. Guitars usually are amplified. The balance must be calculated in the hall with the equipment to be used, but even so, the gentle sound of this instrument does not suggest a thick or heavy background.

    c. Vocal soloists can be powerful enough to hold their own against a full orchestra, but great care must be taken when their part falls below midrange.

    d. The size of a chorus is an important consideration. A group of forty or so can deal on equal terms with strings and woodwinds, particularly when singing in unison or octave doublings. It is very common to double vocal parts in the orchestra—both for soloists and for choral parts, or to highlight or shadow voice lines. Choral passages that are declamatory—rhythmic repetitions—tend to cut through more easily than lyrical ones. Such passages can tolerate accompaniments that have leading lines. Hard consonants in the text project better than vowels.

2. Blending factors can be crucial. A soloist who blends too well with the accompaniment runs the risk of being absorbed into the orchestral fabric. Therefore, contrast between the solo and its accompaniment is important: a percussive instrument accompanied by lyrical ones (or the reverse), a bright instrument accompanied by dark ones (but *not* the reverse), a wind instrument accompanied by strings, and so on. Diversity of activity should be considered: When the soloist is active, the accompaniment is best kept very inactive.

All of this assumes that the orchestra is intended to be in the background. This is not the case at all times in concertos or choral works. Such compositions often play off the soloist and the orchestra by alternations of importance—repetitions by one of what the other just did, or using the soloist as an accompanist for the orchestra. In some compositions, such as Berlioz's *Harold in Italy* and Berg's Violin Concerto, the solo players often become soloists *in the orchestra.* Conversely, some concertos feature soloists in the orchestra that occasionally join the designated soloist on an equal footing (some concertos of Vivaldi, Strauss's *Don Quixote*).

THE CHAMBER ORCHESTRA

The chamber orchestra could be thought of as partway between a large chamber music group and a full orchestra. Many organizations today are called "chamber orchestra." Their literature generally consists of eighteenth- and twentieth-century music. During the nineteenth century, the orchestra grew to (and beyond) the present size of the "full orchestra," but in the early years of the twentieth century, a reaction against very large-scale works resulted in a surge of works for chamber ensembles of various types. Many works written initially for large or very large orchestra were later revised in reduced form (Schoenberg's Five Pieces for Orchestra, Webern's Six Pieces, and so on), usually for practical reasons. Paul Creston published several works in two versions simultaneously, labeled "A" and "B."

The typical chamber-orchestra work calls for one or two each of the standard wind instruments, a percussion group small enough to be handled by one player, and a few stands of string players. Often less-usual instruments appear, such as the English horn, the guitar, or the piano. The chamber orchestra has fewer possibilities for massed effects, such as tone clusters or thick harmonies, than the full orchestra does and cannot as readily achieve blending, owing to diminished resources—instrumental differences are more obvious in this setting. The kind of music that is appropriate for this medium, then, is polyphonic; and transparent textures are more natural than the thick, veiled, and sustained sounds that are found in much Romantic and Impressionist music.

The emphasis is on the heterogeneous, each wind instrument tending to act as a soloist much of the time. Compositions tend to be light in character, with a fair amount of staccato articulation, and not as lengthy as those for full orchestra. This orchestra is ideal as an accompaniment for any instrument, especially the weaker ones.

CONCLUSION

This chapter has provided guidelines for various facets of scoring. They are to be regarded as suggestions and warnings, and not recipes to be mechanically applied. After the essentials of scoring have been learned, the student is advised to attend rehearsals of orchestras (at all levels of ability) armed with copies of the scores being rehearsed. Note the things that give the players trouble—especially balance, coordination, and execution problems. Talk to the players and ask what they find difficult about the parts in terms of performance or notation. Ask the conductor about problems in the scoring.

There is no substitute for score study and comparison of what is seen with what is heard, particularly in *live* performance. Students should always ask themselves why an effective passage is scored the way it is, as opposed to the alternatives.

The scorer is once again urged to be open to new possibilities. New styles demand new sound structures. As with harmonies that formerly were considered ugly, ways of using instruments singly or collectively that would have been considered ugly in the past should be looked upon now as potential raw material for the masterpieces of tomorrow.

TRANSCRIPTIONS

Avison (Charles), Concerti grossi for strings (harpsichord sonatas of Domenico Scarlatti)

Bach, Cantata, "Wir danken Dir, Gott," Sinfonia; and Cantata, "Herr Gott, Beherrscher aller Dinge" (Violin Partita in E major, mvt. 1)

Bartók, Nine Hungarian Peasant Songs (Nos. 7–15 of 15 Hungarian Peasant Songs)

Brahms, Variations on a Theme by Haydn; Hungarian Dances, Nos. 1, 3, and 10

Britten, *Soirées musicales* and *Matinées musicales* (Rossini)

Debussy, *Gymnopédies* (Satie); *Marche écosaisse*

Dvořák, Slavonic Dances, Op. 46

Grainger, *Irish Tunes from County Derry* (strings)

Liszt, *Second Mephisto Waltz;* Schubert Songs ("Die Loreley," "Mignons Lied," "Die Vatergruft," "Die junge Nonne," "Gretchen am Spinnrade," "Der Erlkönig" (voice and orch.); Schubert's *Wanderer Fantasy* (piano and orch.); Polonaise brilliante (Weber; piano and orch.)

Ravel, *Alborado del gracioso; Mother Goose* Suite; *Pavàne pour une Infante défunte; Pictures at an Exhibition* (Musorgsky); *Le Tombeau de Couperin*

Respighi, *Antiche arie e danze per liuto; Gli uccelli;* Passacaglia in C Minor (Bach); 3 Organ Chorales (Bach)

Schoenberg, Piano Quartet in G minor (Brahms); Concerto Grosso Op. 9, No. 7 (Handel); Two Chorale Preludes (Bach)

Tchaikovsky, Suite No. 4: *Mozartiana* (Mozart: Gigue, K. 574; Menuet, K. 355; *Ave verum corpus,* K. 618; Variations, K. 455)

Webern, Ricercare, *The Musical Offering* (Bach)

CHAPTER 9

Wind–Percussion and String Ensembles

THE CONCERT BAND

The concert band (or symphonic band) has a history that is as old as that of the orchestra, extending at least as far back as the military and royal bands of the sixteenth century. Handel's *Royal Fireworks Music* and divertimenti of Haydn and Mozart are among the early examples of wind music (with or without percussion) that are standard concert items today. Overall, band literature designed for formal concerts is less extensive than that for orchestra, but in recent decades the band has become increasingly important in high schools and colleges (in some cases actually taking the place of orchestras), prompting composers to give greater attention to this and related ensembles. Today, the number of publications for band is staggeringly large.

The concert band is distinguishable from the wind orchestra and the wind ensemble. Its instrumentation has become about as standard as that of the orchestra, but the *numbers* of the various instruments have not. Authors vary in the numbers they give, probably because bands vary widely in this respect.

The band can be divided into three or four families, depending on whether the saxophones are considered as a separate one: woodwinds, (saxophones), brass, and percussion. The flutes and the clarinets, like the strings in the orchestra, are grouped in sections of a few or several instruments playing the same part. Other instruments may be represented by one player or by several but are fewer than the flutes or the clarinets. The list on page 310 is typical.

Other instruments may be called for—must often, the E-flat alto clarinet, the bass saxophone, the celesta, or the harp. In the first decades of this century, the cornet was considered the principal soprano brass instrument of the band, and the trumpet was thought to be a less-refined subsidiary to it. Since about 1950, there has been a shift to a greater reliance on the trumpet—so much so that cornets do not appear at all in many recent scores.

Piccolo: 1 player (possibly doubling on flute)

Flute: 6 (in two or three parts—flute 1, flute 2, and so on)

Oboe: 3 (in two parts)

English horn: 1 (doubling on oboe)

E-flat clarinet: 1

B-flat clarinet: 10–18 (in three parts; usually, there are more of clar. 3 than of clar. 2 and more of clar. 2 than of clar. 1)

Bass clarinet: 2

E-flat contralto or B-flat contrabass clarinet: 1

Bassoon: 3

Contrabassoon: 1 (doubling on bassoon)

Alto saxophone: 2 (in two parts)

Tenor saxophone: 1

Baritone saxophone: 1

Cornets: 6 (in three parts)

B-flat trumpets:[1] 4 (in two parts)

Horns: 4–8 (in four parts)

Trombones: 5 (in three parts—tbn. 3 is played on bass trombones)

Baritone horn or euphonium: 2

Tubas (or "basses"): 4

String bass: 1

Timpani

Percussion: 3 players

Piano

Notation

The usual score order is shown in the preceding list. Woodwinds and brass are often separately bracketed. Bracing of staves varies somewhat from score to score. Like instruments are generally braced together: flutes, oboes, clarinets, saxophones, cornets, trumpets, horns, and trombones. The parts for all but the flutes, and possibly also alto saxes and oboes, are usually placed on separate staves. On occasion, however, the flutes may appear on one staff each, as may the oboes. Example 9-1 shows a typical layout. The E-flat contralto and B-flat contrabass clarinets might be written as one part in the score but must have separate parts to play from.

Among the percussion instruments, the mallets may be placed above the nonpitched instruments. Those playing the latter may be given a percussion score to read from.

Some scores specify how many of each instrument are desired. If more than

---

[1]If cornets are not in the organization, there will be 6 or 7 trumpets in two or three parts.

Example 9-1

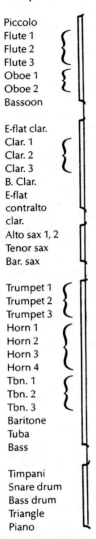

Piccolo
Flute 1
Flute 2
Flute 3
Oboe 1
Oboe 2
Bassoon

E-flat clar.
Clar. 1
Clar. 2
Clar. 3
B. Clar.
E-flat
contralto
clar.
Alto sax 1, 2
Tenor sax
Bar. sax

Trumpet 1
Trumpet 2
Trumpet 3
Horn 1
Horn 2
Horn 3
Horn 4
Tbn. 1
Tbn. 2
Tbn. 3
Baritone
Tuba
Bass

Timpani
Snare drum
Bass drum
Triangle
Piano

one instrument is notated on one staff, the terms *solo* (for one player), *tutti, divisi,* and *unisoni* may be used, as for string sections. If more than one part is on one staff, "a 2" or "a 3" signifies that they play in unison.

The question of whether or not to write the score "in C" (that is, with all notes sounding as written, except for instruments that are normally written an octave higher or lower than sounding) has been debated among band directors.

The argument for it is that it makes difficult scores easier to read. An argument against it is that the director loses the sense of fingering and the "true representation of the sound." Most scores *are* transposed (not in C), but publishers often include a condensed score in concert pitch showing instrumental assignments; in that way, the conductor can have it both ways, to some extent.

Scoring Considerations

Writers on band scoring seem to agree on the following points.

1. Flat keys are easier to play in than sharp keys.
2. Except for the clarinets, and very good players on other instruments, the band cannot achieve the tonal refinement and lower dynamic levels of the orchestral strings, and not even the clarinets can play softly on very high notes. This is a factor to remember when making orchestra-to-band transcriptions.
3. The saxophones, having characteristics of both woodwinds and brass, can serve as a bridge between the two groups, strengthening the woodwinds and softening the brass when playing in unison with them, respectively.
4. There are problems of balance within the clarinet group, owing to a lack of strength in lower pitch areas. Saxophones can help here as a supplement to the lower clarinets.
5. Since flutes tend to play sharp in higher registers and clarinets tend to play flat, doubling them in unison can create intonation problems. Some have advocated a larger flute section so that doubling by the clarinets for strength will not be necessary.
6. The alto is the most popular of the saxes. The soprano is used less frequently than the alto and the tenor, and the bass is rarely used. Percy Grainger, a prolific composer of band music, recommended the use of the full family.
7. Flutes and clarinets are better doubling the cornets or the trumpets an octave higher than doubling them at the unison. In general, thick doublings are not desirable in middle pitch areas.
8. Since there tend to be distinct differences in ability among players in school bands, it is recommended that the more difficult and the more important parts be given to the first and second parts—for example, flute 1, horn 1, and horn 2. The same is true for those instruments that are most likely to be found in bands, especially at lower educational levels: the flutes, the B-flat clarinets, the alto saxes, the trumpets, the horns, the trombones, the baritones, and the tubas. If such a part *is* assigned to an instrument other than one of these, it is advisable to cue it in an appropriate instrument from the preceding list (see the next section, "Cuing"). Cuing should also be used for third and fourth parts, such as horn 3 and horn 4, since players might not be available to play them. For the same reason, if a quartet of horns or saxophones is given the complete harmony, it is wise to assign the most important notes of the chord to the first and second players so that if the other players are missing, the sense of the harmony will be retained (for example, for a major triad, the root and the fifth, or the root and the third, should be retained).
9. The brass are more numerous in the band than in the orchestra; thus, it would be easy for a heavily scored brass section to overpower the woodwinds. Strong doublings and the use of upper registers may be required for the woodwinds to hold their own. At the very least, a large component of the woodwinds should play above the brass in a tutti.

Roy Miller calculates that in loud passages, 3 flutes, 2 clarinets, 2 oboes, or 2 bassoons equal 1 horn, and 2 high flutes equal 1 trumpet or 1 trombone.[2]

In moderate-to-thick textures composers tend to assign functions to homogeneous groups, as they do in the orchestra. The saxophones, which have a special quality, are often used as a group, although they are at times indistinguishable from clarinets or bassoons. They seem to be mixed with other woodwinds much more often than with brass, but they also double brass lines.

In traditional music, such as marches and arrangements, each instrument tends to have a characteristic role.

1. Clarinets and trumpets (cornets) have most of the leading lines and individual solos.
2. The flutes, saxes, horns, trombones, and percussion have about an equal amount of leading lines and accompaniments: The flutes and the piccolos often contribute brilliant flourishes and trills, and the lower and middle brass provide various rhythmic backgrounds along with the percussion.
3. The mallet instruments and the chimes offer brilliant melodic possibilities, often doubling wind instruments.
4. The baritone horn or euphonium, the bass clarinet, and the tenor sax usually are given secondary lines. Such countermelodies are important features of marching-band music.
5. Balance and blending principles (see Chapter 8) are more critical when the spacing is open than when it is close.

It is well to remember that the band, being predominantly composed of winds, does not have the tonal variety of the orchestra. Contrasts are especially important. An active percussion section often provides them, with emphasis on mallets. Within the winds, subgroups and solos are sources of contrast with full sections.

The composer Ingolf Dahl said that he found the experience of writing for band a fearful one because a finely adjusted balance might be destroyed if the performing group had different numbers of players from what he expected;[3] therefore one is advised to determine the forces of a group for whom one is writing *before* beginning work.

Cuing

Cuing is the insertion of some of the notes of one instrument's part into the part of another instrument, usually during rests. See Example 9-2. The cued instrument must be identified, and the notes must be small, and transposed, if needed,

---

[2]Roy Miller, *Practical Instrumentation for the Wind Band* (Detroit: Wayne State University Press, 1963), p. 36

[3]Ingolf Dahl, Lecture, "Sinfonietta for Concert Band: Discussion," *Proceedings of the 13th National Conference of the College Band Directors National Association*, Tempe, Ariz., December 1964.

to sound the same as the cued instrument. Cuing serves one of two purposes: to help the player enter correctly or to allow the player to supply the notes of an instrument that is not available or whose player is not capable of playing it adequately. The second reason is of concern here.

Example 9-2

Cuing should be employed during rests or during passages that can be dispensed with. The choice of instrument to act as the substitute naturally demands that it be available, that it will sound well playing the cue, and that it is reasonably close in timbre, strength, and character to the missing instrument. If the last of these is not respected, a carefully worked-out balance or blend may be negated. The substituted instrument need not always be a member of the same family—for example, a horn could substitute for a middle-to-high bassoon, or a saxophone could replace a baritone horn.

Cuing should also be considered for some percussion: The piano can give a reasonably good imitation of mallet instruments, the harp, or the celesta. (The most available percussion instruments are snare drum, bass drum, cymbals, triangle, and timpani. There may also be a xylophone, chimes, and a bell lyre, which is similar, but inferior, to the glockenspiel).

It is important to show the cues in the score.

More discussion of cuing can be found in Chapter 10.

THE SCHOOL BAND

Below the college level, the issues of instrument availability and playing ability become critical. For the most part, only the most usual instruments can be expected to be present, and close attention should be given to the difficulty factors mentioned in Chapters 2 (for string bass), 3, 4, and 5. Breath control and ranges are best treated conservatively. Phrases should not last over 10 seconds. The playing range should remain about a fifth or so above the lowest note of the professional range (this is least true for the clarinet) and a fifth to an octave lower than the highest note (for example, although the professional range of the flute is c^1 to d^4, the school flutist should not be written outside about g^1 to d^2). Horns should be kept in the treble clef. Important lines are best in middle registers. The use of tenor clef is not advised. Percussion parts should have relatively uncomplicated rhythms and only rudimentary sticking patterns.

THE WIND ORCHESTRA

The wind orchestra attained a certain popularity in the 1950s and 1960s. Its instrumental complement is the same as the symphony orchestra's without the strings, except possibly for string basses. Because of this association with the full orchestra, many important composers of orchestral works were attracted to it. Some of the compositions are called "Symphony"—for example, several of those by Alan Hovhaness. The numbers of instruments required are generally somewhere between those in the full orchestra and those in the concert band. Carlos Surinach's *Paeans and Dances of Heathen Iberia*, for example, has numbers that approach those of the band, such as 6 clarinets, 6 bassoons, and 6 trumpets (among other instruments), and John Williams's Sinfonietta calls for 3 clarinets, 3 bassoons, and 4 trumpets. The distinguishing difference between the wind orchestra and the concert band is that the wind orchestra has no nonbasic instruments such as saxophones, baritone horns, and alto clarinets. Scoring techniques are similar to those used in music for full orchestra.

THE WIND ENSEMBLE

The term *wind ensemble* is sometimes used for groups that have the same forces as the typical concert band. More often, it has no more than two players on any instrument, and some of the nonbasic instruments, such as the alto clarinet, may be missing. If such a group is found at a college that also has a full-size concert band, it is likely to be composed of the better players.

THE STRING ORCHESTRA

The string orchestra is not often found as an independent performing unit, as are the other groups we have discussed. Typically, music written for it is part of a full-orchestra concert, using all of the string section or a portion of it.

The string orchestra has the problem of homogeneity to a far greater degree than do the wind–percussion groups, and the composer must even more carefully guard against monotony of tone color; however, the medium has much to offer in the way of instrumental technique to offset this problem, such as a variety of bowing styles, harmonics, and pizzicato. It does not have the problems that winds have with regard to fatigue, sustaining power, balance, and blending. It can produce heavily thick, homogeneous textures, as well as any number of other thicknesses and spacing configurations without serious balance or blending difficulties.

Strings can play with great intensity, if not with raw power (except for certain things, like multiple-stopped chords), but manipulation of forces can create the illusion of a wide dynamic range—for example, the contrasting of a solo group with the whole orchestra.

This was exploited dramatically by Vaughan Williams in his *Fantasia on a Theme by Thomas Tallis*. The composer divided the strings into two orchestras—one about a third the size of the other—and soloists (drawn from both orchestras). Sections of the music are neatly defined by changes in the number of players used at any moment. The smaller orchestra is to sit apart from the larger one, enhancing the contrast of size. The music imitates Renaissance choral music with block writing in groups ranging from a solo quartet to the whole ensemble in multiple parts.

Dvořák's Serenade for Strings, on the other hand, treats the string orchestra as an amplified string quartet. The amplification takes the form of bass support, divisi, and octave doubling. The basses are not used for independent lines but provide rhythmic impulse with pizzicatos or double the cellos an octave below. As in orchestral music, the violas and the second violins are often divided into two or three parts for added fullness. Octave doubling between the violin sections or within them lends a spacious sweep to the flowing lines.

Strauss's *Metamorphosen* specifies 10 violins, 5 violas, 5 cellos, and 3 basses. Each player is given a separate staff, except for extended unison passages. This method of part assignment provides a means of controlling balance and voice leading in a rather precise way, but the treatment is not very different from that in other works for string orchestra. The usual notation (in sections) might have been feasible in most cases, since there are never twenty-three (the maximum possible) independent parts.

Penderecki's *To the Victims of Hiroshima: Threnody* calls for 24 violins, 10 violas, 10 cellos, and 8 basses (close to the proportions in Strauss), again with each player's part given a separate staff when it is independent. The work, which is highly descriptive, uses very high, unspecified pitches (as well as specified ones), thick tone clusters, glissandos, variable vibrato, and various bowing effects. The sounds it produces are so unusual that it may be difficult to believe that they come from strings. An important part of this effect is the nontraditional use of vibrato: Where it is not specifically required to be either "molto" or "very slow, with a sliding finger," vibrato is usually not used at all (for the glissandos or the many isolated tones) and, of course, is not available when the bow is drawn over the tailpiece or the bridge!

Example 9-3 is a sample of this piece. Here, groups of violins play clusters of pitches with slow vibrato, while some cellos and basses play "notes" on the bridge or the tailpiece.

Example 9-3 Penderecki, *Threnody to the Victims of Hiroshima,* mm. 64–66

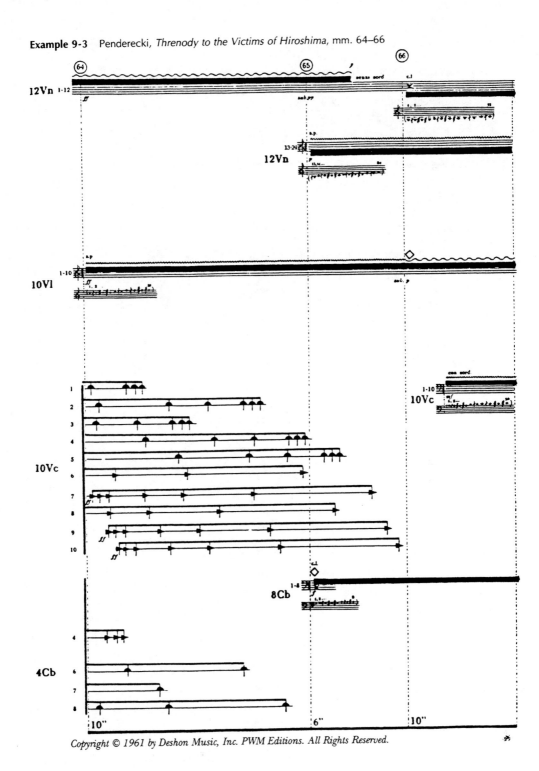

WORKS FOR LISTENING AND STUDY

Colgrass, *Winds of Nagual (1985)*
Dahl, Sinfonietta (1961)
Hindemith, Symphony in B-flat for Concert Band
Holst, First Suite in E-flat
Hovhaness, Symphonies No. 4 and 7 for Wind Orchestra
Husa, *Music for Prague 1968*
Persichetti, Divertimento for Band
Surinach, *Paeans and Dances of Heathen Iberia*
Williams, Sinfonietta for winds and percussion

Transcriptions of Orchestral Works

Barber, First Symphony
Offenbach, Overture to *La Belle Hélène*
Milhaud, *Suite française*
Shostakovich, *Festive* Overture
Wagner, *Lohengrin,* Prelude to act 3
Weinberger, Polka and Fugue (from *Schwanda*)

Works for string orchestra are listed at the end of Chapter 2.

CHAPTER 10

Preparing the Score and Parts

Traditions and habits usually arise out of trial and error, and musical notation is no exception. One of the most practical aspects of the art, it has always had to change in response to the evolution of instruments, compositional styles, and performance practices. This seems to have accelerated since 1970, and in only a few years, a wealth of new approaches has emerged. Every so often, an organization of composers meets to devise standards. Some of the newer methods will be listed under "Newer Practices" in this chapter.

Because notation is ultimately a practical matter, it should be treated as such. Innovations have been devised because composers find the old methods inadequate for new ways of making sound. Although one should be encouraged always to look for the best way to notate one's thoughts, it may be impractical if the new version is so radical that the hoped-for gain in precision is not worth the possible rejection by publishers, conductors, or performers. Many composers do take the risk, however, and some experiments have been generally adopted, whereas others have had only a limited currency.

There are several books on the subject of notation in general, and some of these are listed in the Bibliography. It is assumed that the student has studied the basics of calligraphy; therefore, this chapter deals only with matters that are most pertinent to orchestral writing.

THE SCORE

The Preliminary Pages

The following are recommendations for the content of the preliminary pages, many examples of which can be found in publications. The *title page* usually has the composer's name at the top. The title comes just below that, and the medium for which the composition is written is at the bottom. If the orchestrator and the composer are not the same person, the orchestrator's name should be placed just under the title. Example 10-1 gives a hypothetical example. The title page may be the cover page or the first right-hand page.

Example 10-1

GEORGE FREEMAN

LANDSCAPES

orchestrated by Holly Weston

for

ORCHESTRA

The next page often lists the instruments needed, in score order, with the heading "Instrumentation." This is helpful to many users, including the conductor, the stage manager, the players, and the score reader. It is well to list all percussion instruments and any assignments to players, if there is no setup diagram. It is also desirable to give the duration of each movement and of the entire composition on this page.

Setup diagrams, seating diagrams, or special instructions are generally placed on the page following the instrumentation. There might also be explanations of the notation, translations, vocal texts, or program notes. A table of contents is desirable if there are many movements, especially for stage works. Opera scores also often include casts of characters.

The First Page of Music

Page 1 normally has the title at the top, centered. The composer's name is usually in the upper right, just above the top staff, and the orchestrator, if a separate person, is named just below the composer. If there is text, the author's name can appear at the upper left, just above the music.

At the bottom of the page, the copyright notice is placed, generally in the form "Copyright [year] by [name]."

Example 10-2 shows the typical general arrangement of the instruments in the score. All instruments that are to be used in the piece should, if possible, be shown in their assigned positions (as another way of showing which instruments are to be used), whether or not they have anything to play on this page. If there are many percussion instruments, these can be listed in groups, whether by player or not. Example 10-3 (page 322) is an example. In this case, Tower has shown percussion assignments on a preliminary page, and the players are identified in the left margin by numbers, but their instruments are not (they are identified when they enter). Otherwise, all the names of the instruments are given in the margin, spelled out in full, and in the traditional order shown in Example 10-2. (As mentioned in Chapter 6, Tower uses a less-than-usual positioning of the percussion—below the harp and the piano/celesta.) Any instrument built "in a key," such as trumpet in B-flat or clarinet in A, must be identified as such. If there are two or more wind instruments written on one part, this must be clear—for example, "flutes 1 and 2" or "2 flutes" (not just "flutes").

Example 10-2

Woodwinds
Brass
Timpani
Other percussion
Harp, celesta, piano, organ
Chorus and/or solo instruments
Strings

Family Groups

It is customary to bracket the woodwind, brass, and string groups separately, but many scores do not. Composers vary even more in their treatment of percussion: Some set the timpani off from the rest, as is done in Example 10-3; others bracket all percussion together; and still others use no brackets at all for this family. When nonpitched percussion are written on single-line rather than five-line staves, it is easier to identify their parts at a glance, and a bracket may not be necessary.

Two other ways of showing family groups are to run the bar lines *through*, but not *between*, families, as in Example 10-3, and to leave an empty staff between families. The latter also leaves room for tempo indications. If there is a group of singers in the score, bar lines should not be drawn through their staves, since that would interfere with the text.

Within families, the instruments are arranged in subgroups by type. From the top down, the woodwinds, in order, are flutes, oboes (and English horn), clarinets, and bassoons. The brass subgroups in order are horns, trumpets, trombones, and tuba (some scores put the trumpets first). Within the subgroups, the higher-sounding instruments are placed above the lower-sounding ones. The most usual exception to this is the piccolo when the player is expected to double on second flute. In that case, the piccolo's notes are written on the staff that is given to the second flute, and the part is marked "flute 2, piccolo."

Whether or not families are set off, like instruments almost invariably are—either by the kind of brackets used for the horns in Example 10-3 or by the braces used for the harp and the piano in the same example. Like instruments in this case are those belonging to the same subgroup (for example, flute and piccolo,

Example 10-3   Tower, *Silver Ladders*

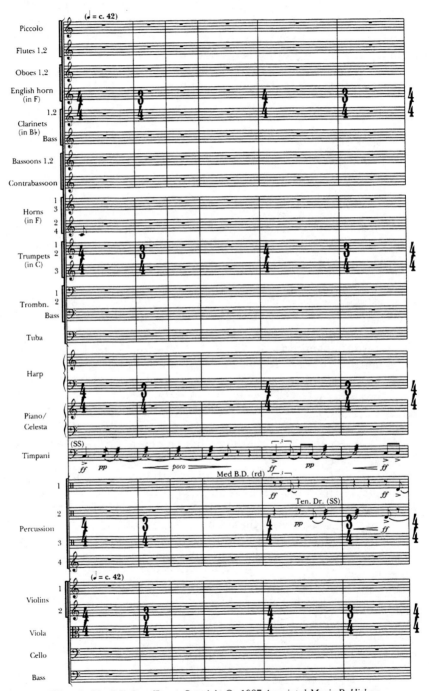

oboe and English horn; in the strings, cellos and basses are often braced). It is traditional to put the first and second trombones on one staff and the third trombone and the tuba on the staff below, and to brace the two staves together. That is not done here. When there are three of the same wind instrument, it is customary to put the first two on the upper staff and the third on the staff below, as is done with the trumpets here.

Within families, subgroups ordinarily proceed from "higher-sounding" to lower-sounding, again based on the lowest notes in the respective ranges (for example, flute–oboe–clarinet–bassoon), but traditionally the horns are placed above the trumpets.

Since the saxophone is not a standard orchestral instrument, it does not have a commonly agreed-upon location. It seems logical to place it among the woodwinds: It has been found below the clarinets, above the clarinets, and even below the brass.

Vocal parts have at times been placed just above the cellos, probably as a holdover from Baroque times, when the conductor played a keyboard instrument from the bass line.

Offstage instruments are often put in a place other than with the family(ies) of the instruments involved—for example, at the top of the score, or at the bottom, or in the "solo instruments" position.

Score order sometimes departs significantly from the arrangements shown, especially in works for small orchestra.

It has been mentioned that bar lines can be used to delineate families by being drawn through, but not between, them (as in Example 10-3). If there are not many representatives of each family, it may be practical to run bar lines all the way through the score without a break. This helps to delineate systems (lines of music) where there are more than one on a page.

Subsequent Pages

After the first page, the score can follow one of two general formats.

1. The "conductor's score," which has the same layout on every page, each instrument appearing in its proper location, whether or not it plays. This makes it unnecessary to give the name in the left margin, although it is helpful to do so, or to name the instrument when it enters for the first time on the page.
2. The "study score," which shows only the instruments that play on a given page: This makes it necessary to name the instruments, either in the left margin or at their entrances, with abbreviations after the first page.

Example 10-4a gives an example of the conductor's-score format; 10-4b gives the same music in study-score format. In this instance, the conductor's score presents a challenge when it comes to identifying the instruments that are playing: The strings are easily recognized because they are all represented at the bottom, but the clarinets are identifiable mostly by their key signature alone. Many conductor's scores use family brackets, which are very helpful, or at least brackets for like instruments (which in this case would help to identify the horns if there were

Example 10-4   Mendelssohn, *Hebrides* Overture, mm. 200–212

Example 10-4   *(continued)*

four of them). This conductor's score puts each woodwind instrument on a separate staff, which has both advantages and disadvantages. Such a format requires more staves per page, with the parts more spread-out and difficult to see as one; yet, it isolates each one with more individual clarity than if there were two parts on a staff.

Two Parts on a Staff

This is most practical when the instruments are of the same kind and when their parts are easily distinguishable (review the discussion of Examples 2-33, 3-2, and 3-3). Instruments that have different transpositions *cannot* be placed on the same staff. If one instrument sounds as written and the other does not, they should be put on the same staff only if their individual parts are identical and they are intended to sound in octaves. By this rule, Example 10-5a is acceptable, but Example 10-5b is not. Example 10-5c is even more objectionable, because the

Example 10-5

English horn sounds a perfect fifth lower than written, but the oboe does not. Such things may be found in scores, but they are unnecessarily difficult to read.

It sometimes happens that two like instruments, written on one staff, are so far apart in pitch that they must be put in separate clefs. This is most likely to happen with horns and is feasible only if the lower notes are distinctly lower on the staff than those of the upper instrument. See Example 10-6.

Example 10-6

Alignment

For the most part, *events that begin at the same time should be vertically aligned.* There is hardly anything that makes a score more difficult to read than symbols out of alignment. Example 10-7a gives an example of poor alignment, and 10-7b shows the correct version. (Computer software makes alignment an easy matter, but the mathematics of time values usually must be calculated by the user.)

If successive notes are spaced in a way that suggests their relative durations, the line will be easier to read: Example 10-8b is thus easier than 10-8a.

Example 10-7

Example 10-8

Rests and Beams

The way rests and beams are used can help or hinder the eye in understanding metrical and rhythmical units. If a metrical unit is partly filled with a rest or rests, the normal unit of subdivision is easier to read than multiples of it. Thus, the eighth rests in Example 10-9a are easier to read than the quarter rests and dotted quarters in 10-9b, and the quarter rests in 10-9c are easier to read than the half rests in 10-9d.

Example 10-9

Whenever a measure has no notes, a whole rest is placed in its center, no matter what the meter signature is. Half rests are aligned in the normal manner. However, it is becoming acceptable to omit rests entirely in such measures in the score, *but not in the parts.*

Beams are like bar lines—they help to group notes in metrical, rhythmical, or phrasing units. Example 10-10a suggests a two-tone grouping in the first two beats, 10-10b suggests a four-note grouping, and 10-10c suggests a one-note, then a three-note, grouping for the same notes.

Example 10-10

Dynamics

At the very beginning of every instrument's part (that is, where its first notes appear), or after a rest of two measures or more, there should be a dynamic marking—in short, the dynamic level of a part should be clear at all times. It is helpful to mark dynamics immediately after any crescendo or diminuendo. (Such details can save much rehearsal time!) A good example of scrupulous marking of dynamics can be found in Sibelius's Violin Concerto.

For instruments, dynamics are ordinarily written below the staff, and indications of *how* to play, such as "con sord." and "a 2," are written above. When two instruments are on the same staff, all indications for the upper instrument should go above, and all those for the lower instrument below. If there is not enough space to do this clearly, other solutions may be adopted, such as putting indications *on* the staff.

For vocal parts, text goes below the staff and all performance indications, including dynamics, go above it.

Articulation

For staves in which only one part is written and for passages in a 2, a 3, and so on (see Chapter 3, "Notating More than One Part on a Staff"), staccato or tenuto marks should be placed on the side of the notehead opposite that of the stem and between the notehead and any slurs, as in Example 10-11a. It follows that the slurs should be on the same side of the notehead as any staccato or tenuto marks. If some of the stems of notes under a slur are upward and others downward, it is easier to see the slur if it is placed *above* the staff. Accents, fermatas, and bow markings go above any slurs.

Example 10-11

When two parts are written at the same time with double-stem notation, articulation marks must be placed outside stems or beams, as in Example 10-11b.

For wind players, the composer can indicate breath marks as shown in Example 10-12.

Example 10-12

Meter Signatures and Tempo Changes

At the beginning of a composition, each staff should have a key signature, if there is one, followed by the meter signature. Thereafter, the key signature appears at the beginning of every line; the meter signature does not, unless the meter changes at that point. An alternative method is to place meter signatures in large figures through the staff area occupied by each family, as in Example 10-3.

Tempo markings and tempo changes, such as "rall." and "accel.," are usually placed just above the top staff and just above the first violin part, also as in Example 10-3. (All changes in *dynamics* must be marked in every part that is affected by them.)

Clef Changes

A change of clef should interfere as little as possible with the reading of notes and rests around it. The new clef should be smaller than normal. If the first note in the new clef comes at the beginning of a measure, the clef should precede the bar line. The clef should be relatively close, wherever the note comes, but if the note is off the beat, the clef is better placed before the rest that begins the beat (if there is one). See Example 10-13.

Example 10-13

Measure Numbers, Rehearsal Letters, and Rehearsal Numbers

In rehearsals, the conductor and the players often need to refer to specific locations in the music. The following are some common ways of marking them.

1. Number every measure.
2. Number every fifth or every tenth measure, etc.
3. Place rehearsal letters (in alphabetical order) at important points in the music, enclosed in a circle or a box. The letters can continue throughout a movement and begin over in the next movement, or, if there are many movements, they may be continued throughout the entire piece; e.g., if the letter *G* is the last letter in the first movement, *H* will be the first one in the second movement.
4. Use rehearsal numbers (1, 2, 3, etc.) instead of letters.
5. Use the measure number instead of a letter or a rehearsal number.

A combination of 1 and 3 is recommended, but each of the five has its advantages and disadvantages. For example, 2 is good for a quick count of measures between widespread locations, and 1 can give a cluttered appearance to the score. Measure numbers are often placed below the lowest staff.

Location markers can be vital when it comes to proofreading both score and parts.

Octave Signs

In the score, *8va* or *15ma* may be used, whenever practical, to keep parts from coming too close to one another. The sign *8ba* is not needed for any woodwind or string part. In the parts, octave signs should not be used for a wind instrument, and in both score and parts, they should not be used in alto or tenor clef.

Literal Repetitions and Doubling

When a figure is literally repeated, especially when it is one beat in duration, the repetitions can be symbolized with the shorthand shown in Examples 10-14a and 10- 4b. A repeated measure can be represented as in Example 10-14c. If there are several repetitions, it is helpful, in the parts, if they are numbered (starting with "2"), as in Example 10-14d. In the parts, a repetition of two or more measures can be represented as in Example 10-14e. If the measures have complicated configurations, it is better to use repeat signs and words—"Repeat five times," for example—but best for the player if they are written out each time.

Example 10-14

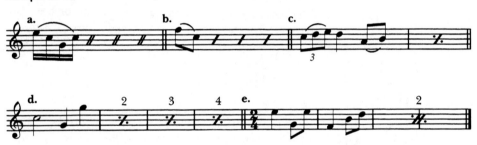

If parts on two or more staves are identical for several measures or more, one of them can be written out in full and the others marked as the violin 1 part is in Example 10-15.

Example 10-15

One line of score is called a system. If there are two or more systems on a page, they should be separated by at least one empty staff and the marks // and \\ at the beginning and the end of the system, respectively.

The Transposed Score

Transposed score was discussed in Chapter 9. Since about 1940, many composers have chosen to write "C scores"—scores in which all notes are written as they are to sound, except those meant to sound an octave higher or lower. If that is done, it should be mentioned either on a preliminary page or in a footnote on the first page. In some scores, all parts are meant to sound as written, including the piccolo, the contrabass, and the glockenspiel.

There are advantages and disadvantages to both C scores and transposed scores. The C score makes a complicated pitch structure easier to comprehend, but an experienced score reader has to resist the habit of mentally transposing parts, a habit acquired at great pains and still needed to read most scores. The transposed score is identical to the parts and thus is more easily used to copy them; it is also more readily associated with fingerings, and so on. The composer, then, should consider whether the pitch complexities of his or her work are severe enough that a C score is advisable. In any case, transposing instruments must have transposed parts.

The Parts

Each nonstring player should receive a separate part. There is good reason, however, for players of like wind instruments to have the part(s) of their colleagues included (on separate staves), so that they may serve as cues, help with coordination, or allow one to substitute momentarily for the other on occasion (say, for breathing purposes). Thus, for example, the second flute player might benefit from having the first flute's part as well as his or her own, and vice versa.

The first page of any part should have the name of the instrument in the upper left corner, the title at the top, centered, and the composer's name to the right. The first line is indented. There should be adequate room between staves for markings and notes that have ledger lines. Subsequent pages need give only the name of the instrument at the top. Often, parts have measure numbers only at the beginning of each line. The advantage of this is that it does not clutter up the music. The disadvantage is that a measure in the middle of a line is not quickly found, especially when it is in a long rest.

The standard size for parts is about 10 by 13 inches, with ten to twelve staves on a page. Like the score, the part should lie flat when placed on the stand.

Page Turns

For all but string parts, there must be rests at the end of a right-hand page so that there is time to turn the page. Even on string parts, this is advisable, because one player must stop playing to turn, and that momentarily reduces the strength of the section by half. Obviously, there should never be a divisi passage at the end of a right-hand page. If a rest sufficient for the turn happens to fall at the beginning of the next page, this should be shown in parentheses in the right margin at the end of the page to be turned so that both players can play all the notes. A common solution to the page-turn problem is to join the pages of the part in accordion fashion (end-to-end) so that the pages can be opened up three at a time. Although this allows three pages to be read before a turn is needed, it is bulky and still does not avoid turns completely.

Cues

The subject of cuing was discussed in Chapter 9. For the purpose of simply helping the player to come in at the right time, cues should be used as efficiently as possible.

1. They should be long enough for the player to get a sense of the line, but not so extensive that they interfere with the part to be played. (Some publications intersperse cue notes among the notes to be played. Although this can occasionally be helpful for coordinating parts, it can be a handicap when it is really not needed, and should be avoided. A better way to show other parts at the same time is to put them on the staff above or below.)
2. Cues should be recognizable. Soprano lines are easier to follow than inner ones, and faster-moving parts are generally more recognizable than slower-moving ones. Also, the closer to the player the cued instruments are on the stage, the more likely they are to be heard.
3. If there are long rests in the part, cues at important spots (usually at rehearsal letters, and the like) save the trouble of counting endless beats. See Example 10-16.

Cues should be used in vocal parts to help the singers find pitches at their entrances.

Cues are sometimes included in the score. This is recommended only if they are used for substitutions (see Chapter 9).

Example 10-16

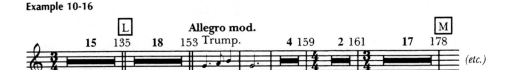

Long Rests

Long rests should be broken up to show important events and changes: any intervening rehearsal marks, changes of meter, and changes of tempo. See again Example 10-16.

If an instrument does not play at any time during a movement, "Movement [number] tacet" should be marked in large letters immediately below the last line of the previous movement or above the first line of the following movement. If the player has nothing to play for the last two lines or so of a movement, the part can be marked "tacet to end," followed by a wavy line through the staff.

Newer Practices

Following are some innovations that can be found in scores. They have not been universally adopted, and some seem to have been abandoned.

1. Portions of staves that have no music are omitted. See Example 10-17. (See also Stravinsky's *Requiem Canticles*.)

Example 10-17

2. If the same clef is used for successive staves, a vertical line shows this, as in Example 10-18 (and *Requiem Canticles*).
3. Only instruments that use more than one clef, such as the bassoon, the horn, the trombone, the viola, and the cello, are given clefs. (See Nono's *Intolleranza*.)
4. If two or more adjacent staves have the same marking, that marking is placed between or before the staves, followed by a brace, as in Example 10-19. (See also *Requiem Canticles* and Berio's *Still*.)

Example 10-18

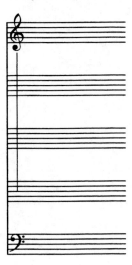

Example 10-19

5. Notes on adjacent staves that are in rhythmic unison share stems, as in Example 10-20 (and *Still*).

Example 10-20

6. Notes on different staves are connected by diagonal lines to show melodic connection, as in Example 10-21. (See Mahler's Symphony No. 7 and Prokofiev's *Alexander Nevsky*.)

Example 10-21

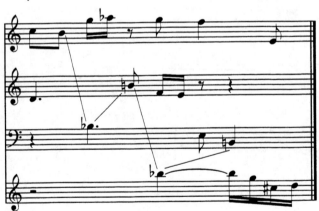

7. The same is done with stems (see Example 10-22 and Stravinsky's *Variations: Aldous Huxley in Memoriam*).

8. A diminuendo or a crescendo is shown across staves as instruments drop out or enter, as in Example 10-23. (See also Henze's Symphony No. 5.)

Example 10-22

Example 10-23

9. Rests are used only when absolutely necessary (Example 10-24 and *Intolleranza*). This format is difficult to read and should be discouraged.

Example 10-24

COMPUTER-MANAGED MUSIC PRINTING

It has become increasingly common for musicians to print music by means of commercially available software running on personal computers. A good source for such material is a yearly publication, *Computing in Musicology* (Center for Computer Assisted Research in the Humanities, 525 Middlefield Road, Suite 120, Menlo Park, CA 95025), which has a section called "Software for Printing Music." This lists reviews of software in journals, gives names and addresses of firms that produce it, and provides dozens of examples of a given musical excerpt, each printed with different software.

Software becomes more sophisticated and efficient year by year. It is possible to produce not only full scores but also individual parts taken from them with little additional work. The following are a few of the programs available.

1. *Finale* (Coda Music Software, Wenger Music Learning Systems, 1401 E. 79th St., Bloomington, MN 55420–1590). Available for the Apple Macintosh and the IBM PC.
2. *MusicPrinter Plus* (Temporal Acuity Products, Inc., 300 120th Avenue N.E., Bldg. 1, Bellevue, WA 98005).
3. *NoteWriter* (Passport Designs, 625 Miramontes, Half Moon Bay, CA 94019). Apple Macintosh.
4. *Encore* (Passport Designs). Macintosh, IBM PC. Scores and parts should be printed on a laser printer.
5. *Score* (Passport Designs). Input is alphanumeric and requires separate passes for pitch, rhythm, and articulation. IBM PC compatibles. *ScoreInput* (Passport also) allows Midi input.
6. *Nightingale* (Opcode Systems, 3641 Haven Ave., Menlo Park, CA 94025). Macintosh.

HAND-WRITTEN MANUSCRIPT

Manuscript paper of various sizes and for various uses can be ordered from the following companies.

1. Associated Music Copy Service (231 W. 54th St., New York, NY 10019)
2. Circle Blue Print (225 W. 57th St., New York, NY 10019)
3. Judy Green Music (1634 Cahuenga Blvd., Hollywood, CA 90028)
4. Valle Music Reproduction (12048 Ventura Blvd., North Hollywood, CA 91604)

These companies also make copies. Information regarding materials that are useful in preparing manuscript is available in recent books on manuscript preparation (see the Bibliography).

CHAPTER 11

Unusual Instrumental Techniques

Gardner Read's *Thesaurus of Orchestral Devices*, published in 1953, gives an extensive list of devices that were relatively unusual for that time: extremely high notes, double- , triple- , and flutter-tonguing, open and stopped horn, various mutes, and many others.[1] Most of those devices can now be included among the *usual* techniques of the instruments, since they have become more commonplace. In 1976, Read updated his catalog under the title *Contemporary Instrumental Techniques*, exhaustively listing new devices by instrumental family along with examples of compositions in which they can be found.[2] Read's book serves as a good supplement to this chapter, which does not have space for every detail of the topic.

As indicated in Chapter 7, the beginning of the twentieth century saw a search for new sounds in the form of new harmonies, new instrumental combinations, new instruments, and new uses of the old ones. Later decades have seen a similar development, especially the fifties and sixties. As before, the more avant-garde composers are the ones who are likely to use new instrumental sounds, which often appear in the context of tone clusters, dense polyphony, aleatoric passages, and taped or synthesized sound. Most examples can be found in solo or chamber music, where the composer is likely to be writing for specific performers whose abilities he or she knows and who may have invented some of the devices.

The rest of the chapter discusses various unusual techniques in each family of instruments.

---

[1]Gardner Read, *Thesaurus of Orchestral Devices* (New York: Pittman, 1953).
[2]Gardner Read, *Contemporary Instrumental Techniques* (New York: Schirmer Books, 1976).

STRINGS

Bowing

1. Playing behind the bridge, which gives a high squeak whose pitch will vary from instrument to instrument. The pitch ascends as one moves from the lowest to the highest string, but fingering is usually not involved. Arpeggios and multiple "stops" are common.
2. Playing on the bridge. This produces a barely audible scrape.
3. Drawing the bow on the opposite side of the fingers. This is feasible mostly on the I and IV strings, and the bow must be drawn close to the nut. The sound is weak, and the pitches that result are not what the player expects. Example 11-1 shows some fingered notes on the violin G string (below) and the approximate pitches of the result (above) when the bow is drawn behind the fingers. Using this as a guide, one can calculate the results on other strings or on other instruments. (For example, since the first fingered note shown is a perfect fourth above the open string and the sounding note is an octave and an augmented fifth above that, the comparable notes on the cello's D string would be *g* and *d♯¹*, respectively.)

Example 11-1   Bowing on the other side of the fingers

The lower notes are the notes produced with normal bow placement. The upper notes are approximately what are heard.

Violin, G String

4. Bowing *under* the strings. Strings I and IV can thus be played simultaneously.
5. *Scratch tone.* Bowing with great bow pressure and slow bow speed, which completely distorts the normal tone. With control, the player can produce a fairly clear pitch one octave lower than normal.
6. Playing on the tailpiece. This does not make much sound when the hair of the bow is used. Striking the tailpiece col legno can give a clicking and drumlike effect, especially on the lower instruments, but also can damage both the bow and the tailpiece.
7. Striking the bow against the strings without drawing it across them (in Mahler, "mit dem Bogen geschlagen"). It is effective with multiple stops and produces a brittle, rattling effect.
8. Striking the wood of the bow against the body of the instrument. It is not recommended, for obvious reasons.

Fingering

1. Damping the tone with the left-hand fingers to stop the decay.
2. Fingering without using the bow. The sound is a very weak slapping sound.
3. Striking the strings with the right hand. If the strings are not plucked at the same time, no clear pitch is produced—just a thump.

4. Playing with left-hand fingernails depressing the strings. This is feasible to the extent that the players allow their nails to grow long enough (nails must be kept short enough to allow the flesh of the fingertip to stop the string for normal playing). The result is a nasal sound.

5. Depressing the string only partway with the left-hand fingers. This gives a less-focused sound.

6. Tapping the body of the instrument at various places with the fingers or the hand. This yields various resonances and pitches but should be used sparingly. It is very effective on the lower instruments. Rubbing the body, especially with rosined fingers, should be discouraged.

7. Glissando with vibrato. A sobbing effect.

8. Scraping the string along its length with a fingernail. This produces a whistling sound whose pitch is relative to the range of the instrument.

Intonation

1. Microtones. This requires no special technique, but a good ear.

2. Scordatura: Abnormal tuning of one or more strings. Usually, the lowest string is tuned down. The tone becomes flabbier the lower it is detuned. The pitch can be altered while the string is being played, making a gliss. (If every one of the stringed instruments were tuned differently, it should be possible to sound a wide range of notes, all playable as open strings, which are clear and ringing. To the author's knowledge, this has not ever been done since Benjamin Franklin's String Quintet!)

Pizzicato

1. *Snap pizz.* The string strikes the fingerboard with a snapping buzz.

2. Plucking with the fingernail or a plectrum, producing a nasal, guitarlike sound.

3. *Slap pizz.* The pizz. is accompanied by a sharply percussive sound—most effective on the bass.

4. The *legato pizz.* (see Example 11-2) requires the first note to be plucked; the following notes are just fingered. It is more effective upward than downward, but either way the notes must follow quickly to be heard at all.

Example 11-2

5. Tremolo. A note is rapidly repeated by plucking with alternate fingers.

6. The *buzz pizz.* is accomplished by allowing the string to vibrate against a left-hand fingernail.

7. Plucked harmonics. The left-hand finger must be raised immediately after the note is plucked. On the viola and the violin, the effect is feasible only with the first natural harmonic (one octave above the open string). It resembles an electronic chime.

Other effects have been developed for the double bass, whose large dimensions and resonance allow them better than do the other instruments. See Turetzky in the Bibliography.

Penderecki's *Threnody* for strings offers a study in new effects, along with an explanation of the notational symbols used. See Example 9-3.

WINDS

Many techniques are possible on both woodwinds and brass.

Pitch

1. *Microtones* require special fingerings, embouchure control, or both, that can be left to the player to manage. The trombone is the most natural instrument for this, since its pitches are not limited by fixed tube lengths.
2. *Multiphonics.* Woodwind instruments are capable, within limits, of sounding more than one pitch at the same time. (See Bartolozzi in the Bibliography.) It is recommended that only the desired pitch *area* be given. The effect is generally dissonant, rough, and unstable. It is possible to slur from one to another, and even to trill. Chordal effects can be gotten from both woodwinds and brass by playing one note and humming another, so that combination tones (other notes that are harmonically related) are also heard.
3. The *timbral trill* is a rapid alternation between two fingerings for the same pitch. This is possible mostly for higher notes. The fingerings give different timbres and may also give slightly different pitches.
4. The *double trill* is the same trill played with both hands—possible on woodwinds, especially the clarinet, that have trill keys. The trills move at different speeds.
5. A note below the range of the instrument can be played by inserting a tube of cardboard or rolled-up paper, or the like, in the bell. The tone loses some quality and power, and it is not feasible to play upper notes while the extension is in place.

Embouchure Modification

1. *Air tones* are produced by blowing into the instrument while bypassing the usual vibrating body—the edge of the flute's embouchure plate, the reeds of the other woodwinds, and the tensed lips of the brass player. The sound is a gushing whoosh or hiss. It can be combined with other effects, such as flutter-tonguing, as well as normally played notes.
2. *Whistle tones* are playable on the flutes and the clarinets by modifying the airstream so that the sound is a pale ghost of the normal tone.
3. *Smorzato* is an intensity vibrato on the clarinet and double reeds that is made with the jaw.
4. *Buzz tones* are possible on the flutes (other than the piccolo): The player blows into the mouthpiece instead of against the edge, using the lips as a brass player does. The pitches go below the usual range.
5. *Slap tongue* involves a forceful release of the tongue, adding a percussive ending to the tone.

6. *Smack tone* or kiss. The double-reed or brass player sucks noisily on the reed/mouthpiece.
7. Whispering, growling, singing, or speaking into the instrument.

Manipulation of the Instrument

1. *Key or valve clicks or slaps.* The key(s) or valve(s) is (are) forced down hard enough to make a sound, with or without breath. Pitches can be heard if all holes are covered. It is especially effective on the flute and the saxophone.
2. Playing on the reed or mouthpiece alone. On reeds, this gives a squawking sound with unstable pitch. Brass mouthpieces yield a prominent buzz.
3. Attaching reeds or mouthpieces to other instruments. The results are often novel and surprising.
4. Playing on parts of instruments. The reed or a section of the instrument can be removed. The head joint of the flute can be played separately, with the right hand closing the opening or with fingers inserted to modify the pitch. The trombone can be played with either the slide section or the F slide out. Both are less resonant than normal.
5. *Mouthpiece, barrel, or slide pop.* The hand is slapped against the mouthpiece by itself, the open barrel, or an open portion of the trombone.
6. The valve slide of a brass instrument can be pulled out, making a popping noise. On the trombone, this can be quite loud.
7. Brass instruments can be tapped (usually on the bell) with various objects, or a comb can be rattled inside the bell.

PERCUSSION

The technique of most percussion instruments has been so widely explored that a good deal of what would have been considered novel in 1953 is fairly standard now and has been covered in Chapter 5. Many of the present novelties involve new striking implements, such as switches (as early as Mahler) and brooms. Other sources of novelty are everyday objects, some of which have become almost standard, such as glasses, anvils, and brake drums. Another is the striking of one instrument with another. The sky continues to be the limit!

THE HARP

Some techniques were mentioned in Chapter 6. Here are some others.

1. "Falling hail" (from Salzedo): Slow fingernail glisses in both directions at once.
2. Scraping the strings lengthwise with a fingernail.
3. Muting with one hand while playing with the other.
4. Putting the pedal halfway between the slots, causing the string to buzz.
5. A true pitch gliss by detuning the string with the tuning key. This should not extend more than about a semitone upward or a major second downward.
6. Microtonal tunings are, of course, possible on the harp with the tuning key, but microtonal *changes* with the pedal are not.

7. Placing paper or similar fabric between the strings so that they buzz against it.
8. Vibrato created by alternations of pressure at the upper end of the string (indicated by "V" and a wavy line.

THE PIANO

The sight of a pianist reaching inside the piano has become rather common in performances of new music. The instrument, being so large and resonant and having so many parts, is a rich source of interesting sounds. The following are some inside-the-piano techniques.

1. Plucking strings with or without the key being depressed and with the flesh of the fingertip, with the fingernail, or with a plectrum.
2. Striking, plucking, or stroking the strings glissando-fashion. Any keys that are depressed will cause those notes to resonate, no matter which strings are plucked or struck. Hands or mallets can be used with good effect.
3. Touching strings lightly at nodes and playing the note with the key, producing a harmonic. This has become common and is quite effective, but it cannot be accomplished quickly.
4. Objects can be laid over, woven into, or wedged between the strings to alter their pitch and timbre. John Cage's Sonatas and Interludes for Prepared Piano are early examples of the possibilities: The instrument can be made to sound remarkably like a whole array of percussion instruments of varying pitch, timbre, and resonance.
5. A rosined cord can be threaded into the strings to "bow" them.
6. Various surfaces, both inside and outside the instrument, can be rapped with the knuckles.

AMPLIFICATION

Any instrument can be amplified, using contact or freestanding microphones, and the sound can be modified by a synthesizer. Plain amplification is sometimes used to reinforce a relatively weak instrument, such as the harpsichord, or for instrumental effects that are not sufficiently strong in themselves. It should be noted that amplification also alters the original *timbre* and *direction* of the sound. With regard to the latter, if the speakers are placed overhead and to the side of the stage, or at least at one side of the stage, the amplified sound might be separated unnaturally from the rest of the orchestra.

AFTERWORD

It is well to be aware of possible problems with some newer devices.

1. Many produce sounds that are difficult to integrate with rest of the orchestral fabric, and thus are often used alone. They might sound like mere effects, on display as at an exhibition.
2. Most orchestral players have to learn some of these techniques without benefit of hav-

ing heard them or seen them demonstrated. (Indeed, many string players still do not adequately execute "sul ponticello" or "sul tasto"!)

3. Some devices may be either too soft or too little different from normal playing to be effective in the orchestra.

These problems are mentioned not to discourage but to remind the student that although any kind of sound is potentially useful in music, it must be part of an integrated whole for the result to be satisfactory, and one must resist the temptation just to show off one's knowledge. In most cases, it is wise for the composer to ask a professional to demonstrate the effect before attempting to use it and, equally important, to determine if it might damage the instrument. But a new sound that is playable and "right" in its context is very much to be welcomed!

Fingering Charts
for Stringed Instruments

VIOLIN

Numbers are for fingers in each position.

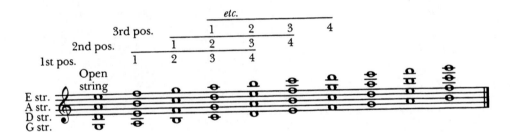

VIOLA

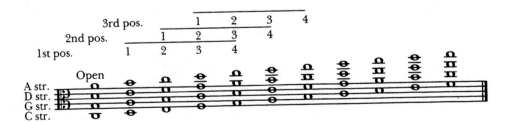

CELLO

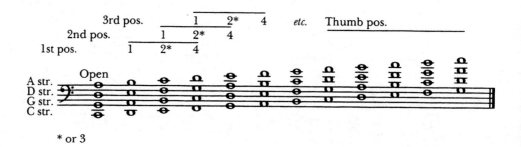

* or 3

BASS

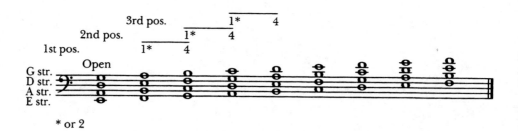

* or 2

APPENDIX **B**

Woodwind Fingering Charts

FLUTE

Schematic fingering diagram (approximate location of keys):

T [B♭ B♮]
1
2
3
G♯
B♭ tr
1
D tr
2
D♯ tr
3
D♯
C♯
C
B

T	T	T	T	T	T	T	T	T	T	T	T	B♮			T	T	T	T	T
1	1	1	1	1	1	1	1	1	1	1	1	1	1				1	1	1
2	2	2	2	2	2	2	2	2	2	2					2	2	2	2	2
3	3	3	3	3	3	3	3	3	3						3	3	3	3	3
									G♯										
—	—	—	—	—	—	—	—	—	—	—	—	—	—	—	—	—	—	—	—
1	1	1	1	1	1	1					1				1	1	1	1	
2	2	2	2	2	2										2	2	2		
3	3	3	3	3			3								3	3			3
B	C	C♯		D♯	D♯	D♯	D♯	D♯	D♯	D♯	D♯	D♯	D♯	D♯		D♯	D♯	D♯	D♯

```
     T   T   T   T   B♮       T   T   T   T   T           T   T   T           T
     1   1   1   1   1   1        1   1   1   1   1            1   1
     2   2   2                2   2   2           2   2   2                2   2
     3   3                    3   3       3   3   3   3            3   3           3
     _   G♯  _   _   _   _   _   _   G♯  _   _   _   G♯  _   _   _   G♯  _   _
                 1                    1   1   1            1   1        1   1   1
                                      2   2                                    2
                                      3                3
    D♯  D♯  D♯  D♯  D♯  D♯  D♯  D♯  D♯  D♯  D♯  D♯  D♯  D♯  D♯      D♯ tr
                                      3
                                      D♯
```

This and the other charts give only one fingering for each note, whereas for many notes, there are alternative fingerings that can be used for better connections between notes, better intonation, or better quality. The fingering given is "basic."

Note: "T" = Thumb. Symbols above the line are fingerings for the left hand and those below the line for the right hand. "1" is the first finger, and so on.

OBOE

Schematic diagram:

```
81 82
   1
   B tr
   D tr
   2
   C♯ tr
   3
   G♯
   B
   D♯
   B♭
   F
   A tr
   G♯
   1
   D tr
   2
   F
   3
   C
   C♯
   D♯
```

First fingering chart:

```
1   1   1   1   1   1   1   1   1   1   1   1   1   1   1   /   /   /
2   2   2   2   2   2   2   2   2   2   2   2   2               2   2   2
3   3   3   3   3   3   3   3   3   3   3                       3   3   3
Bb  B   _   _   _   D#  _   _   _   _   G#  _   _   _   _   _   _   D#
1   1   1   1   1   1   1   1   1   _       1   _   1   1   1   1
2   2   2   2   2   2   2   2                                   2   2   2
3   3   3   3   3   3       F                                   3   3   3
C   C   C   C#                                                 C#
```

Second fingering chart:

```
81  81  81  81  81  82  82  82  82  82  /   /   81  81  81  81  81  81
1   1   1   1   1   1   1   1   1   1               /   /   Btr 1   1   1
2   2   2   2   2   2   2   2           2   2   2   2   1
3   3   3   3   3                       3   3   3       2   3   3   3
                        G#              B   G#  G#                  B   B
_   _   _   _   _   _   _   _   _   _   _   _                   _   _   G#
1   1   1       1       1   1                   1   1           2   2
2   2                                   2   2   2               3   3
    F                                   3   3   3                   D#
                                        D#  D#
```

Note: "/" = half-hole; "81" = octave key 1; "82" = octave key 2.

CLARINET

Schematic diagram:

```
        8
        T
        A
        G#
        1
        2
        Eb tr
        3
        B tr
     Bb tr C#
     F# tr F
        E
        Eb F#
        1
        2
```

B tr
3
F#
G#
E
F

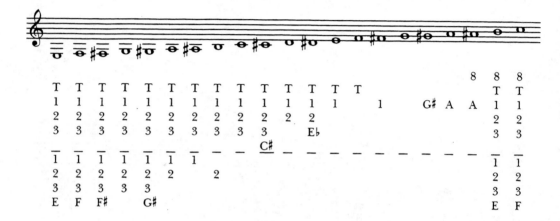

```
                                                                                8   8   8
T   T   T   T   T   T   T   T   T   T   T   T   T   T                            T   T
1   1   1   1   1   1   1   1   1   1   1   1   1              1        G#  A   A  1   1
2   2   2   2   2   2   2   2   2   2   2   2                                     2   2
3   3   3   3   3   3   3   3   3   3      Eb                                     3   3
                                      C#
1   1   1   1   1   1   1                                                        1   1
2   2   2   2   2   2       2                                                    2   2
3   3   3   3   3                                                               3   3
E   F   F#          G#                                                          E   F
```

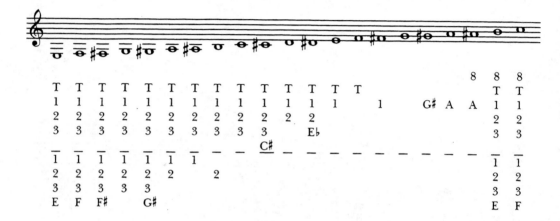

```
8   8   8   8   8   8   8   8   8   8   8   8   8   8   8   8   8   8   8   8   8
T   T   T   T   T   T   T   T   T   T   T   T   T   T   T   T   T   T   T   T   T
1   1   1   1   1   1   1   1   1   1   1
2   2   2   2   2   2   2   2   2       2   2   2   2   2   2   2   2   2
3   3   3   3   3   3   3   3   3               3   3   3   3   3       3   3
                                C#      Eb                      C#
1   1   1   1   1                           1   1   1               1   1
2   2   2   2       2                       2   G#  B tr           2   B tr
3   3   3                                       G#  G#  G#  G#  G#  G#
F#          G#
```

Note: "T" = thumb; "8" = octave key.

BASSOON

Schematic diagram:

```
              1
    Bb        D s
    F# tr B   B s
              C
    D         A s  2
              C#
```

cr
3
Eb
Db
—
C# tr
1
Bb
E 2
F#
Bb tr
Ab
3
F
F#
Ab

	Bb					D														C#		
B	B	C	C	D	D		cr	cr	cr	cr	cr	cr	cr	cr	cr	cr	cr	cr	cr	cr	cr	cr
1	1	1	1	1	1	1	1	1	1	1	1	1	1	1	1	1	1	1	/	/	/
2	2	2	2	2	2	2	2	2	2	2	2	2	2	2	2	2			2	2	2
3	3	3	3	3	3	3	3	3	3	3	3	3	3	3	3		3		3	3	3

E̅	E̅	E̅	C#̅ E̅	E̅	Eb̅ E̅	E̅	—	F#̅	—	—	Bb̅	—			F#̅		
1	1	1	1	1	1	1	1	1	1	1	1	1		1	1	1
2	2	2	2	2	2	2	2	2	2	2	2			2	2	2
3	3	3	3	3	3	3	3	3	3					3	3	3
F	F	F	F	F	F	F	F		Ab								Ab

			D C#								A C#	A C#	B	B	B	D	D F#	C# F#
1	1	1	1	1	1	1	1	1		/	/	1	1	1	1	1		
2	2	2	2	2	2	2			2	2	2	2	2	2				2
3	3	3	3	3			3	3	3	3	3	3	3		3	3	3	3

—	Bb̅	—	—	—	—	—	—	Bb̅	—	—	Bb̅	Bb̅	—			F#̅ C#
1	1	1			1	1	1	1			1	1	1			Ab
2	2			2	2	2	2	F		2	2	2			
				3	3				3	3	3		3	3	3
											F	F	F	F	F	F

Note: "s" = speaker key; "cr" = crook key; "/" = half-hole.

SAXOPHONE

Schematic diagram:

```
8
F  Eb
T
1    D
2    F
3
G#
Bb
────────
E
C
Bb
1
2
F# tr
3
Eb
C
```

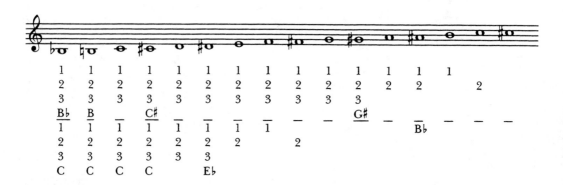

Fingering Charts
for Brass Instruments

Except for the trombones, only one fingering is given for each note, whereas there are alternative fingerings for many notes. The fingering is "basic."

HORN IN F/B-FLAT

Notation is for F horn. T puts the horn into B-flat.

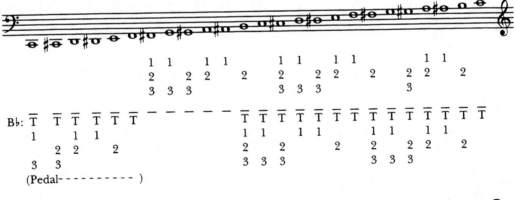

TRUMPET

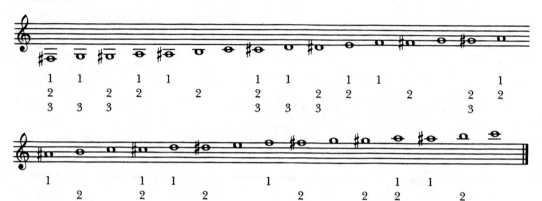

TROMBONE (TENOR AND BASS)

Note: "X" = not available; "F" = with F valve; "E" = with E valve.

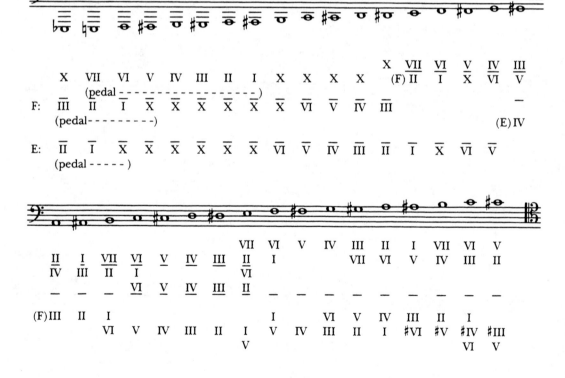

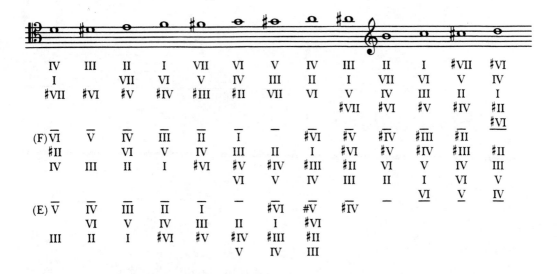

IV	III	II	I	VII	VI	V	IV	III	II	I	♯VII	♯VI
I		VII	VI	V	IV	III	II	I	VII	VI	V	IV
♯VII	♯VI	♯V	♯IV	♯III	♯II	VII	VI	V	IV	III	II	I
								♯VII	♯VI	♯V	♯IV	♯II
												♯VI

(F) V̄I	V̄	ĪV	ĪII	ĪI	Ī	‒	♯V̄I	♯V̄	♯ĪV	♯ĪII	♯ĪI	
♯II		VI	V	IV	III	II	I	♯VI	♯V	♯IV	♯III	♯II
IV	III	II	I	♯VI	♯V	♯IV	♯III	♯II	VI	V	IV	III
					VI	V	IV	III	II	I	VI	V
										V̲I	V̲	I̲V̲

(E) V̄	ĪV	ĪII	ĪI	Ī	‒	♯V̄I	#V̄	♯ĪV	
	VI	V	IV	III	II	I	♯VI		
III	II	I	♯VI	♯V	♯IV	♯III	♯II		
				V	IV	III			

BB♭ TUBA

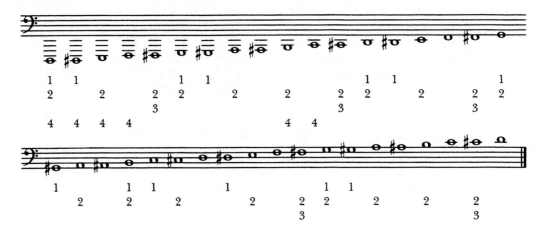

1	1			1	1			1	1			1
2		2		2	2		2	2	2		2	2
			3					3			3	
4	4	4	4			4	4					

1		1	1		1		1	1	
	2	2	2	2	2	2	2	2	2
						3			3

Foreign Terms

PITCH NAMES

In German, *B* is the English B-flat and *H* the English B-natural. The ending *-es* is the English *flat* and *-is* the English *sharp*. Thus, the German *Des* is D-flat and *Fis* F-sharp in English, with the exceptions that E-flat is *Es* in German and A-flat is *As*. The German for *double flat* is *eses*, and for *double sharp*, it is *isis*. The French and the Italians use solfège syllables instead of letters for pitch names: C is *do* for the Italians and *ut* for the French; D is *re* for both, and so on to B = *si*. The word *flat* is *bémol* for the French and *bemolle* for the Italians, and *sharp* is *dièse* for the French and *diesis* for the Italians. For double sharps and flats, the French precede the respective words with *double* and the Italians with *doppio*.

Examples:

ENGLISH	GERMAN	FRENCH	ITALIAN
G-sharp	Gis	sol dièse	sol diesis
B-flat	B	si bémol	si bemolle
c-double sharp	Cisis	ut double-dièse	do doppio diesis

WORDS

A

ab Off

Abstrich Downbow

acciaio Steel

accordoir Tuning key

acuto High

a filo At the edge

agitar Shake

agité Shaken

agogo A type of cowbell

à la corde Bowed on the string

al centro At the center

alla corda Bowed on the string

allein Alone

Alt Alto

alta High

Altflöte Alto flute

Althorn Alto horn

Altklarinette Alto clarinet
alto Viola, alto
Altsaxophone Alto saxophone
Amboss Anvil
am Rande At the edge
anche Reed
ancia Reed
appeau Bird whistle
arcata in giù Downbow
arcata in su Upbow
archet Bow
archi Stringed instruments
arco Bow
arpa Harp
au bord At the edge
aufgehängt Suspended
Aufstrich Upbow
Auto Huppe Auto horn
avec plateaux Crash cymbals

B

baccheta Stick
baguette Stick
baguettes de bois suspendus Wooden wind chimes
baguettes de verre suspendus Glass wind chimes
baguettes metalliques suspendus Metal wind chimes
Bambusrohre Bamboo wind chimes
Bambustrommeln Boobams
Baritonsaxophon Bariton saxophone
bas Low
baskische Trommel Tambourine
basque Trommel Tambourine
Bassetthorn Basset horn
Baßflöte Bass flute
Baßklarinette Bass clarinet
basso Low, bass
basson Bassoon
Baßsaxophon Bass saxophone
Baßtrompete Bass trumpet
batintin Gong
battente Beater
battere To strike

batteria Percussion
batterie Percussion
Becken Cymbals
Becken frei Suspended cymbals
Becken hängend Suspended cymbals
beide Both
Besin Wire brush
bicchieri di vetro Glasses
bisbigliato Whispered
blasen To blow
Bläser Wind instruments
Blechinstrumente Brass instruments
Blechtrommel Steel drum
bloc Block
blocchi Blocks
blocchi di legno cinese Woodblocks
bloc chinois Woodblock
bloc de bois Woodblock
bocca Mouth
bocchino Mouthpiece
Bogen Bow
Bogenstange The wood of the bow
bois Wood
bord Rim
bordo Rim
bottiglie Bottles
bouche Mouth
bouteilles Bottles
Bratsche Viola
Brettenklappe Slapstick
brosse Brush
Brummtopf Lion's roar
bubolo Jingles
bugle alto Alto horn
bugle à pistons Flugelhorn
buttiba Friction drum

C

Cabaza Cabasa
caccavella Friction drum
cadenas Chains
caisse Drum, shell
caisse claire Snare drum
caisse roulante Side drum, parade drum

calabasse   Cabasa
campana   Bell
campanaccio   Cowbell
campana di legno   Temple block
campane tubolari   Chimes
campane da gregge   Cowbells
campane da pastore   Cowbells
campanelle de vacca   Cowbells
campanelli   Glockenspiel
campanelli da mucca   Cowbells
caoutehouc   Rubber
carillon   Glockenspiel
carta sabbiata   Sandpaper blocks
carta vetrata   Sandpaper blocks
cascabel   Sleigh bells
cassa   Drum, shell
cassa chiara   Snare drum
cassa di legno   Woodblock
cassa di metallo   Cowbell
cassa grande   Bass drum
cassa rullante   Military drum, parade drum
cassa sordo   Military drum, parade drum
cassetina   Woodblock
castagnetta   Castanet
castagnette de fero   Metal castanet
Castagnetten   Castanets
catene   Chains
catuba   Bass drum
cencerros   Cowbells
centre   Center
centro   Center
cepillos metal   Wire brushes
ceppi cinesi   Temple blocks
ceppi de carta vestro   Sandpaper blocks
cerchio   Rim
chaîns   Chaines
charleston   Hi-hat
chevalet   Bridge (of a stringed instrument)
chiave   Key
chiave per accordare   Tuning key
chinesische Becken   Chinese cymbals
chinoise   Chinese
chiuso   Closed, stopped
chucoté   Whispered

cimbali antichi   Antique cymbals
cimbalini   Antique cymbals
cimbalo   Cymbal
cimbalos crapulosos   Suspended cymbals
cimbalos dedos   Finger cymbals
cimbalo suspendo   Suspended cymbal
cinelli   Cymbals
cinelli dito   Finger cymbals
cinesi   Chinese
clagnebois   Xylophone
Clapper   Slapstick
claque bois   Xylophone
clarinette   Clarinet
clarinette alto   Alto clarinet
clarinette basse   Bass clarinet
clarinette contre-alto   Contralto clarinet
clarinette contrebasse   Contrabass clarinet
clarinetto   Clarinet
clarinetto alto   Alto clarinet
clarinetto contra-alto   Contralto clarinet
clarinetto contrabasso   Contrabass clarinet
clarinetto basso   Bass clarinet
clavier   Keyboard, keyboard instrument
clef   Key
cliquette   Slapstick
cloche de vache   Cowbell
cloche double   Agogo bells
cloche en lame de metal   Bell plate
cloches   Chimes
cloches plaques   Bell plates
clochettes   Glockenspiel, cup bells, bell tree
clochettes à main   Handbells
col   With the
colle mazzette   With soft beaters
colle unghie   With the fingernails
colpi   Strokes
col pugno   With the fist
con   With
con cordes   Snares on
con le dita   With the fingers
con le mani   With the hands
contrabasso   Contrabass
contrafagotto   Contrabassoon
contrebasse   Contrabass

contrebasse à pistons   Tuba
contrebasson   Contrabassoon
coperto(i)   Covered, muffled
cor   Horn
cor anglais   English horn
corde   String, snare
cor de basset   Basset horn
corde de tamburo lasciare   Snares off
cordes pincés   Plucked instruments
cordier   Tailpiece
coreani   Temple blocks
cornet à pistons   Cornet
cornetta   Cornet
cornetta a pistoni   Cornet
corno   Horn
corno di bassetto   Basset horn
corno di vacca   Cowhorn
corno inglese   English horn
coulisse   Slide
couvert   Covered, stopped
crécelle   Ratchet
cri-cri   Bird call
cuero   Leather
cuir   Leather
cuivré   Brassy
cuivres   Brass instruments
cupola   Crown
cymbale   Cymbal
cymbale doigté   Finger cymbal
cymbales avec plateaux   crash cymbals
cymbales de concert   Crash cymbals
cymbales digitales   Finger cymbals
cymbale sur tiges   Sizzle cymbal
cymballettes   Jingles

D

dämpfen   Mute, muffle
Dämpfer   Mute
Daumen   Thumb
d'eponge   Of sponge
destra   Right
detimbrée   Snares off
deux   Two
dito   Finger

doigt   Finger
Donnerblech   Thunder sheet
Donnermaschine   Thunder machine
Doppelgriff   Double stop
Doppelzunge   Double-tongue
doppio colpo   Double-tongue
doppio corda   Double stop
double articulation   Double-tongue
doubles cordes   Double stops
douce   Soft
Drahtburste   Wire brush
droite   Right
due   Two
dumpf   Muffled
Dur   Major
duro   Hard

E

echelette   Xylophone
ein   One
einfell   Single-headed
eisen   Iron
embouchure   Mouthpiece
enclume   Anvil
Englischhorn   English horn
entspannt   Loosened
eolifono   Wind machine
èponge   Sponge
étouffé   Choked, damped
eufonio   Euphonium

F

Fagott   Bassoon
fagotto   Bassoon
Faust   Fist
Fell   Drumhead
feltro   Felt
fer   Iron
ferro   Iron
feutre   Felt
fiati   Wind instruments
fieltro   Felt
Filzschlägel   Felt stick
Fingerzimbeln   Finger cymbals
fischi   Whistle

fischiare   To whistle
fischietto a pallina   Police whistle
flagello   Slapstick
flageolet   Harmonic
Flageolet   Harmonic
Flaschen   Bottles
Flatterzunge   Flutter-tongue
flauto   Flute
flauto a culisse   Slide whistle
flauto basso   Bass flute
flauto contralto   Alto flute
flauto piccolo   Piccolo
flessatono   Flexatone
flicorno   Flugelhorn
flicorno basso   Euphonium
flicorno contralto   Alto horn
Flöte   Flute
Flügel   Grand piano
flüsternd   Whispering
flûte alto   Alto flute
flûte basse   Bass flute
Fortepedal   Damper pedal
fouet   Slapstick
frapper   To strike
fregare   To rub, brush
frei   Free, suspended
freihängend   Suspended
Frosch   Frog (of the bow)
frotter   To rub
frullato   Flutter-tongue
frusta   Slapstick
Fußbecken   Hi-hat
fusta   Slapstick

G

Gabelbecken   Metal castanets
Garn   Yarn
Geige   Violin
gerader Dämpfer   Straight mute
gestopft   Stopped
gestrichen   Bowed on the string
gettando   Jeté
gezupft   Plucked
giapponese   Japanese

Glas   Glass
Gläserspiel   Glasses
Glaspapier   Sandpaper
Glasstäbe   Glass wind chimes
Glas-Windglocken   Glass wind chimes
gli altri   The others
gli uccelli   Bird whistle
Glocken   Chimes
Glockenplatten   Bell plates
Gongstrommel   Steel drum
gran cassa   Bass drum
grande   Large
grand tambour   Bass drum
gran tamburo   Bass drum
grave   Low
gregge   Cowbells
grelots   Sleigh bells
Griffbrett   Fingerboard
Grille   Birdcall
grillo   Birdcall
grillon   Birdcall
grosse caisse   Bass drum
Grosse Trommel   Bass drum
guitcharo   Guiro
gummi   Rubber

H

Hackbrett   Dulcimer
halb   Half
Hals   Neck (of a stringed instrument)
Handglockenspiel   Handbells
Handtrommel   Tambourine, bongo
Hanf   Yarn
Hängebecken   Suspended cymbals
Harfe   Harp
harpe   Harp
hart   Hard
hautbois   Oboe
hautbois d'amour   Oboe d'amore
Herdenglocken   Cowbells
hoch   High
hochet   Rattle
Holz   Wood
Holzblock   Woodblock

Holzblocktrommel　Woodblock
Holzharmonika　Xylophone
Holzkasten　Woodblocks
Holzklapper　Slapstick
Holzrand　Rattle
Holzraspel　Reco-reco
Holzschlägel　Wood stick
Holztrommel　Log drum
Holz-windglocken　Wood wind chimes
Huppe　Klaxon horn

I

immer　Always, sempre
incudine　Anvil
Indisch　Indian
instruments à cordes　Stringed instruments

J

Jazzbesen　Wire brushes
jeu de cloches　Chimes
jeu de clochettes　Glockenspiel
jeu de timbres　Keyed glockenspiel

K

Kastagnetten　Castanets
Kesselpauken　Timpani
Ketten　Chains
Kinder-　Toy
Kinderklavier　Toy piano
Klappe　Key (on a woodwind instrument)
Klapper　Slapstick, ratchet
Klappholz　Slapstick, ratchet
Klarinette　Clarinet
Klaviatur　Keyboard
Klavier　Keyboard, piano
klein　Small
kleiner Bass　Euphonium
kleine Trommel　Snare drum
klingen lassen　Let vibrate
Klöppel　Stick, bass drum beater
Knarre　Ratchet, rattle
Knie　Knee
Knochenklapper　Slapstick
Kontra-Altklarinette　Contralto clarinet
Kontrabass　Contrabass

Kontrabassklarinette　Contrabass clarinet
Kontrafagott　Contrabassoon
Konzert-Trommel　Snare drum
Kork　Cork
Kornett　Cornet
Krotalen　Crotales
Kuba-Pauken　Timbales
Kuhglocke　Cowbells
Kundstoff　plastic
künstlische Flageolett-Ton　Artificial harmonic
Kürbisraspel　Guiro
kurz　Short

L

labbri　Lips
Landknechtstrommel　Long drum
lang　Long
langue　Tongue
lasciare vibrare　Let vibrate
lasci vibrare　Let vibrate
lastra　Sheet
lastra del tuono　Thunder sheet
lastra di latta　Thunder sheet
lastra di metallo　Metal plate
Leder　Leather
légère　Light
leggiera, o　Light
legnetti　Claves
legni di rumba　Claves
legno　Wood
legno del' arco　The wood of the bow
leicht　Light
Leise-Pedal　Soft pedal
lero-lero　Reco-reco
levres　Lips
libres cymbales　Suspended cymbals
Liebesoboe　Oboe d'amore
lingua　Tongue
Lippen　Lips
l'ongle　Fingernail
Lotosflöte　Slide whistle
lourd　Heavy
Löwengebrüll　Lion's roar

M

macchina dal ventro Wind machine
macchina di tuono Thunder machine
machine à vent Wind machine
machine à venti Wind machine
madera Wood
maglio Heavy mallet
mailloche Bass drum beater
main Hand
manche Neck (of a stringed instrument)
manico Neck (of a stringed instrument)
mano Hand
maraca de métal Metal rattle
maraca di metallo Metal rattle
marache Maracas
margine Edge
Marimbaphon Marimba
marteau Hammer
martello Hammer
mascella d'asino Jawbone
mazza Bass drum beater
mazzette Bass drum beater
medio Medium
Mehrklang Multiphonic
Messing Brass
meta Half
Metallblock Anvil
Metallfolie Thunder sheet
Metallgefässrassel Metal rattle
Metallkasten Anvil
Metallraspel Metal scraper
Metallschlägel Metal beater
mettre To place, put on
mezzo Medium
Militartrommel Military drum
mineur Minor
mit With
Mitte Center
mittel Medium
Mittelpedal Sostenuto pedal
Moderatorpedal Soft pedal
mokugyo Temple block
Moll Minor

molle Soft
molto Much, very
morache Wooden rasp
morbido Soft
moteur Motor
moyen Medium
multifonico Multiphonic
multiphonique Multiphonic
Mund Mouth
Mundstück Mouthpiece
Muschelpendelrassel Shell wind chimes
Muschelwindglocken Shell wind chimes
muta Change

N

nacchera Castanets
nacchera cilindrica Woodblock
Nachtigallenpfeife Water whistle (nightingale)
Nagel Fingernail
narucco Wooden wind chimes
naturale In the normal manner
Nietenbecken Sizzle cymbals
nocche Knuckles
noix de coco Maracas

O

offen Open
ohne Without
ongle Fingernail
organo di legno Xylophone
oscillato Motor on
ôter Take off
ottavino Piccolo
ottone Brass

P

pandereta brasiliana Jingles
papier de verre Sandpaper
Paradetrommel Parade drum
patuoilles Xylophone
Pauken Timpani
Paukenschlägel Timpani stick
pavillon Bell
peau Skin, drumhead
pédale centrale Sostenuto pedal

pedale centrale Sostenuto pedal
pedale del piano Soft pedal
pedale di risonanza Damper pedal
pédale forte Damper pedal
Pedalton Pedal tone
Peitsche Slapstick
Peitschenknall Slapstick
pelle Skin, drumhead
Pendelrassel Wind chimes
percuotere To strike
percuter To strike
petit Small
petite flûte Piccolo
petite trompette Piccolo trumpet
petit tambour Snare drum
pfeifen To whistle
Pianino Upright piano
piano à queue Grand piano
piano des enfants Toy piano
piano droit Upright piano
pianoforte à coda Grand piano
pianoforte dei bambini Toy piano
pianoforte vertical Upright piano
piatti Cymbals
piatti à pedale Hi-hat
piatti da concerto Crash cymbals
piatto chiodat Sizzle cymbal
piatto cinese Chinese cymbal
piccole campani Cup bells
piccolo Small
piccolo cassa Small drum
Pikkolotrommel Piccolo snare drum
pincé Plucked
Pistolenschoss Pistol shot
pistolettata Pistol shot
Piston Cornet
pistoni Pistons, valves
pistons Pistons, valves
plaque de métal Steel plates
plaque de tonnerre Thunder sheet
Plattenglocke Bell plate
plectre Plectrum
Plektrum Plectrum

plettro Plectrum
pointe Tip of the bow
Polizeiflöte Police whistle
pollice Thumb
pompa mobile à coulisse Slide
Posaune Trombone
pouce Thumb
poussé Upbow
profond Low
profondo Low
provençal tambourin Tabor
punta Tip of the bow

Q

Quadrupelgriff Quadruple stop
quadrupla corda Quadruple stops
quadruples cordes Quadruple stops
quica Lion's roar
quijada Jawbone

R

raganella Ratchet
Rahmentrommel Frame drum
rail d'acier Steel bar
Rand Edge
râpe Quiro
raspa di metallo Metal scraper
raspe Guiro
Raspel Guiro
Rasseln Rattles, maracas
Ratche Ratchet
Reibtrommel Lion's roar
Reifen Rim
richiamo de uccelli Birdcall
ricoperta, o Covered or wound with
rivoltella Pistol shot
Rohrblatt Reed
Röhrenglocken Chimes
Röhrenglockenspiel Chimes
Röhrenholztrommel Cylindrical woodblock
Rolliertrommel Tenor drum
Rollschellen Sleigh bells
Rolltrommel Tenor drum
Rommelpot Lion's roar

rossignol   Water whistle (nightingale)
roulement   Roll
ruggio di leone   Lion's roar
ruggito   Lion's roar
rugissement de lion   Lion's roar
Ruhrtrommel   Field drum
rullo   Roll
Rumbakugeln   Maracas
Rute   Switches
Ruthe   Switches

S

sablier   Maracas
Saiten   Snares, strings
Saitenhalter   Tailpiece
Sandblöcke   Sandpaper
Sandbüchse   Maracas
Sandpapier   Sandpaper
sans   Without
sassofono   saxophone
sassofono baritono   Baritone saxophone
sassofono basso   Bass saxophone
sassofono contralto   Alto saxophone
sassofono soprano   Soprano saxophone
sassofono tenore   Tenor saxophone
saxhorn contrebasse   Tuba
saxhorn tuba   Euphonium
saxophone alto   Alto saxophone
saxophone baryton   Baritone saxophone
saxophone basse   Bass saxophone
saxophone soprano   Soprano saxophone
saxophone ténor   Tenor saxophone
scampellio da gregge   Cowbells
Schallbecher   Bell (of an instrument)
Schallbecken   Cymbals
Schallenbecken   Cymbals
Schallenglöckschen   Cup bells
Schallstück   Bell (of an instrument)
Schalltrichter auf   Bells up
Schelle   Jingles
Schellen   Sleigh bells
Schellenrassel   Tambourine without head
Schellenreif   Tambourine without head
Schellentrommel   Tambourine

Schlagbecken   Crash cymbals
Schlägel   Beater
schlagen   To strike
Schlagrassel   Jawbone
Schlagstab   Claves
Schlagzeug   Percussion
Schlitztrommel   Slit drum, log drum
schmetternd   Brassy
Schmirgelblock   Sandpaper block
Schnarre   Rattle, ratchet
Schnarren   Snares
Schwammschlägel   Sponge sticks
scie musical   Musical saw
scordate   Snares off
scovolo di fero   Wire brushes
scovolo di fil   Wire brushes
sec   Dry, choke
secco   Dry, choke
sega   Saw
sega cantante   Musical saw
sehr   Very
senza   Without
siffler   To whistle
sifflet à coulisse   Slide whistle
sifflet à roulette   Police whistle
sifflet d'oiseau   Bird whistle
sifflet sirène   Siren whistle
Signalpfeife   Siren whistle
silofone   Xylophone
silofono   Xylophone
silomarimba   Xylomarimba
singende Säge   Musical saw
sirena   Siren
sirena à mano   Siren
sirène   Siren
sirène à bouche   Mouth whistle
Skordatur   Scordatura
smorzare   Dampen
soffiare   To blow
sonagli   Sleigh bells
sonaglieri   Jingles
sonaglio   Rattle
soneria di campane   Chimes
sonnailles de troupeau   Almglocken

son pédale   Pedal tone
son rèel   Real pitch
Sopran   Soprano
Sopransaxophon   Soprano saxophone
sordina   Mute
sordina d'esercizio   Practice mute
sordina diritta   Straight mute
sordinare   Muffle
sordino   Mute
sospeso   Suspended
souffler   To blow
sourdine   Mute, soft pedal
sourdine d' exercise   Practice mute
sourdine droite   Straight mute
spazzola   Brush
spazzolle di jazz   Wire bushes
spazzolino   Switch
spegnere   Dampen
Spieler   Players
Spielsäge   Musical saw
Spitz   Tip of the bow
Springbogen   Saltando, jeté
spunga   Sponge
Stabglockenspiel   Chimes
Stahl   Steel
Stahltrommel   Steel drum
stappare le bottiglia   Pop gun
Steg   Bridge (of a stringed instrument)
Steilkastagnetten   Finger cymbals
Stempelflöte   Slide whistle
sticcada   Xylophone
Stimme   Voice
Stimmeisen   Tuning key
stimmen   To tune
Stimmung   Tuning
Streichinstrument   Stringed instrument
stromento   Instrument
stromento à tastiera   Keyboard instrument
strumenti à corde   Stringed instruments
strumenti à pizzico   Plucked instruments
sul, sulla   On, on the
suoni metallici   Brassy
suono di bottiglia   Tuned bottles
suono di osso   Slapstick

suono flautato   Harmonic
suono-pedale   Pedal tone
suono reale   Real pitch
sur   On
suspendue   Suspended

T

tabella   Slapstick
Taberett   Tabor
tabletta   Slapstick
taletta   Slapstick
tallone   Frog (of a bow)
talon   Frog (of a bow)
tambour   Snare drum
tambour à corde   Lion's roar
tambour à friction   Lion's roar
tambour d' acier   Steel drum
tambour de basque   Tambourine
tambour de bois   Log drum
tambour d'empire   Parade drum
tambour de provence   Tabor
tambour en peau de bois   Wooden tom-tom
tambourin   Tenor drum, tabor
tambourin de provence   Tabor
tambour indien   Indian drum
tambour militaire   Military drum
tambour provençal   Tabor
tambour roulante   Field drum
tambour sur cadre   Snare drum, frame drum
tamburello   Tambourine
tamburello basco   Tambourine
tamburello senza cimballi   Frame drum
Tamburin   Tambourine
tamburini   Timpani
tamburino   Tambourine
tamburo   Drum
tamburo acuto   Piccolo snare durm
tamburo à fessura   Slit drum, log drum
tamburo alto   Snare drum
tamburo basco   Tambourine
tamburo basso   Field drum
tamburo chiara   Snare drum
tamburo d'acciaio   Steel drum
tamburo di basilea   Parade drum

tamburo di frizione   Lion's roar
tamburo di latta   Steel drum
tamburo di legno   Woodblock
tamburo di legno-pelle   Wooden tom-tom
tamburo grande   Bass drum
tamburo indiano   Indian drum
tamburo militare   Military drum
tamburone   Bass drum
tamburo orientale   Chinese drum
tamburo piccolo   Snare drum
tamburo provenzale   Tabor
tamburo rullante   Field drum
tamburo senza corde   Tenor drum
tampon   Bass drum beater
tarole   Shallow snare drum
tarolle   Shallow snare drum
Taste   Key (of a keyboard instrument), fingerboard
Tastininstrument   Keyboard instrument
tasto   Key (of a keyboard instrument), fingerboard
Teller   Plates (cymbals)
Tempelblock   Temple block
Tenorsaxophon   Tenor saxophone
Tenortrommel   Tenor drum
Tenortrompete   Tenor trumpet
Tenortuba   Baritone horn
teschio cinese   Woodblock
tief   Low
timbales   Timpani
timbales cubani   Timbales
timpanetti   Timbales
tôle   Thundersheet
tonerre à poignée   Thundersheet
Tonhöhe   Pitch
touche   Fingerboard
trémolo (dental)   Flutter-tongue
trepei   Triangle
très   Very
Triangel   Triangle
Triangelstab   Triangle beater
triangolo   Triangle
tromba   Trumpet
tromba bassa   Bass trumpet

tromba piccola   Piccolo trumpet
tromba tenore   Tenor trumpet
Trommel   Drum
trompe d' auto   Auto horn
Trompete   Trumpet
trompette   Trumpet
trompette basse   Bass trumpet
trompette ténor   Tenor trumpet
tuba ténor   Baritone horn
tuba tenore   Baritone horn
tubes de bambou   Bamboo wind chimes
tubes de cloches   Chimes
tubi di bambù   Bamboo wind chimes
tubolari   Chimes
tumba   Conga
tuono a pugno   Thundersheet
Türkische Becken   Crash cymbals
Türmglockenspiel   Chimes

U

Übungsdämpfer   Practice mute
uccelli   Bird whistle
unghia   Fingernail
usignolo   Water whistle (nightingale)

V

Ventil   Valve
vents   Wind instrument
verga   Wire brushes, switches
verges   Wire brushes, switches
verghe   Wire brushes, switches
verres   Glasses
via   Away, off
vibrafono   Vibraphone
Vibraphon   Vibraphone
Vieschelle   Cowbell
Violine   Violin
violon   Violin
Violoncell   Cello
violoncelle   Cello
voce   Voice
Vogelpfeife   Bird whistle
voix   Voice

W

Waldteufel   String drum
weg   Away, off
weich   Soft
Windglocken   Wind chimes
Windmaschine   Wind machine
Wirbel   Roll
Wirbeltrommel   Tenor drum

X

Xilofon   Xylophone

xilofono   Xylophone
xilomarimba   Xylomarimba
xylophon   Xylophone

Z

Ziehpfeife   Slide whistle
zilafone   Xylophone
zilafono   Xylophone
Zimbeln   Antique cymbals
Zug   Slide
Zunge   Tongue

APPENDIX E

Ranges, Transpositions, and Checklist

The symbol ◊ indicates elementary-school levels. The symbol ● indicates high-school levels.

STRINGS

1. *VIOLIN*

2. *VIOLA*

3. *CELLO*

4. *BASS*
(Written an octave higher than sounding)

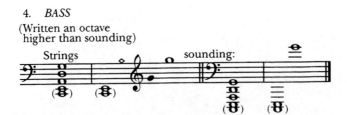

WOODWINDS

1. *PICCOLO*
(Written an octave
lower than sounding)

2. *FLUTE*

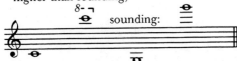

3. *ALTO FLUTE*
(Written a perfect fourth
higher than sounding)

4. *OBOE*

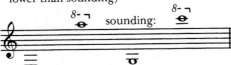

5. *ENGLISH HORN*
(Written a perfect fifth
higher than sounding)

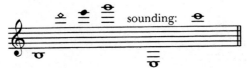

6. *Eb CLARINET*
(Written a minor third
lower than sounding)

7. Bb CLARINET
(Written a major second
  higher than sounding)

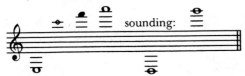

8. A CLARINET
(Written a minor third
  higher than sounding)

9. BASS CLARINET
(Written a major ninth higher than
  sounding in the treble clef, a major
  second higher in the bass clef)

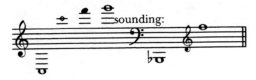

10. BASSOON

11. CONTRABASSOON
(Written an octave
  higher than sounding)

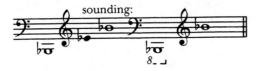

12. *SAXOPHONES*
all written:

ALTO
(Written a major sixth
  higher than sounding)

sounds:

TENOR
(Written a major ninth
  higher than sounding)

sounds:

BARITONE
(Written an ocatave
  and a major sixth
  higher than sounding)

sounds:

BRASS

1. *HORN*
(Written a perfect fifth
  higher than sounding)

sounding:

2. *D TRUMPET*
(Written a major second
    lower than sounding)

3. *B♭ TRUMPET*
(Written a major second
    higher than sounding)

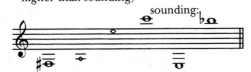

4. *TENOR TROMBONE*

5. *TENOR–BASS*
    AND BASS TROMBONE
    (with E or F attachment)

(F)   (E)

6. *TUBAS*

8- ⌐

PITCHED PERCUSSION

1. *TIMPANI*

32", 30"   29", 28"   26", 25"   23"   20"

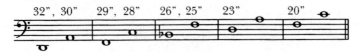

2. *ROTO-TOMS*

3. *GLOCKENSPIEL*
(Written two octaves
  lower than sounding)

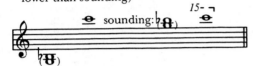

4. *XYLOPHONE*
(Written one octave
  lower than sounding)

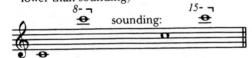

5. *MARIMBA*

6. *VIBRAPHONE*

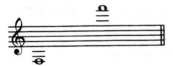

7. *CHIMES*

8. *STEEL DRUMS*

9. *CROTALES*
(Written two octaves
 lower than sounding)

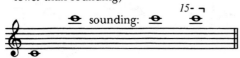

10. *HANDBELLS*

11. *GONGS*

SCORING CHECKLIST

1. Does every note in the original sound?
2. Is every articulation in the original rendered?
3. Are dynamics marked in all instruments at each entrance and where there are changes?
4. Are all instruments named on each system? (recommended)
5. Is the number of instruments given (e.g., 2 flutes, 3 trumpets in C)?
6. Is the key of the clarinets, the saxophones, and/or the trumpets given?
7. Are the initial tunings and subsequent changes given for the timpani and the harp? (recommended)
8. Are instruments in "correct" score order?
9. Are horns 1 and 3 given high parts, and 2 and 4 low parts? Are horns 1 and 2 on the upper staff? (recommended)
10. Are notes properly aligned?
11. If two or more wind instruments are written on one staff, is it clear *at all times* which are/is to play ("1." vs. "a 2," etc.)? (Do not use "divisi" or "unisoni" except where appropriate in band scoring.)
12. For strings, is "pizz." corrected by "arco," is "pont." corrected by "normale," is "con sord." corrected by "senza sord.," is "div." corrected by "unis.," is "solo" corrected by "tutti," and are double or multiple stops or divisi clearly indicated?
13. For strings, is it clear that notes under a slur indicate *one* continuous bow stroke?

14. Is the time signature given only at the beginning and where it changes?
15. Are dynamics marked (where possible) below the staff (for instruments) and all other playing indications above the staff?
16. Are all notes within the instrument's range?
17. Are transposed notes correct? (Check accidentals in the original carefully.)
18. Are instruments with different transpositions written on the same staff?
19. Is the balance appropriate?
20. Is a part unnecessarily difficult or impossible in some way?

Bibliography

ORCHESTRATION AND ARRANGING

ADLER, SAMUEL, *The Study of Orchestration* (2nd ed.). New York: W. W. Norton & Co., Inc., 1989.

ANTRAVAIA, THOMAS J., "Scoring Techniques in Arranging for the Junior High School Band." Master's thesis, San Diego State College, 1967.

BENNETT, ROBERT RUSSELL, *Instrumentally Speaking*. Melville, N. Y.: Belwin-Mills Publishing Corp., 1975.

BLATTER, ALFRED, *Instrumentation/Orchestration*. New York: G. Schirmer, Inc., 1980.

BURTON, STEPHEN DOUGLAS, *Orchestration*. Englewood Cliffs, N.J.: Prentice-Hall, 1982.

CACAVAS, JOHN, *Music Arranging and Orchestration*. Melville, N.Y.: Belwin-Mills Publishing Corp., 1975.

CARSE, ADAM, *The History of Orchestration*. New York: Dover, 1964.

———, *The Orchestra from Beethoven to Berlioz*. New York: Broude Bros., 1949.

DEL MAR, NORMAN, *The Anatomy of the Orchestra*. Berkeley and Los Angeles: University of California Press, 1984.

ERICKSON, FRANK, *Arranging for the Concert Band*. Melville, N.Y.: Belwin-Mills Publishing Corp., 1983.

GREEN, ELIZABETH, *The Dynamic Orchestra*. Englewood Cliffs, N.J.: Prentice-Hall, 1987.

HANSEN, BRAD, *The Essentials of Instrumentation*. Mountain View, Calif.: Mayfield, 1991.

JACOB, GORDON, *The Elements of Orchestration*. Reprint. Westport, Conn.: Greenwood Press, 1976.

KENNAN, KENT, and DONALD GRANTHAM, *The Technique of Orchestration* (4th ed.). Englewood Cliffs, N.J.: Prentice-Hall, 1990.

LANG, PHILLIP J., *Scoring for the Band*. New York: Mills Music, Inc., 1950.

MCKAY, GEORGE FREDERICK, *Creative Orchestration*. Boston: Allyn & Bacon, 1963.

MANCINI, HENRY, *Sounds and Scores*. Northridge Music, Inc., 1973.

MILLER, ROY M., *Practical Instrumentation for the Wind Band* (4th ed.). Detroit: Wayne State University Press, 1963.

PEYSER, JOAN, ed., *The Orchestra: Origins and Transformations*. New York: Scribner's, 1986.

PISTON, WALTER, *Orchestration*. New York: W. W. Norton & Co., Inc., 1955.

READ, GARDNER, *Contemporary Instrumental Techniques*. New York: Schirmer Books, 1976.

———, *Style and Orchestration*. New York: Schirmer Books, 1979.

RIMSKY-KORSAKOV, NICOLAI, *Principles of Orchestration*. Reprint. New York: Dover, 1964.

ROGERS, BERNARD, *The Art of Orchestration*. New York: Appleton-Century-Crofts, Inc., 1951.

STILLER, ANDREW, *Handbook of Instrumentation*. Berkeley and Los Angeles: University of California Press, 1985.

WAGNER, JOSEPH, *Band Scoring*. New York: McGraw-Hill, 1960.

YODER, PAUL, *Arranging Method for School Bands*. New York: Robbins Music Corp., 1946.

INSTRUMENTS

BAINES, ANTHONY, *Brass Instruments, Their History and Development*. London: Faber & Faber, 1976.

———, ed. *Musical Instruments through the Ages*. London: Penguin Books, 1961.

BARTOLOZZI, BRUNO, *New Sounds for Woodwinds* (2nd ed.). Oxford: Oxford University Press, 1982.

BLADES, JAMES, *Percussion Instruments and Their History* (rev. ed.). London: Faber & Faber, 1984.

BRINDLE, REGINALD SMITH, *Contemporary Percussion*. London: Oxford University Press, 1970.

BRYMER, JACK, *The Clarinet*. New York: Schirmer Books, 1976.

CHAPMAN, F. B., *Flute Technique*. Oxford: Oxford University Press, 1973.

COAR, BIRCHARD, *The French Horn*. DeKalb, Ill.: Dr. Birchard Coar, 1947.

DALE, DELBERT, *Trumpet Technique* (2nd ed.). Oxford: Oxford University Press, 1985.

FASMAN, MARK J., *Brass Bibliography*. Bloomington: Indiana University Press, 1990.

GEIRINGER, KARL, *Instruments in the History of Western Music* (3rd ed.). New York: Oxford University Press, 1978.

GLEASON, HAROLD, *Method Of Organ Playing* (7th ed.), ed. Catherine Crozier Gleason. Englewood Cliffs, N.J.: Prentice-Hall, 1988.

GREGORY, ROBIN, *The Horn*. New York: Praeger, 1969.

HOLLAND, JAMES, *Percussion*. Yehudi Menuhin Music Guides. New York: Schirmer Books, 1978.

HOLLOWAY, RONALD A., and HARRY R. BARTLETT, *Guide to Teaching Percussion* (3rd ed.). Dubuque, Iowa: Wm. C. Brown, 1978.

INGLEFIELD, RUTH K., and LOU ANNE NEILL, *Writing for the Pedal Harp*. Berkeley and Los Angeles: University of California Press, 1985.

JOPPIG, GUNTHER, *The Oboe and the Bassoon*, trans. Alfred Clayton. Portland, Oreg.: Amadeus Press, 1988.

KLEINHAMMER, EDWARD, *The Art of Trombone Playing*. Evanston, Ill.: Summy-Birchard Co, 1963.

LANG, PHILLIP, and HARRY SPIVAK, *Dictionary of Percussion Terms* (rev. ed.). New York: Lang Percussion Co., 1988.

LANGWILL, LYNDESAY G., *The Bassoon and Contrabassoon*. New York: W. W. Norton & Co., Inc., 1965.

LAWRENCE, LUCILLE, *The ABC's of Harp Playing*. New York: G. Schirmer and Sons, n.d.

LAWRENCE, LUCILLE, and CARLOS SALZEDO, *Method for the Harp*. G. Schirmer and Sons, n.d.

LEHMAN, PAUL R., *The Harmonic Structure of the Tone of the Bassoon* (rev. ed). Seattle: Berdon, Inc., 1965.

MASON, J. KENT, *The Tuba Handbook*. Toronto: Sonante Publishers, 1977.

MAZZEO, ROSARIO, *The Clarinet: Excellence and Artistry*. Sherman Oaks, Calif.: Alfred Publishing Co., 1981.

MUELLER, KENNETH A., *Teaching Total Percussion*. West Nyack, N.Y.: Parker Publishing Co., Inc., 1972.

PEINKOFER, KARL, and FRITZ TANNIGEL, *Handbook of Percussion Instruments*, trans. Kurt Stone and Else Stone. London: Schott, 1969.

PINO, DAVID, *The Clarinet and Clarinet Playing*. New York: Scribner's, 1980.

RAINEY, THOMAS E., JR., *The Flute Manual*. Lanham, Md.: University Press of America, Inc., 1985.

REED, H. OWEN, and JOEL T. LEACH, *Scoring for Percussion*. Englewood Cliffs, N.J.: Prentice-Hall, 1969.

REHFELDT, PHILLIP, *New Directions for Clarinet*. Berkeley and Los Angeles: University of California Press, 1978.

ROTHWELL, EVELYN, *Oboe Technique*. London: Oxford University Press, 1962.

RUSSELL, RAYMOND, *The Harpsichord and Clavichord* (2nd ed.). New York: W. W. Norton & Co., Inc., 1973.

SACHS, CURT, *The History of Musical Instruments*. New York: W. W. Norton & Co, Inc., 1940.

SALZEDO, CARLOS, *Modern Study of the Harp*. New York: G. Schirmer, Inc., 1948.

SCHULLER, GUNTHER, *Horn Technique*. London: Oxford University Press, 1962.

SHERMAN, ROGER, *The Trumpeter's Handbook*. Athens, Ohio: Accura Music, 1979.

SPENCER, WILLIAM, *The Art of Bassoon Playing*. Evanston, Ill.: Summy-Birchard Publishing Co., 1958.

STEVENS, ROGER S., *Artistic Flute Technique and Study*, ed. Ruth N. Zwissler. Hollywood, Calif.: Highland Music Co., 1967.

TOFF, NANCY, *The Flute Book*. New York: Scribner's, 1985.

TURETZKY, BERTRAM, *The Contemporary Contrabass*. Berkeley and Los Angeles: University of California Press, 1974.

WHITENER, SCOTT, *A Complete Guide to Brass Instruments and Pedagogy*. New York: Schirmer Books, 1990.

WICK, DENNIS, *Trombone Technique*. London: Oxford University Press, 1971.

WILLIAMS, PETER, *A New History of the Organ from the Greeks to the Present Day*. Bloomington: Indiana University Press, 1980.

ACOUSTICS

BACKUS, JOHN, *The Acoustical Foundations of Music* (2nd ed.). New York: W. W. Norton & Co., Inc., 1977.

BALDWIN, JOHN BARD, "Some Acoustical Properties of Triangles and Cymbals and Their Relation to Performance Practices." Ph.D. diss., Michigan State University, 1970.

BENADE, ARTHUR H., *Fundamentals of Musical Acoustics*. London: Oxford University Press, 1976.

———, *Horns, Strings, and Harmony*. Garden City, N.Y.: Anchor, 1960.

CAMPBELL, MURRAY, and CLIVE GREATED, *The Musician's Guide to Acoustics*. New York: Schirmer Books, 1988.

HUTCHINS, CARLEEN M., ed., *Musical Acoustics, Part I*. Stroudsburg, Pa.: Dowden, Hutchinson & Ross, Inc., 1975.

MEYER, JÜRGEN, *Acoustics and the Performance of Music,* trans. John Bowsker and Sibylle Westphal. Frankfurt/Main: Verlag das Musikinstrument, 1978.

RIDGEN, JOHN S., *Physics and the Sound of Music* (2nd ed.). New York: John Wiley & Sons, 1985.

SLAWSON, WAYNE, *Sound Color*. Berkeley and Los Angeles: University of California Press, 1985.

WHITE, HARVEY E., and DONALD H. WHITE, *Physics and Music*. Philadelphia: Holt, Rinehart and Winston, 1980.

NOTATION

CUNDICK, ROBERT, and NEWELL DAYLEY, *Music Manuscript*. Orem, Utah: Sonos Music Resources, 1974.

HARDER, PAUL O., *Music Manuscript Techniques*. Boston: Allyn & Bacon, Inc., 1984.

READ, GARDNER, *Music Notation* (2nd ed.). Boston: Crescendo Publishers, 1969.

———, *20th-Century Microtonal Notation*. New York: Greenwood Press, 1990.

STONE, KURT, *Music Notation in the Twentieth Century*. New York: W. W. Norton & Co., Inc., 1980.

Index of Instruments

Index
of Orchestration

Index of Composers

Amram, David, 268

Bach, J. S., 180–85, 260
Bartók, Béla, 46, 167, 235, 258–65
Beethoven, Ludwig van, 76, 194–200, 225, 277–78,
    298, 300, 303
Berg, Alban, 235, 259, 306
Berio, Luigi, 268, 334
Berlioz, Hector, 77, 164, 193, 230, 306
Bizet, Georges, 275
Boulez, Pierre, 268
Brahms, Johannes, 63, 76, 206–24, 284–88, 296, 304
Britten, Benjamin, 266

Cage, John, 345
Carter, Elliott, 101, 151, 156, 268, 269, 298
Copland, Aaron, 113, 123, 172, 267, 280
Creston, Paul, 307
Crumb, George, 114, 150, 173

Dahl, Ingolf, 313
Debussy, Claude, 50, 52, 124, 235–58, 278–79, 300
Del Tredici, David, 268
Dvořák, Antonin, 73, 304, 316

Elgar, Edward, 175

Foss, Lukas, 270
Franck, César, 50, 56, 81, 162, 163, 228
Franklin, Benjamin, 342

Gershwin, George, 303
Grainger, Percy, 312

Handel, George Frideric, 180–85, 309
Haydn, Franz Joseph, 185–92
Henze, Hans Werner, 336
Hovhaness, Alan, 315

Ligeti, György, 268, 269, 270

Mahler, Gustav, 39, 56, 174, 175, 176, 225–35, 258,
    272, 298, 303, 341, 344
Mendelssohn, Felix, 200–205, 296, 324–26
Mozart, Leopold, 269
Mozart, W. A., 185–92, 301

Nono, Luigi, 151, 334, 338

Orff, Carl, 128

Penderecki, Krzysztof, 268, 316, 317, 343
Pousseur, Henri, 268
Prokofiev, Sergei, 336

Ravel, Maurice, 29, 56, 63, 123, 235–58, 298, 300
Read, Gardner, 340
Rimsky-Korsakov, Nicolai, 28, 77, 164, 167, 219,
    225–35, 290–93
Rodrigo, Joaquín, 276
Rossini, Gioachino, 199, 203

Scarlatti, Domenico, 289, 297
Schoenberg, Arnold, 55, 167, 258–65, 272,
    293, 307
Schubert, Franz, 303–4
Schumann, Robert, 76, 81, 85, 282–83, 301

Date Due